The Theory of Fashion Design

To dress a woman . . . is to envelop nature in a significant contour which accentuates her grace.—Paul Poiret

The Theory
of Fashion Design

Fashion Institute of Technology   *Helen L. Brockman*

John Wiley & Sons, Inc., New York · London · Sydney

15 14 13 12 11

Library of Congress Catalog Card Number: 65-25852
Printed in the United States of America
ISBN 0 471 10586 4

To Hertha, Moisha, Toula, and Joseph,

who represent

the gifted graduates of our school

to whom I owe so much

Foreword

Unique and interesting in its approach, this book will be of value to those interested in any aspect of fashion. The analysis is comprehensive yet handled with such simple directness that the average reader can enjoy and profit by this analytical excursion into the world of fashion. The author has delineated the processes of designing apparel in a clear, precise style of writing that will be a rewarding experience for all who use this book.

The book begins with a realistic profile of the designer at work and continues in the second chapter with a discussion of the many practical limitations on fashion design which challenge and inspire designers to develop styles that are contemporary, artistic, and in good taste. The factual information contained here can be useful to anyone interested in the evaluation and selection of clothing in today's diversified market. Here and throughout the book, the many fashion sketches and diagrams accurately illustrate the subject matter and thus give the reader a clear impression of each topic discussed. The illustrations are one of the delights of this book.

The biographical accounts of the designers who have been the trend setters in this century and the historical analysis of cultural aspects as they have developed and influenced fashion are important contributions to this study of fashion theory. The material presented on these two subjects is not lengthy, but has been chosen carefully for its importance in the evolution of fashion.

The artistic and technical, the theoretical and practical are blended for a realistic approach to designing as the principles and elements of design are described. The chapter on Application of Fine-Arts Principles provides an excellent guide for the creators of fashion and is equally useful to those who deal with the selection of clothing or fashion for any purpose. This guide or tool is basic to all fashion work.

In the second half of the book the author gives an accurate picture of designing from sloper to flat pattern to well-designed apparel, presenting a comprehensive array of styling techniques. Her precise tracing of steps in the various processes is well done and the accompanying diagrams make the steps easy to follow. For anyone studying techniques of apparel design these concise and logical steps will be invaluable.

A glance at the table of contents will show that many will find this book a "must": those who are studying to be teachers, and teachers who want to make their course work more challenging and exciting; those who are studying in the broad field of fashion merchandising as well as those in the field of fashion design. Others who will benefit are those studying clothing selection, clothing construction, and fashion trends and history. This is a book for both those who teach and those who work in fashion.

MARION A. NIEDERPRUEM

Amherst, Massachusetts
August 1965

Preface

Fashion is the product of a unique combination of designer and consumer who have no direct contact with one another, and buyer who acts as their two-way interpreter, reflecting consumer taste for the designer's guidance and offering new fashion trends for the consumer's selection. Unless the designer can present new fashion that the buyer believes in and the consumer is willing to accept, all three partners suffer a loss. It is important, therefore, that both buyer and consumer know the designer's problems, recognize the limitations inherent in the design function, and understand the principles of good design and good taste. The buyer must also develop a sensitivity to the factors that influence consumer acceptance, and the consumer must recognize the problems inherent in the production and merchandising of fashion, and learn enough about the technical aspects of design to be able to put commercial patterns to creative use.

The aim of this book is to increase mutual understanding among the partners, and for this reason its dual concerns are fashion theory and design development. In the first half of the book theoretical aspects of fashion are emphasized, including the influences of sociology, economics, and history, and fine-arts principles and merchandising policies. The second half deals with the application of the principles of design in the styling of garments, from the standpoint of fabric, structure, and trimming. This entire range of material applies both to the study of fashion creation and the study of apparel selection.

For students of fashion design, the chapters on garment structure constitute core text material, whereas for students of home economics and retailing, these chapters on structure offer practical analyses of a wide range of styling techniques. The chapters on fashion influences furnish basic text material for courses in apparel selection, and apparel-design students will find that these chapters serve as excellent bridges to related subjects that are basic to a designer's cultural development.

Teaching without a textbook wastes time; learning without a textbook is difficult, particularly in technical areas where many students are unable to take intelligible notes while watching a demonstration. And for a student who has been absent from class, a textbook furnishes the best presentation of the missing step in the necessarily continuous process of learning.

I undertook to write this book because of the obvious need. The development of proper material in this largely uncharted field has been a constant and intensely absorbing challenge. I must express great appreciation to the hundreds of students who have been my laboratory during the years the book was in process. I am also deeply grateful for the help and encouragement of my graduate students in the industry and my colleagues at the Fashion Institute of Technology who have advised and assisted me, reading chapters and helping to clarify ideas.

All the patterns for skirts, waists, dresses, sleeves, and collars used in the chapters on structure were drafted from the block patterns or slopers for which detailed development steps are shown. All were made to fit a Wolf form, Size 7, 1960 model. A junior rather than a misses form was used because its more curved body lines often make it more difficult to handle than the misses form, and a small size was chosen simply because smaller patterns occupy less space. For ease in drafting, all slopers and patterns were drawn to centimeter scale (one centimeter equaling one inch), using a miniature French curve made especially for this purpose. Because of the accuracy that this method makes possible, all of the patterns can actually be used if enlarged to body size.

All the illustrations in the book represent actual garments copied from magazine and newspaper clippings collected over the past thirty years. These illustrations were sketched for the book by a former student, Lorraine Tercovich Guinta. I am particularly indebted to this talented young woman for her consistently excellent and sensitive interpretation which adds so much to the attractiveness and usefulness of the book.

HELEN L. BROCKMAN

New York City
August 1965

Contents

ILLUSTRATION CREDITS

Fashion sketches by Lorraine Guinta.
Year-by-year sketches on pages 68–75 adapted from illustrations in Vogue *magazine.*
Photographs of fabric by Klein Brothers.
Print fabrics on pages 311–313 supplied by Fred Levi Studio.

Photographs of the dress form by Lionel White.
Jacket and frontispiece design by Betty Mayers.
Photograph of author on jacket by Grey Hodges.

Chapter One

The Designer at Work

Chanel on the Staircase of
Her Salon on the rue Cambon
Paris, 1954

THEORY MEANS "WHY" in addition to "what and how." This book is entitled *Theory of Fashion Design* because its prime objective is to analyze *why*. It offers explanations for the trends by which fashion is motivated and it searches out reasons for the limitations that exist in the many techniques through which apparel is designed. Although "theory" implies a scientific approach to design, it does not alter the high status of design as an art, or decrease the excitement of its intuitive expression. The knowledge of *why* actually deepens the satisfaction because it broadens the understanding.

This book focuses on fashion from two directions, presenting the forces that influence fashion on one hand, and explaining the principles by which these forces can be effectively used on the other. It explores the varied facets of taste and knowledge and training and skill that constitute the designer's background and it analyzes the techniques of structure and the capabilities of fabrics and trimmings that the designer must use as tools in the creation of new and exciting fashion.

This introductory chapter presents a brief description of the role of the designer, who like an actor appears before the curtain to set the stage and acquaint the audience with what the play is going to be about.

What exactly does a designer do? It is no wonder that this question is so often asked because what a designer does may include such a variety of things that it is difficult to find two designers whose "varieties of things" are identical. A designer as a rule works for a wholesale apparel house or manufacturer. Manufacturing consists of several interrelated processes, and perhaps a good way to explain what a designer does is to describe the overall wholesale setup.

The block diagram on this page shows the functions of a wholesale apparel manufacturer. The large circle in the center represents the head of the company, and the three large areas that make up the bulk of the diagram represent the three major functions of the company: design, production, and sales. The small square boxes represent minor functions that are interrelated as shown.

The head of the company directs the general operations necessary to run the company: payroll, personnel, accounting, the boss's secretary, the girl at the switchboard, and so on. The head of the company also is in charge of all its departments.

The design department is headed by the designer who is responsible for producing a collection of newly designed models, generally four times a year: the fall and winter collection, the resort or holiday collection, the spring collection, and the summer collection.

The production department is responsible for mass producing the original models of each collection in various sizes and colors to fill orders.

The sales department markets the models created by the design department, and thus acts as middleman between designer and buyer.

Publicity and promotion functions, often handled by agencies or publicity experts, present outstanding numbers from a line to potential customers, enabling the house to compete suc-cessfully with other houses that market a similar type of apparel.

Orders and shipping, a dual-function department, works as the liaison between the sales and production departments. It collects and collates the customer orders and gives them to the production department in a sequence that facilitates their completion to meet the cancellation dates set by the customer.

Procurement of piece goods affects both the design and production departments. The designer depends on this department to procure a wide selection of new and interesting fabrics. Newly developed and improved fabrics often

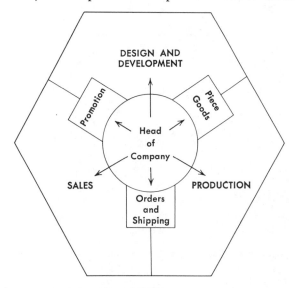

form the basis for new designs that can be produced at more competitive prices. The production department depends on this department for the procurement of fabrics necessary to complete orders on time.

Interdependence among these manufacturing departments demands cooperation if the house is to show a profit and stay in business. The designer, the head of production, and the head of sales are the three important department heads in the firm, although in many popular-price houses the piece-goods buyer has a position of equal importance. The head of the company may act as head of one of these main departments, and in a partnership each partner usually heads a department. The designer must work in cooperation with the other department heads, since all departments are directly concerned with, or indirectly affected by, the design function.

The Designer's Job. As head of a department, the designer has executive as well as creative functions and is expected to take charge of the personnel of the design room (or sample room), to assume part of the responsibility in the selection of fabrics, to procure the necessary trimmings, and, when sent to Europe, to select models to be brought back for copying or inspiration. The primary function of the designer, of course, is the responsibility for the seasonal collections of new models or "lines," each of which may contain from 60 to 120 garments or "pieces."

Six Steps in the Design Process. Perhaps a good way to present a picture of the designer at work is to trace a garment "line" from its inception as a series of ideas in the designer's mind through the manufacturing processes until the garments reach the retail store from which the customer is able to purchase them. We shall choose a misses daytime dress line in the popular-price category because this is the largest of all categories and one in which a young designer often finds a job.

STEP 1. CREATION. The first step in preparing the individual garments that make up a line is the creation of their designs. Each garment must have individual styling, and although it may be similar to other garments in the line, as well as to the garments in the preceding line, it will have new individual features of its own. Its similarities will reflect the silhouette in fashion (a silhouette that is being followed generally by all manufacturers of misses and women's apparel). The similarity of the garments in a line also stems from individual house requirements for producing the particular type of styling that its retail-store customers demand. In addition to these two specific limitations on free creativity, there are other general limitations that affect all designers of apparel: (a) the necessity for good taste and good proportion; (b) the necessity for effective use of the qualities inherent in the fabric; (c) the necessity for good fit. All these factors are covered in detail in later chapters. To perform these miracles of styling, the designer uses the tools of structure, trimming, and fabric; the designer who understands their possibilities and limitations and the principles that govern them has the greatest creative freedom in styling.

STEP 2. EXPERIMENTATION OR MODEL DEVELOPMENT. Within the limitations listed, the designer plans a line. The number of models or "pieces" in a line depends on the type of garment, the price range of the house, the method of distribution, and the number of lines that the house makes. A certain number of garments will be planned for each type of fabric selected and for each of the various categories of garment in which the house specializes. A certain proportion of the line will be basic and conservative, and a certain proportion will be high style. The designer usually helps to select the fabrics and to plan the color ranges to be featured, and chooses the belts, buttons, and other trimmings to be used. The choice of fabric and trimmings is influenced by price as well as appropriateness.

The techniques by which a designer works to develop a line vary. One designer may make sketches that are turned over to an assistant to be developed, first in muslin and then in the chosen fabric. Another designer may work entirely with muslin or with the chosen fabric, using a dress form or even a live model, draping and pinning the pieces together to get the desired "look," and then giving the partially completed work to an assistant to be finished. Or a designer may work "on the flat," as it is called when a new style is developed simply by making changes in a basic pattern according to geometric rules. The choice of method used depends on the designer's preference and the type of garment and styling. Whatever the method, the result must be a garment that fits a live model who will "show" it to buyers as they come to the showroom to choose among the various "numbers" on the line and place orders for those "pieces" that they feel are right for their particular stores. Every designer makes a great many unsuccessful numbers. Designing is truly experimental. A good number has a fortunate combination of the right fabric, the right cut, the right trimming, and can be sold for the right price with the right margin of profit.

STEP 3. STYLE SELECTION. The line is appraised and "weeded" before it is shown. Often half the numbers are discarded as "dogs." The most attractive are frequently discarded because they cannot be fitted into one of the price lines featured by the house. For example, if the price lines are $29.75 and $39.75, as they might be for garments retailing for $49.50 and $69.50, the overall cost of production (materials plus labor plus overhead) of a garment that will go into the $29.75 price line cannot be more than $29.75. A garment must either fit into this lower price line or look expensive enough to go into the $39.75 price line; otherwise it is discarded.

Weeding Practices. The method used to weed a line depends on the policy of the house. The sample model (on whom the line was made) may show the line to the head of the company, who reviews each piece and decides for himself whether it can sell for the price that it must bring to be a profitable item. In one successful firm in which this method is used, the model is asked how she likes the numbers about which the head of the company is in doubt. Models frequently develop great sensitivity to the line, for they show garments day after day and often overhear the buyers' frank reactions to the various numbers. In large firms the salesmen, who also have great sensitivity to buyer reaction, are frequently asked to participate in weeding the line. There are also houses in which the line is weeded on the advice of a favorite buyer who is consistently successful with their merchandise. Weeding, by whatever method used, generally reduces the line to relatively few garments, as is necessary for economical production. It takes only a few really good numbers for a house to have a successful season. As the price of the line increases, the number of pieces in it also increases. Very high-price lines contain a great many numbers since exclusiveness can thus be promised to customers, a sales factor that outweighs other considerations in the high-price market.

STEP 4. PATTERN DEVELOPMENT. Once the line is "set," it is necessary to make patterns for each garment in it in every size offered, 6–16 being common in misses sizes, for example. Pattern development is such an expensive process that production patterns are not made until the line has been weeded. The more-or-less rough pattern used in the sample room for cutting the original sample is made to fit a live model who seldom is a perfect size. Models more often have the idealized proportions used in fashion drawings, with broad shoulders, narrow hips, and long legs, and thus the clothes, as they model them, have a look of greater elegance and chic.

The more expensive houses use very tall girls, popular-price houses may use smaller models, and in the low-end market garments are shown on hangers.

The Pattern Maker. As head of production or under his supervision, the pattern maker cuts an accurate or "perfect" pattern for each sample on the line. He does not rip up the sample garment, but by looking at it and taking measurements, and perhaps by also looking at the original sample-room pattern, he is able to develop a pattern for whatever regular size the house uses for "duplicates," generally Size 10 or Size 12 in the misses range. The pattern maker has a duplicate cut and made in the sample room to "prove" the new pattern. The duplicate is then modeled by a "duplicate model" who is a perfect size, and it is compared with the first sample that is modeled by the "sample model," to see that the duplicate fits properly and has not lost too much of the smartness of the original sample. Unless the designer has a good understanding of garment construction and thus has designed the sample with seams in certain necessary locations, the pattern maker may have made drastic changes in the lines of the garment so that it can be cut in a standard way and laid out economically in production. If the first duplicate is not satisfactory, the pattern maker changes his pattern and has another duplicate cut, made, and compared with the sample garment.

The Pattern Grader. When the duplicate is satisfactory, the pattern grader, who is the pattern maker's assistant, then uses the perfect or "master" pattern to make the other required sizes, by mathematically and mechanically reducing or enlarging each pattern piece. From Size 10, for example, the pattern pieces are reduced to produce Sizes 8 and 6, and they are enlarged to produce Sizes 12 and 14. One reason for keeping a line as small as possible is the expense entailed in producing the sets of patterns that each number requires. Money is saved when the same set of patterns can be used for more than one number in the line or when certain pieces of the pattern, such as the skirt or the sleeve, can be used in more than one number, a practice followed whenever possible to reduce the cost of production. After the pattern is "graded" (the range of sizes made), a duplicate may be made in one or two of the sizes to prove them also. Finally, a "marker" is made for the complete pattern set for each number. It is similar to the direction sheet of a commercial pattern that shows economical layouts for various widths of fabric, but in this case the layout probably will be from 50 to 100 feet in length since it must contain all the pieces for all the sizes in which the number is made, and laid out, of course, as economically as possible.

STEP 5. PRODUCTION. The designer and the pattern maker generally work at the showroom location, whereas the factory or production department usually occupies less-expensive quarters elsewhere. The cost of space in the area of the city where the showroom is located is often prohibitive. The factory may be owned by the apparel firm, or it may be owned by a contractor who works for several noncompeting apparel firms and thus is better able to keep the workers busy the year around. For contract work the garments may be cut out and wrapped in individual bundles on the home premises, otherwise the bolts of fabric and the master markers are shipped to the factory where the entire work of cutting and assembling the garments is done.

Piece Work. Factory work, which is generally "piece work," is managed and payment for it controlled in this way. A serially numbered ticket with five identical, perforated parts is used for each garment made. One section of the ticket is attached to the garment for identification. The other four sections of the ticket go to the workers who assemble the garment: the operator, who stitches it together; the finisher, who does the handwork required; the presser, who gives the garment its final pressing; and the examiner, who checks the garment when it is finished, cleans off threads, attaches labels, tags, and so on. Each part of each ticket is worth an individually set amount agreed on at the beginning of the season by the company and an elected union representative or shop steward. Thus each worker is paid according to the number of tickets of each serial number that he has accumulated by the end of the work week. Factory employees on piece work have work only when there is "work in the house." They may be laid off when a season is poor.

Week Work. An operator who shows exceptional ability is frequently promoted to sample hand, working in the design room on the samples, where the employees are generally assured steady employment at a regular weekly salary.

STEP 6. DISTRIBUTION. The sales department consists of the head of sales, who is usually the owner of the business, and the salesmen who work under his direction. Often there is also a directress who is in charge of the showroom and the models, and who maintains the line in up-to-the-minute shape and keeps up the book of sketches and swatches.

Buyers from retail stores in all parts of the country are invited to visit the showroom for the presentation of the seasonal showings. Between showroom visits buyers are able to replenish stock in these three ways:

(a) A buyer may reorder numbers that are "runners," phoning if necessary with a written confirmation to follow.

(b) Company salesmen regularly visit the established customers, taking some of the numbers from the line—especially new models added since the line opened—a book of well-executed sketches, and a complete set of swatches for the entire line. In low-price houses most of the contact with buyers may be made in this way.

(c) As a rule a retail store is affiliated with a buying office, a headquarters organization through which groups of retail stores, each in a different city, join in a loose federation to obtain up-to-date information on the market. When buyers come to New York, the buying office with which their store is affiliated may brief them on "resources," as the wholesalers are called, or accompany them into the market to furnish help if desired. Buying offices keep in regular contact with the market by seeing the various lines. They furnish their member stores with information on new items and new resources, and they often buy for their member stores between the regular buyer visits.

Shipping and Receiving. The order department receives buyer orders. An order always bears two dates: the date after which shipment can begin and the date before which it must be completed to avoid cancellation. As orders are received, they are numbered, collated, and sent to the production department. When the garments have been completed by the factory, they are sent to the shipping department where they are grouped according to customer order number and shipped out. On arrival at the receiving department of the retail store by which they were ordered, they are checked in, examined, and delivered to the department that placed the order.

Buyer Reaction. An initial order may not be very large. A buyer often waits to see "how the stock comes through," and how it sells on the floor. The numbers that prove popular are reordered in greater quantity, whereas numbers that do not sell satisfactorily go on the markdown rack. A buyer learns what types of garments sell best, and from which manufacturers they come, by analyzing the stock records that are kept by the department to show how many of what sizes and colors of each style are sold each day. Armed with this information, a buyer will return to a manufacturer for profitable styles or types of garments: softly detailed print dresses, costume suits with contrasting over-blouses, or sophisticated cocktail dresses, for example. Retailers as well as wholesalers are in business to make a profit.

The Beginner in the Design Field. Seldom is the first job of a beginner that of designer. The responsibilities that a designer must assume are so great that any manufacturer with much at stake requires a person of experience as head of the design department. Occasionally, a small or struggling house will hire a novice, but as a rule the beginner is hired as an assistant to the designer and may perform a variety of services depending on the size of the house, the number of assistants in the sample room, and the particular way in which the design function is organized. The different jobs that constitute the work performed in an average sample room are described here to acquaint the beginner with the skills and abilities prerequisite to successful employment as a sample-room assistant.

SKETCHING.   A sketcher may be called upon to do either or both of the standard types of sketching. *Working sketches* are pencil sketches for the sample room, made from the designer's roughly planned garment. They must interpret the silhouette precisely and indicate the placement of seamlines and trimmings. *Illustrations* are smart fashion sketches of garments in the line for the showroom book, with indications of color and fabric of the garment.

PATTERN MAKING.   A designer may employ an assistant to make patterns for the samples that are made in the sample room. Patterns are made by the flat-pattern technique, by draping in muslin, or by a combination of the two methods. The pattern produced must be complete and reasonably accurate, although all sample-room work is experimental and changes in a sample occur throughout its development.

SAMPLE MAKING.   A sample maker usually cuts and constructs the sample garment, although occasionally a finisher is provided, and a presser gives the garment a final pressing. The sample maker works with the designer or assistant designer to fit the sample perfectly to the model who will wear it. Often the pattern-making and sample-making functions are combined, and one assistant then carries a sketch through to the completed garment.

DUPLICATE MAKING.   A duplicate maker uses the master pattern to cut the duplicate in fabric. A duplicate must be made with extreme accuracy and attention to the pattern markings, since the pattern maker works from it to correct any inaccuracies that have been found in the pattern in the course of cutting and making the garment.

MISCELLANEOUS DUTIES.   These include shopping for findings and trimmings, running errands, helping the models dress during the busy seasonal showings, assisting at the switchboard, and so on. In a big house these duties may require the entire time of one person, otherwise they generally form part of the assistant's job.

The Theory of Fashion Design

Designer Success. Because buyers return to their established resources for specific types of styling, a designer can be successful at one house but unsuccessful at another. In successful designing the designer's natural taste must find expression, otherwise the work cannot bring the necessary stimulus of satisfaction. Fortunately, there are many fields in apparel design for the beginner to choose among. The following outline briefly summarizes them:

Age-Size Divisions in Apparel
    Women and half-sizes
    Misses and junior
    Junior petite and subteen
    Children, toddlers, infants

Price Divisions in Apparel
    Better garments—high price
    Popular or budget—medium price
    Basement or low-end—low price

Use Divisions in Apparel

    Outerwear
        Daytime dresses
        Cocktail and evening wear
        Sportswear separates
        Coats and suits
        Specialized types
            Uniforms
            Active sportswear
            Bridal wear
            Maternity wear
            Theatrical costumes

    Intimate wear
        Sleepwear
        Robes, housecoats
        Lingerie, slips
        Foundation garments, girdles, bras

    Accessories
        Shoes, bags, gloves, neckwear, etc.

    Millinery

SECTION 1

Forces That Influence Fashion

Chapter Two

Practical Limitations on Creativity

THE GLAMORIZED IMAGE of a designer so often portrayed in films as a mad genius who dreams up extravagant creations in fabulous fabrics seldom exists in reality. A more realistic view of the work of a designer has been presented in Chapter 1. Most designers must assume the heavy responsibility entailed in producing each year several seasonal collections that will unfailingly meet competition and thus enable the house to stay in business. Any designer must accept certain practical limitations on the free creative process in order to design collections that feature the types of clothes for which the house has built a reputation. Four important limitations that furnish guide lines for the designer are explored in this chapter.

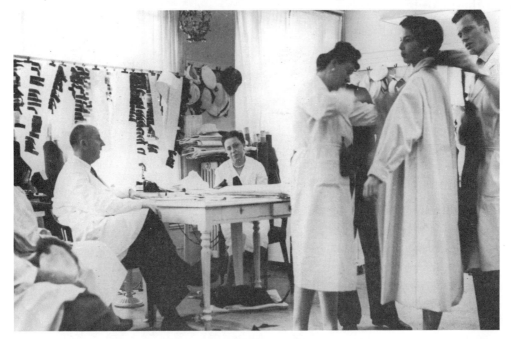

Dior and His Directress
Supervise a Workroom Fitting

Preview of Practical Guide Lines for the Designer. AGE-SIZE RANGE. The age-size range in which garments are produced places immediate restriction on creativity, since each size range appeals to a different type of customer and requires a particular approach to styling. Age-size ranges are discussed more fully on the facing page.

PRICE RANGE. The price range in which garments are produced affects styling in two ways. As garment price becomes lower (a) the narrower margin of profit that the manufacturer can take forces economy in fabric, trimming, and design complexity, since all these factors affect cost; and (b) the number of pieces sold increases and garment styling must have greater mass appeal to attract the broader segment of the consumer market. This facet of styling is explored on the following pages.

SUITABILITY TO OCCASION OR USE. The dress market is now subdivided into specific types of occasion clothes—for daytime wear, for casual leisure wear, and for cocktail and evening wear. An understanding of dress types helps the designer to build diversity into a line, just as it helps the buyer to purchase a balanced selection. Occasion types are analyzed on pages 16 and 17.

HOUSE IMAGE. Every successful wholesale house is patronized regularly by buyers who return each season because they have success with garments from this resource. Thus the general character of the garments must remain stable. Styling must consistently reflect the established house image if the house is to retain its customers. An analysis of the taste factors on which house images depend concludes the chapter.

TYPICAL STYLING IN THE FOUR STANDARD RANGES

Junior

Misses

Women's

Half-Size

RELATIONSHIP OF ADULT SIZE RANGES

Junior	Misses	Women's	Half-Size
5	6	. .	. . .
7	8	. .	. . .
9	10	. .	. . .
11	12	. .	. . .
13	14	34	14½
15	16	36	16½
. .	18	38	18½
. .	. .	40	20½
. .	. .	42	22½
. .	. .	44	24½

Relationship of Size Range to Styling

Evolution of Figure Types. The misses size range, originally Sizes 10–18, began as an extension of children's age-sizes. Size 16 fitted an adult who was shaped like an average 16-year-old. The women's size range (36–44) had been originated much earlier when the Buttericks began to make patterns sized according to bust or chest circumference. For many years women who were smaller, larger, or shorter than the normal misses or women's sizes could not be fitted properly. Since the First World War the apparel industry has been occupied with size standardization and diversification, developing size ranges geared to customer requirements. In 1960 the Wolf Form Company advertised 28 standard types of dress form, each in a range of sizes.

How Size Range Affects Styling. Diversification of figure types has reoriented age-size concepts. The junior and junior petite have replaced the misses as the ideal college girl and teenage miss; the misses has replaced the women's as the standard concept of an adult female; and women's and its more squarely built half-size counterpart have come to represent adult females who are too large to be accommodated by misses sizes. Generally, the misses size range places neither mechanical nor esthetic limitations on design. The junior figure is a shorter version of the misses—the regular junior Size 11 of Wolf Form Company, for example, has the front-waist width of a misses Size 12, the back-waist width of a Size 10, and the back-waist length of a Size 8. The limitation on junior styling is one only of taste—styling that is appropriate for youth. Women's and half-sizes pose both mechanical and esthetic limitations on design, since the figure must be made to look taller and slimmer-waisted, and heavy women both need and prefer conservative styling. Types of styling suitable for young juniors and for youthful women's and half-sizes are analyzed on pages 26 and 27 of this chapter.

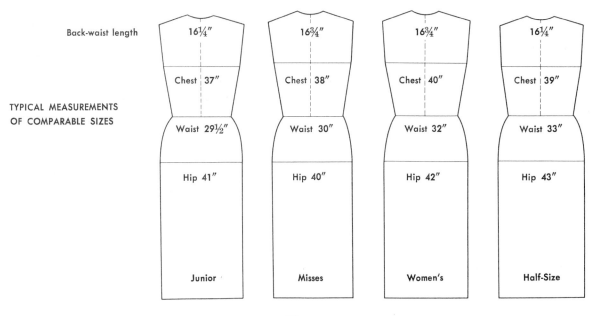

Back-waist length

Junior	Misses	Women's	Half-Size
16¼″	16¾″	16¾″	16¼″
Chest 37″	Chest 38″	Chest 40″	Chest 39″
Waist 29½″	Waist 30″	Waist 32″	Waist 33″
Hip 41″	Hip 40″	Hip 42″	Hip 43″

TYPICAL MEASUREMENTS OF COMPARABLE SIZES

Relationship of Price Range to Styling

A DRESS HOUSE tends to specialize in one of the three general price-range divisions into which the market is divided. In this respect the apparel industry differs from the accepted industrial pattern where a giant company like General Motors makes high-price models, medium-price models, and low-price models. In the apparel industry a manufacturer of high-price dresses may also carry a medium-price line, and a medium-price house may also make a small high-price line. But manufacturers of low-price garments seldom diversify in this way because both their production methods and their marketing procedures are different from those of medium- and high-price markets, and a substantially different group of buyers are their customers.

Share of the Market. A high-price garment takes a greater wholesale mark-up than a medium-price garment, and a medium-price garment takes a greater mark-up than a low-price garment. Retail mark-up follows the same pattern as wholesale mark-up. Thus a dress in the high-price market with a wholesale price of $95.75 will retail for about $200.00 (a mark-up of 50 per cent). A dress in the low-price market, with a wholesale price of $3.75, may retail for $5.69 (a mark-up of $33\frac{1}{3}$ per cent). This apparent imbalance tends to be offset by the proportional number of garments sold. Note on the facing page that at least 65 per cent of garments sold are in the low-price market, whereas very few are in the high-price market.

How Price Affects Styling. The illustrations on the facing page show typical styling that is used in the different price segments of the market. The customers for these market segments and the value factors that they find appealing are listed. Note that high fashion dominates only the tiny high-price segment of the market. More wearable styling is the generally desired look in the comparatively large medium-price market. In the low-price market, the greatest design skill is required to produce fashions that will be widely acceptable under the highly restrictive limitations that this field imposes.

MARKET COMPARISONS

High-Price Market

SHARE OF MARKET

Less than 2 per cent of garments

REPRESENTATIVE CUSTOMERS

Exclusive specialty shops
Better-dress departments

VALUE FACTORS

High-fashion styling
Exclusiveness
Quality fabrics
Name designers

DESIGNER JOB OPPORTUNITIES

Approximately 20 per cent of beginner jobs

Medium-Price Market

SHARE OF MARKET

Approximately 30 per cent of garments

REPRESENTATIVE CUSTOMERS

Specialty shops
Budget departments
Better chain stores

VALUE FACTORS

Wearable styling
Brand-name reliability
Fashion fabrics

DESIGNER JOB OPPORTUNITIES

Approximately 65 per cent of beginner jobs

Low-Price Market

SHARE OF MARKET

More than 65 per cent of garments

REPRESENTATIVE CUSTOMERS

Basement departments
Volume chain stores
Catalog houses

VALUE FACTORS

Fashion at a price
Hanger-appeal styling
Novelties and fads
Appealing fabric patterns

DESIGNER JOB OPPORTUNITIES

Approximately 15 per cent of beginner jobs

Relationship of Functional Suitability to Styling

DURING THE VICTORIAN ERA a fashionable woman's wardrobe contained little except custom-made gowns intended for afternoon and evening wear, all of them complex, voluminous, and as expensive as possible to demonstrate the social and economic status of the wearer. The first functional breakthrough came at the time of the First World War, when Poiret and Chanel introduced a new concept of fashion in which simplicity was featured rather than complexity and ostentation. The rising popularity of women's sports, the entrance of great numbers of young women into business offices during the 1920's, and the increasing availability of suitable fabrics all contributed to the new broadened concept of women's apparel which began to include daytime business clothes and more realistic sportswear in addition to the established categories of afternoon dresses and evening gowns.

Occasion Types of Clothes Diversify the Ready-to-Wear Market. During the 1930's many retail stores established special departments for ski wear, beach wear, and spectator sportswear as customer acceptance began to be based on suitability of a garment to its intended use rather than on its lavish workmanship and fabric. Schiaparelli designed the first evening suit in the mid-1930's and it immediately fostered an entirely new and less-formal concept of dress-up clothes including the cocktail dress, the dinner dress, and the hostess gown. After the Second World War the important new category of casual leisure wear developed out of the shirttail and jeans outfits first worn by the subteen set. This category has grown to become one of the most popular types of apparel across the entire country. Its essentially young and casual look is so pervasive that it is an important influence in all apparel styling.

OCCASION-TYPE GROUP INTERRELATIONSHIPS. The nine occasion-type groups of garments that now dominate the dress market are shown on the facing page. They are arranged in a circle to illustrate that the change in functional suitability from one division to the next is so slight that it is usually possible to find garments in any one group that are suitable also for use in one or the other of the adjoining groups.

DEGREE OF FORMALITY DETERMINES OCCASION-TYPE SUITABILITY. The degree of formality of a dress can serve as a criterion for its functional suitability. Formality derives from a combination of the cut of the garment and the fabric used for it. "Cut," as used in this connection, means the tightness of fit and the amount of flesh exposed. The more formal a garment is, as a rule, the more décolleté. A formal evening gown may be cut very low, whereas a dinner dress tends to be cut higher and often has a matching jacket. Casual leisure wear, at the other extreme, generally covers the upper third of the body and exposes or accentuates the middle or lower third with bare midriffs and short shorts or skin-tight pants. Daytime wear features the least exposure. The afternoon dress is the most décolleté since it occupies the position adjacent to the cocktail dress in the diagram. Generally, the daytime categories strive for moderation and understatement, and the cocktail and evening groups strive for glamor. The casual leisure wear groups strive for a look of uncontrived comfort suited to the activities of play and leisure.

FUNCTIONAL OCCASION-TYPE DIVISIONS OF THE DRESS MARKET

9 to 5   Daytime

Spectator

Afternoon

GENERAL DAYTIME WEAR

Sportswear
Separates

Cocktail
and Dinner

Informal
Evening

Play Clothes

CASUAL LEISURE WEAR

COCKTAIL AND

EVENING WEAR

Hostess Gowns
and Pyjamas

Formal
Evening

17

Influence of Silhouette on Styling

THE SILHOUETTE is the fundamental factor in apparel styling since it dictates the outline shape that a garment gives to its wearer. Exaggeration in silhouette is synonymous with high fashion, whereas in the medium- and low-price markets the silhouette is toned down or normalized. Changes in the silhouette are initiated by the haute couture, and the interpretation of the incoming silhouette trend acts as the controlling influence within the limits of which a designer works with cut, fabric, and trimming to build the "house image."

Silhouette Trends. The sketches on this page illustrate the "looks" or outline shapes that have been in fashion during this century. Either the wide shoulder and fitted waistline of the triangular hourglass have been high fashion, or the unfitted waistline and natural shoulder of the rectangular shift have been in the ascendancy, except for brief periods of time when the pendulum was swinging from one extreme to the other; and during these seasons, the normal silhouette became high fashion.

Styling Requirements. Both the extreme hourglass and the extreme shift are too high fashion to appeal to the majority of women. The modified hourglass and A-line silhouettes are far easier to wear and can probably account for more than half of any season's successes, and the normal silhouette has consistent appeal, especially in larger sizes and in lower-price lines. Skirt length and shoulder width are the most sensitive barometers of fashion. They date a garment immediately, and for this reason they always incline in the direction of the trend at all price levels.

SILHOUETTE TYPES AND THE FASHION LOOKS THEY PRODUCE

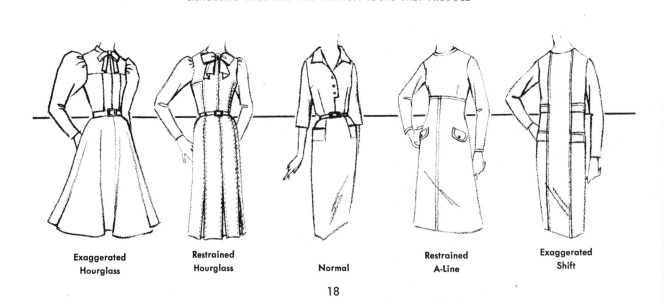

Exaggerated Hourglass   Restrained Hourglass   Normal   Restrained A-Line   Exaggerated Shift

House-Image Taste Factors

High Style   ←——————— to ———————→   Conservative

    Extreme silhouettes   Modified silhouettes
    Exciting, extreme fabrics   Wearable fabrics
    Sophisticated trimmings   Scaled-down trimmings

Tailored   ←——————— to ———————→   Soft

    Crisp, mannish fabrics   Gentle, feminine fabrics
    Darts, gores, pleats   Gathered and draped effects
    Belts, buttons, pockets   Soft ties, bows, embroidery

Casual   ←——————— to ———————→   Dressy

    Durable and wearable fabrics   Fragile and rich fabrics
    Easy, comfortable styling   Body-conscious styling
    Functional trimming   Frankly pretty trimming

Young   ←——————— to ———————→   Youthful

    Faddish fabrics and colors   Soft prints, flattering colors
    Wide choice of silhouette   Normal silhouette, easy fit
    Simple styling   Figure-flattering lines
    Gay and novelty trimmings   Quiet, expensive trimmings

House Image.   A garment manufacturer's success is established when enough retail customers prefer to shop in stores where his line is sure to be available. Bobbie Brooks, Jonathan Logan, and Nellie Don are three examples of manufacturers who have been so successful in this respect that their "brand names" are nationally known. If a manufacturer is to develop his product into a household word, in this profitable way, the characteristic look of his clothes—his *house image*—must be so stable that it is recognizable season after season. House images are compounded from the individual mixtures of the taste factors that are shown in the outline (and analyzed on the following pages). In the outline the salient design elements of these taste ranges are listed as more-or-less opposite extremes between which exists a wide range of intermediate possibilities. Each pair of factors is considered separately in the analysis, but in practice all operate simultaneously in complex interrelationships with one another. It is the uniquely individual compound of these relationships that makes the house image of one manufacturer different from that of all others. A designer can be successful in one house but unsuccessful in others, since success so often depends on the ability to project the established house image.

IMPORTS	ADAPTATIONS

High-Style—to—Conservative

A

Very Sheer Broadcloth

Cotton Print

IMPORTS AND THEIR adaptations are shown side by side to illustrate the high-style–to–conservative principle. Imports are useful to designers in two rather different ways. Adaptations, as shown in A, bear considerable resemblance to the original; and style details, as shown in B, give a look of the current trend to garments that otherwise are very conservative. Changes are made in most imports to make adaptations that are easier to wear as well as less expensive to produce. A two-piece garment is changed to a one-piece or vice versa, the closing is moved from back to front, sleeves are added, or the skirt is made wider. The "look" of the import can be retained, however, so long as the salient design features are carried over in easily recognizable form. Imports that can be used for copying down and for inspiration have the most influence on fashion trends.

B

Worsted Crepe and Moiré Ribbon

Rayon Flat Crepe

Silhouette: Extreme to Modified. Imports define the silhouette trend, dictating whether the hourglass (C) or the shift (D) is high fashion, and whether the skirt is short, medium length, or long. These criteria are followed by the industry to whatever degree is compatible with the individual house image. Modifications are

C

Velvet Jacket, Taffeta Skirt

Schiffli Embroidery on Wool

Range in Styling

D

Fine-Quality Linen   Linenlike Blend

E

Mohair   Silk Linen

F

Duvetyn   Salt-and-Pepper Tweed Blend

made to normalize the silhouette because the average customer cannot wear exaggerated silhouettes with assurance. Most women prefer clothes that make them feel comfortable rather than conspicuous.

Fabrics: Extreme to General Purpose. Extreme fashions depend greatly on fabrics that will produce their exaggerated silhouettes. General-purpose fabrics are less crisp or soft or thick or thin, as a rule, and generally less expensive. When they are used the silhouette automatically becomes less extreme. It is not possible, for example, to produce in rayon flat crepe the silhouette that distinguishes the import shown in B, or in a linenlike blend to reproduce the exaggerated look of the import in D. Fabrics are chosen specifically for the silhouette, the styling, and the price range that the house image dictates.

Trimmings: Sophisticated (Scaled Up) to Conservative (Scaled Down). Exaggerated silhouettes and extreme fabrics demand sophisticated, scaled-up trimmings for artistic balance. As the styling is made more conservative, the trimmings also must be scaled-down in proportion to the garments, as all six pairs of sketches illustrate.

Tailored-to-Soft

TAILORED SOFT

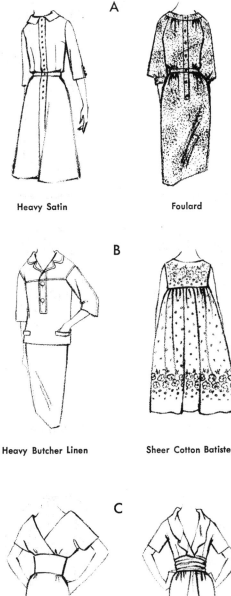

A

Heavy Satin   Foulard

B

Heavy Butcher Linen   Sheer Cotton Batiste

C

Silk and Worsted   Crepe Romaine

THE TAILORED-TO-SOFT range in styling is illustrated by the "twin" dresses shown on these two pages. Both twins in each illustration are suitable for the same occasions, representing the individual preferences of women for either more crisply tailored or more softly feminine styling. Among daytime dresses both tailored and soft styling are equally easy to find, but in cocktail and evening wear the tendency is toward more feminine styling, and casual clothes tend to be more tailored. The type of occasion for which a garment will be worn limits to some extent the tailored-to-soft range of styling.

Fabrics: Crisp to Gentle. Extreme fabrics (A, B, C) furnish the base upon which both extremely tailored and extremely soft styles are built. Very soft fabrics are adapted to styling that features draped effects or uses soft ease controlled by a yoke. Exceedingly soft fabrics are not suitable for tailored styles, although feminine styling can take advantage of their particular quality of drapability. Extremely crisp fabrics, on the other hand, are quite unsuited to soft effects, but are ideal for tailored styling. Fabric and styling collaborate in good design.

Range in Styling

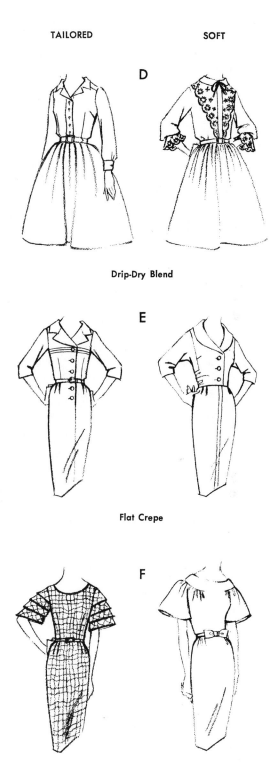

Style Lines: Tailored to Soft. Extreme fabrics dictate their own best styling, but general-purpose fabrics (D, E, F) can be styled in a rather soft or a rather tailored manner. Sketch D shows the same fabric in both tailored and soft versions of the shirtwaist dress, for example. Generally, darts and shaped seamlines and sharply defined pleats are tailored, whereas gathered and draped effects are soft. Gathered skirts are softer than pleated skirts; unpressed pleats are softer than pressed pleats; full skirts are softer than sheath skirts. Unmounted sleeves are softer than plain set-in sleeves, and eased or gathered sleeves are softer than fitted sleeves.

Trimmings: Tailored to Soft. Garments that use the conservative normal silhouette and general-purpose fabric will look either tailored or soft, depending on the trimmings used. Bows are softer than buttons, pockets, or tab details. Bow belts are softer than buckle belts, self-belts are softer than leather belts. Ruffles make a softer finish for edges than binding or welt stitching. Fabric, styling, and trimmings must be sensitively combined for the resulting style to have strong sales appeal.

D

Drip-Dry Blend

E

Flat Crepe

F

Flat Crepe

Casual-to-Dressy

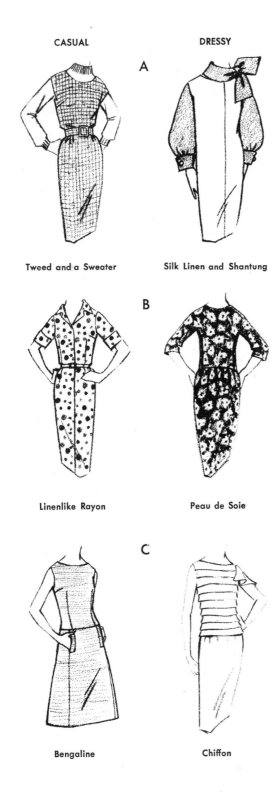

CASUAL

DRESSY

A

Tweed and a Sweater

Silk Linen and Shantung

B

Linenlike Rayon

Peau de Soie

C

Bengaline

Chiffon

CASUAL AND DRESSY are terms used to express both wide and subtle differences in styling, ranging from the broad difference between a spectator outfit and an afternoon dress to the subtle difference between two dresses of the same occasion type. Thus the dresses illustrated in A and B would be found in different wholesale lines and in different retail-store departments, whereas the dresses in C might be bought from the same house and hang side by side on a rack in the same department.

Fabrics: Casual or Dressy. Fabric surface pattern and texture often combine to indicate most appropriate styling. In A, for example, the svelt silk linen, with its crisp, semisheer shantung blouse, is the antithesis of the bold, bulky tweed that is properly coupled with a sweater. In B, the rich peau de soie, patterned with a strong sophisticated floral, is properly styled as a cocktail dress, whereas the slubbed rayon, patterned with subdued coin dots in a monochromatic color range, is appropriate as a summer daytime classic. The two short evening dresses in C might easily have been styled by the same designer, but the softness of chiffon makes it suited to more dressy styling than the comparatively rugged-

Range in Styling

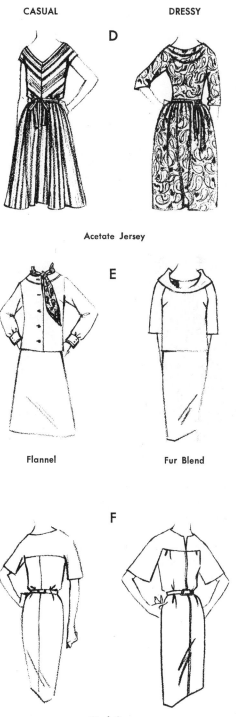

CASUAL   **DRESSY**

D

Acetate Jersey

E

Flannel   Fur Blend

F

Wool Crepe

looking ribbed bengaline. In all cases, fabric pattern combines with fabric type to dictate the styling. Fabric pattern alone may often have a strong influence in determining proper garment styling, as illustrated by the dresses in D, both of which use the same acetate jersey as ground fabric. Bold stripes can never be considered dressy, and when their impact is increased by mitered seaming at center front, they are appropriate for this very casual style, and the restrained paisley print is equally appropriate for an afternoon dress.

Styling and Trimming: Casual or Dressy. When fabric is not a factor, styling and trimming must combine to produce the desired casual or dressy look. In E, for example, in which both outfits are made from soft, thin wool, the casual look of the one comes from its "shirt" styling coupled with the colorful scarf that is tucked into the casually unbuttoned neck. The dressy look of the other comes from its body-conscious shaping together with the draped collar and jeweled pin. In F the casual dress reflects a pullover sweatshirt in styling, whereas the dress beside it has a more precise fit and dressy detail at the neckline.

Young-to-Youthful

IN AN ERA when youth is ascendant, as it has been since the Second World War, the "misses" category has indeed come to represent a size range rather than an age. Women shop in misses departments along with their daughters and granddaughters. Only when a woman is too large to wear a misses size must she patronize the women's or the half-size departments—and there, too, the matronly concept is played down while youthful styling is accentuated. At the

SUMMER COTTONS

Young Styling. Dainty floral Liberty lawn with baby-dress styling. Little-girl puff sleeves and tiny pearl buttons are appropriate trim.

Youthful Styling. Soft light and shadow print on cotton voile. Lacy spaghetti self-trim on round neck and pockets. Restrained flare in skirt.

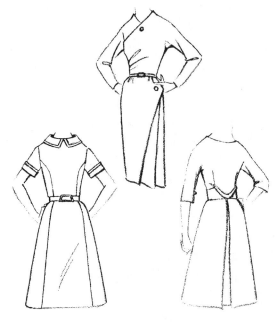

BASIC WOOLS

Young Styling. Swinging skirt with princess-line styling. Collar and cuff "set." Bold silver belt buckle.

Youthful Styling. Overskirt effect lengthens the figure. Self-detail in trapunto work effectively slims the waistline. An "away" neckline suitable for wearing costume jewelry.

Range in Styling

same time, junior styling has grown increasingly sophisticated. Between these two ever narrowing extremes of young and youthful lies the true young-adult misses. For this reason, it seems appropriate to show three sketches, rather than two, in the groups on these pages, although the captions will discuss only young and youthful styles, ignoring the sophisticated misses. The young junior look approaches the misses look from the left, and the youthful women's look approaches it from the right.

DRESSY SILKS

Young Styling. Dress of white polka dots on red with reverse red on white trim. Balloon sleeves and scaled-up pussycat bow.

Youthful Styling. Elegant dyed-lace appliqué on silk crepe. Pretty cowl collar frames the face while the control of lace at midriff slims waistline.

TAILORED CLASSICS

Young Styling. Typical shirtdress with full dirndl skirt, young front yoke and tucking detail. Peter Pan collar and wide belt.

Youthful Styling. Buttondown, fly-front sheath skirt. Dart tucks rather than darts control ease at the waistline. Small flat collar and good V-neckline.

Chapter Three

Fashion Trends and Trend Setters

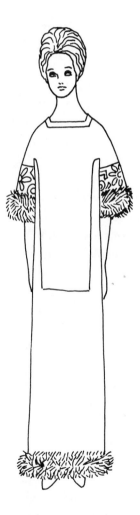

Poiret's Shift, 1910
The First New Look
of Our Century

IN THIS CHAPTER the changing trends of fashion over the past hundred years (1860–1960) are examined through biographical accounts of the lives of the members of the French couture who have set fashion trends over an appreciable span of years and to a definitive degree. These great fashion leaders are presented personally in this way to emphasize the fact that fashion trends are based on forces beyond individual control, regardless of depth of training and breadth of talent. Chapters 3 and 4 constitute a unit, one chapter presenting the trend setters at their work, the other presenting the forces that first have placed them in their position of influence and then have caused them to lose it.

Leaders and Followers of Fashion. The desire to lead and the desire to follow combine to make fashion. Although fashion moves with a predictable rhythm of alternate innovation and conformity, its changes are not necessarily related to practicality, and writers often erroneously attribute fashion trends to the whims of the Paris couture or to the desire of apparel manufacturers to force women to buy new clothes. The fact is, however, that fashion cannot be forced on women, and fashion designers are successful only when they look to see where women wish to go and then lead them there. To quote Carmel Snow, one of the great fashion editors of our time, "The direction of fashion change comes out of the air we breathe. Success in fashion design results from having a finger on the pulse of the times." Cecil Beaton, in his book *The Glass of Fashion,* explains fashion acceptance in a similar way, "When we take up the new, it is only because we have a secret need for it and have unconsciously prepared for it."

Women with a dominant desire to be leaders are the first to accept a new fashion. They are the individualists who have most successfully overcome their desire for the safety of standardization. A natural flair or sense of taste is stronger in some individuals than in others, and fashion leaders generally have strong natural taste. Their inborn fashion sense outweighs the habit of conformity to accepted standards characteristic of our day. They derive great satisfaction from being first and from being copied by others. This satisfaction can best be maintained by continually making changes, and thus a fashion leader is incessantly searching for innovations in order to maintain the satisfaction she derives from her position of leadership. She constantly strives to differentiate herself, while the members of her group who are less sure of their taste seek to copy her and thus identify themselves as fashionable. Fashion acceptance for the majority of women thus becomes the process of copying a group leader, for conformity and its concomitant social status. The minimum amount of acceptable fashion change each season is that in which fashion leaders can detect something new; the maximum amount of acceptable change is that which just falls short of being too alarming for the leaders to accept.

Natural Taste and Fashion Sensitivity. Our senses furnish us with the ability to react to our environment—to enjoy it when it is in "good taste," to be offended by it when it is not. Our senses become more acute and thus increase our capabilities for discrimination and enjoyment when they are sharpened by our reliance on them. They deteriorate and become dull when they are merely taken for granted. The eye, for example, develops a natural preference for things that are in harmony with the principles of proportion, balance, and unity when it is encouraged to look critically not only at paintings and sculpture, but also at home furnishings, apparel, window displays, and magazine advertising—always with the question, "Do I like it and, if so, why?"

THE EYE LIKES FASHION CHANGE. Sight is perhaps the most acute of our senses and is thus the most responsive to movement and change. Flames in a fireplace and clouds in the sky delight the eye with their constantly changing patterns of movement. Our senses become fatigued without the variety of change. The nose loses its sensitivity to any constant odor; the ear becomes deaf to an incessant sound; the tongue finds a constantly repeated taste increasingly tasteless. And the eye soon becomes indifferent to an unvaried stimulus and requires something different—a new look—to stimulate it. Everyone enjoys fashion change, but only the individualistic leaders dare to be different. From this group come the innovators, the designers who create new styles as well as the fashion leaders who make the new styles fashionable by their acceptance of them. A fashion can thus be defined as a style that is accepted by enough women to make deviation from it noticeable or obvious.

Pre-Couture Fashion. *In ancient and medieval times,* fashion as we know it was not a factor in women's lives because styles of women's clothes remained practically unchanged for centuries at a time. Changes in style of women's apparel did not begin to accelerate until the modern world began to evolve after the dark middle ages. Then voyages of discovery to unknown lands inhabited by strange races of people with different cultures, different customs, and different costumes brought a new restlessness to all phases of Western culture. During the Renaissance, as this period is now called, styles in dress began to change much more rapidly. As new things became available, more new things were desired. Nothing motivates change so well as change itself.

By the middle of the seventeenth century, Louis XIV had established the court of France and assumed leadership in the renaissance of culture. This "Grand Monarque," or "Sun King," as his subjects fondly called him, ruled for 70 years. He made France the chief political power in Europe and established Paris as the fashion capital of the world. He built a magnificent palace at Versailles and surrounded himself with the most interesting personalities of his time—all those who could paint well, write well, talk well, or look well were brought together to live at Versailles. This group became his "court," and those in his court were "in society" and became arbiters of taste. The French court thus became the epitome of all that was "in fashion." The queen and the women of distinction who made up her entourage, women of self-assurance

because of their exalted social position, were the first to accept and, by their acceptance, sponsor new fashions. Textile industries were built up in Lyons and other French cities to supply the court with tapestries and brocades, ribbons and laces, and dressmakers began to collaborate with these fabulous women of assured taste who presided at court and ruled fashion.

During the eighteenth century, the descendants of the Sun King ruled France. When Louis XIV died in 1715, his great grandson Louis XV became king. He was succeeded in 1774 by his grandson Louis XVI. The extravagances of the court during this century have been blamed for the French Revolution of 1789 in which Louis XVI followed his queen, Marie Antoinette, to the guillotine in 1794. Fashion changed in 1783, in response to a general revulsion against excess. The extravagant shepherdess costume with huge panniers was replaced by the slim Empire gown immortalized by David in his portrait of Madame Recamier.

At the beginning of the nineteenth century, Napoleon I became emperor of France. Under the leadership of his Empress Josephine, society remained society, as fashion continued to reflect the attire of the court. Finally, at the close of the reign of Napoleon III and his Empress Eugénie (1852–1870), the court phase of fashion leadership faded away, as at last the Third Republic of France replaced the monarchy, to reflect the growing tendency toward more liberal government throughout the Western world.

The Industrial Revolution, which had begun in the eighteenth century, was a strong positive force in broadening the social base on which fashion rested. Society began to include the wealthy industrial class whose newly acquired wealth enabled them to live as expensively as the members of the royal circles to which they sought access. Fashion became a status symbol for the *nouveau riche*. Paris in 1800 had long been the fashion capital of the world, and thus it was Paris that drew the wives of the increasingly wealthy industrialists, planters, and financiers from other European countries, England, and America. With their lavish patronage, the submissive dressmaker was replaced by or evolved into the couturier, who possessed not only creative imagination and exquisite taste, but also had a good head for business and a flair for showmanship. A dressmaker cut and sewed and fitted each garment; a couturier became the director of a salon and employed assistants who carried out his ideas. The "haute couture" of today is composed of these salons where made-to-measure tailoring for a select clientele is combined with the production of models for export.

The Beginning of the French Couture. Charles Frederick Worth was the first member of the French couture to gain wide recognition. Born an Englishman in 1826, he was forced by family reverses to quit school and go to work when he was only 11 years old. At 20 he left London for Paris where his working experience "in trade" enabled him to obtain within a short time a position as clerk in a good establishment, selling men's overcoats and ladies' accessories such as shawls. The mannequin who modeled the accessories for him was beautiful; they fell in love and were married. He began designing dresses for her which were made by the establishment's seamstress, who was employed to make up fabrics that were sold by the yard. His styles were admired by the customers who came to the store to select fabrics and have dresses made by the seamstress—all dresses in the one identical style for which she had a pattern. Worth began to sketch new ideas for the seamstress, the delighted customers brought their friends, and before long Worth became a partner in the establishment. He later went into business for himself. This is the story, in capsule form, of the beginning of the House of Worth, a story told in charming detail in a book written by the grandson of the founder.

THE HOUSE OF WORTH. Worth went into business for himself in 1860 at the age of 34. With the help of his beautiful and clever wife, who modeled for him, he attracted more and more socially prominent women as clients until at last Empress Eugénie wore his clothes. Such prestige attached to her patronage, both because of her position as empress and the elegance of her personal taste, that other members of the royalty throughout Europe and in England were anxious to be dressed by Worth. At one time his clientele included nine "crowned heads." Each season he prepared a book of exquisite hand-colored sketches to be sent to each of his royal clients—otherwise he did no advertising, nor did he need any. So anxious were women of society to be dressed by the same couturier who dressed royalty that he was able to select his clientele, turning away those who lacked the ability to wear his clothes with sufficient distinction. Styles were originated for the most exclusive of his clients and copied for the wives of wealthy businessmen, a class of society that grew tremendously with the industrialization that was taking place in the latter half of the nineteenth century.

CHARACTERISTICS OF THE ERA. Other couture houses opened in Paris, and by 1900 Paris set the styles for the continent, England, and North and South America. The wives of wealthy industrialists and planters as well as the great actresses of that era bought their entire wardrobes in the couture houses of Paris. For example, in 1896 four of the haute couture, including Worth and Paquin, each did a business of five million francs, or the equivalent of the amount of business done by Dior during his most successful years. Dresses in that era were made of unbelievably costly fabrics, trimmed with magnificent handmade laces and an enormous amount of elaborate detail. They were one-of-a-kind creations, requiring untold labor, each fitted to the individual wearer.

**Worth Gown from the
Brooklyn Museum Collection**

The Actress as Fashion Leader. After Worth *père* died in 1896, his sons, Jean and Gaston, continued in the House of Worth, successfully adapting their ways to the new era that was developing. The age of "elegance" had faded away. Life at court was no longer a reality. The actress began to replace the empress as fashion leader, with the couture houses competing for her business. Actresses of that era were women of great personal taste and magnetism who wore clothes superbly well. Their profession brought them before the public and thus offered the designers who dressed them excellent showcases for new fashion. The leading actresses at the turn of the century—Bernhardt, Réjane, Duse—commanded tremendous respect as actresses; they were personages of supreme glamor as well and their clothes thus had great influence. They recognized the contribution made by the couture to their appearance and gave credit to their designers in playbills and in photographs of them that appeared frequently in fashion magazines.

Dolls and Mannequins. When Worth started in business each dress was individually designed for each client, but during the latter half of the nineteenth century an innovation was introduced that brought a revolution to the fashion business—the making of certain models for export. To publicize these models, gowns were made in miniature for dolls. A doll thus dressed was shipped to London, for example, where orders for the model were taken and mailed back to the Paris house where the doll originated. The model was reproduced to the customer's measurements and mailed back to her in London. This was the first departure from the usual practice of showing the client fabrics and sketches from which she chose the fabric and the style in which the dress was to be made. From the beginning Worth had used a live mannequin—his beautiful wife—to display actual gowns for his clients to choose from in his salon. This practice was soon adopted by all the couture houses. The mannequins, however, came from the same working class as the seamstresses or midinettes. Until the 1920's the occupation of mannequin or model had no glamor. Exclusive Worth did not advertise in fashion publications as many of the other houses did, nor did he send mannequins to the races to show his clothes as was the accepted practice—the races at Longchamps taking on the function of a fashion show where mannequins paraded in the latest creations of the house that sponsored them, without regard for their suitability to the occasion.

The Demimonde and Fashion. The latter half of the nineteenth century is known as the Victorian Era because Queen Victoria was the titular head of the British Empire during the period of 1837–1901, when Great Britain was an extremely powerful nation, politically and economically. Extravagance and bad taste in art forms and the so-called "double standard" in behavior were characteristics of the Victorian Era. In Paris the double standard was exemplified by a frank acceptance of the demimonde (half world) of fabulous kept women. (This facet of society is delightfully explained in *Gigi*, a short novel by Colette, which was made first into a play and then into an enchanting film.) That Worth dressed some of the most famous of the demimondaine is an excellent example of French realism.

OTHER COUTURE HOUSES OF THE VICTORIAN ERA. The second great couture house to open in Paris was founded by a woman, Madame Cheruit, who was by birth a Levantine and the wife of a Paris banker. Next, Redfern immigrated to Paris from London and opened the House of Redfern in 1881. Madame Jeanne Lanvin opened her salon in 1890. She had begun her career informally by making such beautiful dresses for her own little daughter that people who saw them asked for copies for their own children. As her daughter grew, Madame Lanvin made clothes for older girls, and eventually for women. She was a lover of fine arts as well as a woman of great personal taste and elegance. She maintained her high position in the haute couture as long as she lived, being especially famed for her beautiful evening "robes de style." She was chosen by the French government in 1926 to act as the head of the Costume Pavilion for the great French Exposition of Culture held in Paris. Madame Lanvin's daughter, the Countess of Polignac, assumed management of the House of Lanvin at her mother's death in 1946, and it was she who brought Castillo, who previously had been with Elizabeth Arden in New York, to Paris to be the designer. The name of the house was then changed to Lanvin-Castillo. In 1960 this house was the oldest member of the French haute couture.

A number of other couture houses opened before the end of the nineteenth century, among them the House of Callot Soeurs in 1895. There were three Callot sisters, of whom Madame Gerber became the best known because she handled the designing. M. D. C. Crawford, of *Women's Wear Daily,* credits her with being the top fashion leader in Paris from 1900 until 1920 when the house closed, and says that she created the first draped skirt and "did more for the kimono sleeve than anyone outside Japan." Vionnet was to become her most illustrious pupil.

Another of the great couture houses that was headed by a woman was the House of Premet. Madame Premet was a woman of unerring taste who was patronized by the most fashionable women in Paris. Her designer, Madame Lafranc, shortened skirts in 1914 to the shortest they had ever been, a scandalous eight inches from the floor. Madame Lafranc was an original and gifted creator who died unfortunately just as she was gaining recognition. Madame Charlotte who replaced her lost out to Chanel as a trend setter although she had great success, especially with the *garçonne* type of dress so popular in the mid-1920's.

The Fashion Press and Trend Setters. During the Victorian Era, French and English fashion magazines began to flourish, *Godey's Lady's Book* being particularly famous. These fashion publications were the only sources of fashion information available to the great middle class of women who were not able to go to Paris.

Little dressmakers in small towns and large dressmaking establishments in cities reproduced for their clients the elegant and elaborate fashions shown in the magazines, fashions often altogether unsuited to the client's way of life since they copied the fashions suited to the leisurely existence of European royalty.

In New York the magazine *Vogue* began publication in 1894. As its name indicated, it gave women information on what was "in vogue." Reports on Paris fashion became a feature of *Vogue* in 1906, at first consisting only of descriptions of outfits seen by the reporter at fashionable restaurants, the theater, the opera, and at the races or on the Champs Elysées (the Fifth Avenue of Paris). Soon sketches accompanied the descriptions, but the couture house from which a gown came was never mentioned. Socially prominent women were photographed "at the races" or in studio portraits by the famous Baron de Meyer, but the source of their gowns was never divulged. The unwritten social dictum of that era demanded that nothing which could be construed as advertising should be connected with members of society. For this reason it is impossible to associate the members of the Paris couture with the gowns they designed before 1910, at which time they began to permit the fashion press to view their collections. From 1910 fashion magazines were able to report on designers and their collections, and thus made it possible to identify the designer who was setting the trend.

POIRET. The first member of the Paris haute couture who can be definitely established as a trend setter is Poiret. He introduced a new look in fashion and at the same time he introduced a new type of design personality. He did not merely design clothes for women, who up to that time were accustomed to having a certain amount of choice in what was designed for them.

Poiret "dressed" his clients, dictating to them, enslaving them, and thus completely enchanting them. When the press referred to him as the Sultan of Fashion, it was not an undeserved compliment.

Poiret's Training and Apprenticeship. Paul Poiret was born in Paris in 1880, in rather ordinary circumstances. As a child, he recounts in his frank autobiography, he was sensitive, literary, in love with the theater, to which he went every night, fond of poetry, and interested in women's clothes. When he finished secondary school, he was apprenticed to an umbrella maker where he was very unhappy. At night he spent his time sketching original designs and dressing a doll mannequin with scraps from the umbrella covers. He finally took his sketches to some of the couture houses, and one of them, Doucet, eventually hired him as a sketcher. In two years at Doucet he made enviable progress, but he was so unmanageable that he was fired. His final infraction of the rules occurred when he allowed the actress who was his mistress at that time to take his sketches for her gowns to a cheaper house to be made up. From Doucet, Poiret went into the army for the three years of military service required of all male citizens of French birth. When he returned to civilian status in 1901, he found a job at the House of Worth, then being directed by Jean and Gaston, the sons of the founder. Gaston, the practical one, hired Poiret to make a line of ordinary clothes or, as he expressed it, a department of "fried potatoes." Jean headed the department of "delicacies." Jean hated Poiret's little "tailor-mades," as he called them, which were so original, so bold, and so chic. In 1904 Jean apparently prevailed over Gaston and Poiret was fired.

Poiret Opens His Own Salon. Poiret's mother then lent him enough money to start a modest salon of his own. He decided to get married too and, to the surprise of everyone, he chose a country girl. He rapidly transformed his wife into one of the most stunning women in Paris—a marvelous showcase for his new and exciting creations. Her excellent slim figure required no corsets and with her to lead the way he proceeded "to liberate all women from their shackles of bone and steel," as he expressed it. His wife was always his best mannequin. Her rather oriental features and dark distinguished beauty were a perfect setting for the new look that he had created in fashion.

**Poiret's Minaret Silhouette
from Bon Ton Magazine, 1913**

Poiret's Philosophy of Fashion. With Poiret the elegance of chic simplicity began to replace the elegance of display that had been in vogue since the time of Louis XIV. Poiret expressed his philosophy of dress in an article published in *Vogue* in October 1913. "I feel satisfied if my garments give an impression of simple charm, when all of the details completely disappear in the general harmony of the whole. The ignorant mistake the rich for the beautiful, the costly for the elegant. I make war upon these glittering atrocities. To dress a woman is not to cover her with ornaments, it is to underline the meaning of her body and bring it out and magnify it, to envelop nature in a significant contour which accentuates her grace." Thus Poiret interpreted the change in the position of women and helped them in their emergence from the strictly ornamental position they had occupied to that time. He knew where they were going and was able to lead them there.

Poiret's Contributions to Fashion. Poiret was a man of broad interests, great imagination, and magnificent taste. He is generally credited with having the most original mind that the couture has produced. He traveled widely and was the first to take mannequins, rather than dolls, with him to show his clothes. He toured Europe with nine mannequins who made such a sensation in Russia that he kept them locked in their hotel rooms at night for safety. He made two trips to the United States and his unfavorable and often amusingly accurate descriptions of American customs make delightful reading. He lectured on fashion in various American cities and entranced his audiences by cutting garments from bolts of beautiful fabric and designing gowns on a live model as he spoke. When in 1913 he created the minaret or lampshade tunic and the hobble skirt, both their fashion acceptance and his fame were the greatest that any designer had ever experienced. At the beginning of the First World War, in September of 1914, he was called back into military service, where he spent a particularly unhappy time, being as he was a law unto himself and utterly unsuited to the discipline of army life. Since the occupation listed on his official army papers was "tailor," he was put to work repairing army uniforms. This was most unsuccessful, for Poiret could not sew. Instead he designed a new uniform for the French Army, requiring considerably less fabric and less labor than the one then in use, and eventually he was put in charge of the entire uniform production of the country. Still he was in constant difficulties due to his completely individualistic personality.

Poiret's Fall from Power. When at the end of the war Poiret returned to his position as head of the House of Poiret, he experienced great frustration because his clothes were no longer considered outstanding or even particularly smart. Fashion had changed during the war years. Chanel and jersey and the *garçonne* look infuriated him. He could not understand the new look and he was never able to regain his former position of dominance. His evening gowns, where his sense of oriental splendor could be utilized to advantage, were best. The extravagant costume balls that he gave at his magnificent villa received great publicity, but his fashion influence dwindled, his customers forsook him, and by the end of the 1920's he was forced to live on the charity of family and friends. He died a pauper in 1944.

Poiret's Influence. No couturier has ever equaled the influence that Poiret had over his generation, not only in apparel but in fabrics, interior decoration, and the art of living. He was a rarely and widely gifted man, an artist and an epicure in the grand fashion, a true genius whose benefits were reaped by others while he bore the expense. He was magnificently extravagant, with a passionate distaste for the ordinary. He introduced the kimono sleeve and the first modern straight-line dress. He loved color and revitalized the fabric industry by introducing new brilliant hues: cerise, purple, vermilion, emerald green, royal blue. He founded the Martine School for Crafts in Paris

in 1912, which added impetus to the new directions that were beginning to be felt in interior design, bringing it from a craft up to the status of an art. His fatal shortcoming seems to have been his inability to differentiate between actuality and the creations of his imagination. He was not a realist.

Poiret in New York, 1920
(Trend designs on pp. 68–69)

The history of fashion would certainly have been different had Poiret been able to continue his career instead of being forced into the army at the peak of his trend-setting popularity. His view of fashion was a mirror of his time—the transition period from elegance to simplicity. Whether he could have changed with the rapidly changing times and introduced the functional understated look that replaced his strong, colorful, rather oriental approach to fashion is doubtful. Designers with as strong an individual concept of fashion as he had generally are not able to retain a position of leadership after the rhythm of fashion change sets in. When Poiret was called to war, it was inevitable that someone else would replace him and set the trend of fashion, and it was Premet who achieved this status by audaciously shortening the skirts to 8 inches off the floor. This trend was so welcome, so suited to modern life, that skirts have never been long for any appreciable period since that time. Premet was not able to follow up her one great contribution, and it was Chanel who, by the end of the war in 1918, was the designer being copied by the other members of the couture.

CHANEL. Gabrielle Chanel was born in 1890. Her mother died when she was a baby and her father went off to America, leaving her in the care of two old aunts who raised horses for the French Army on a farm near Auvergne. This rural existence was not attractive to young Gabrielle and when at 15 she was permitted to visit her grandfather in the city of Vichy, she turned her footsteps toward Paris instead of returning to her old aunts in the country. Until Chanel writes the full account of her eventful life, most of the personal side of it will remain untold, although many colorful stories have been told about her. It is probable that she and a sister first opened a shop in Deauville, and that she first designed millinery. In a French fashion magazine of 1912, a hat is shown "designed by Gabrielle Chanel." During the first year of the war, she evidently moved to Paris, since sketches of her clothes are shown in *Vogue* in 1916, with captions implying that she was already well established and successful there.

Chanel and Jersey. One of a succession of illustrious friends of Chanel manufactured knitted jersey fabrics, and the story is that he allowed her free access to all the jersey that she wanted, and thus she popularized this fabric. That she started the trend for jersey is indicated by quips in *Vogue* such as "Chanel, Jersey & Co." or "soon it will be 'of-course-jersey'" that were used as captions for her clothes. Jersey was an accepted fabric before Chanel popularized it, according to M. D. C. Crawford of *Women's Wear Daily,* having been introduced by Lily Langtry who was the Marilyn Monroe of the

Gay Nineties. She named it for her home on the English island of Jersey. Certainly jersey was ideally suited to Chanel's understated fashions, and it has thus become known as her fabric.

Gabrielle Chanel, 1937
(Trend designs on pp. 69–70)

Chanel and Other Anecdotes. Another one of Chanel's illustrious friends was Archduke Dimitri of Russia, and her use of Russian embroidery is said to have resulted from this friendship. Russian and other oriental embroideries had been fashionable, however, since Bakst and the Russian Ballet had arrived in

Paris in 1909. Poiret had popularized them and it is doubtful that Chanel was unaware of this trend when she made the acquaintance of the Russian Archduke. Another nobleman, the English Duke of Sutherland, is said to have offered to divorce his wife if Chanel would marry him, to which she replied characteristically, "There are many English duchesses, but there is only one Chanel." In the mid-1920's, while vacationing in the perfume country in southern France, trying to recover from the shock of the sudden, untimely death of one of her boyfriends, Chanel was mixing various scents in one of the perfume factories to pass the time when she hit upon a mixture that exactly satisfied her. She christened it Chanel Number 5, because she considered 5 her lucky number, always, for example, holding her first showing each season on the fifth day of the month. Perhaps one reason that she has never joined the Paris Couture Syndicale is that this governing body sets the dates for its members' showings.

Chanel's Philosophy of Fashion. Chanel, always a law unto herself, also has always been her own best model. She is small and built like a boy. She was the prototype of the fashionable look in postwar Paris, with its flat-bosomed silhouette bounded by straight lines. This look in fashion was closely related to the cubist movement in art popular at that time. It was an innovation not copied from any previous period, an outward expression of the new freedom that women were winning for themselves. As Chanel expressed it, "Clothes do not matter. It is the way you look that counts." It was smart to look neither feminine nor rich. Simplicity was the keyword. Chanel's feeling of design suited the period perfectly, "Always dress to make yourself feel young—this means being free and easy and unpretentious in your clothes. You have to breathe and move and sit without being con-scious of what you have on." With Chanel-designed clothes, the wholesale apparel business thrived. Her simplified clothes lent themselves to mass production as the elaborate creations before her could not do. With Chanel the dressmaker went out and Seventh Avenue came in.

Chanel's Look Goes Out. In the 1920's, Chanel was the most successful designer in Paris. By 1923 she had lost out as trend setter because the type of understated smartness that she had brought to the pinnacle of fashion was inevitably replaced by a new trend. She continued to be marvelously successful long after her trend-setting days were over, although the direction of fashion moved further and further away from the look that made her famous. In 1939 when she felt that the trends were a contradiction of her ideal, she closed her establishment—permanently, it was presumed.

Chanel and Her Look Come Back. Fifteen years later, in 1954—the year that Dior brought out his famous A-line silhouette and fashion again fit in with Chanel's theory of what fashion ought to be—she made a comeback at the age of 64. The collection that she showed on February 5, 1954, picked up her own trend of fashion where she had dropped it in 1939; the same smart, understated, easy-to-wear look that had returned to fashion. Her first collection was not well received; only six of her garments were bought by American buyers. Bettina Ballard, then *Vogue* fashion editor, describes Chanel's comeback in her book, *In My Fashion.* She believed in Chanel, featured her collection in the Paris Report in *Vogue,* and again in her annual report at the Fashion Group Luncheon. Buyers and the press "discovered" Chanel in her fall collection, and by 1960 she was generally considered to be one of the three great forces in the Paris couture—the other two being Balenciaga and Saint-Laurent.

MADELAINE VIONNET. A designer's designer rather than a trend setter, Madelaine Vionnet stands between Poiret and Chanel chronologically. She too was French by birth, married and moved to England when she was 18 years old, had a child who died at birth, divorced her husband, and began her fashion career in a London workroom. At 20 she returned to Paris where she continued working as a midinette in the workroom of Doucet. Later she went to Callot Soeurs where under the direction of the great Madame Gerber she showed so much talent that she rose to the high position of head fitter and eventually was sent to manage the branch of Callot Soeurs in London. Finally, after fifteen years' apprenticeship, Vionnet opened her own salon in Paris in 1914. The timing of this venture was unfortunate, however, since war was declared in August of that year. Her finances were not sufficient to withstand the war's generally depressing effect on business, and she was forced to close. During the war years she toured Italy where she became acquainted with the art and architecture and culture of that country. Then in 1919, when she was 40 years of age, she reopened her salon in Paris.

Vionnet's Contributions. At first Vionnet designed for a private clientele. The first Vionnet sketches appeared in *Vogue* in 1920 with the caption, "The rare art of exclusive Vionnet." Almost at once she became the designer by whom other designers were inspired, as she was one of the most originally creative spirits ever to work in fashion. Her greatest contribution was the bias cut. Before Vionnet, garment pieces were normally cut on lengthwise grain of a fabric. (With bias cuts lengthwise grain runs on the diagonal.) Vionnet made other innovations, many of them developed from the principle of the bias cut, such as the asymmetrical neckline, the halter neckline, the cowl neckline, and the skirt with handkerchief points which at the time of its greatest vogue appeared in the collection of every couture house in Paris. She made the first costume in which the lining of the coat was made from the same fabric as the dress. Her first great success was the dress that slipped on over the head without benefit of hooks and eyes—the zipper did not appear as a fastener for dresses until 1934. Her "success" dress was made of a new fabric, crepe de chine, and it had no lining, depending on cut alone to give it shape. The flapper look of the 1920's had its inception in this new approach that Vionnet brought to dressmaking.

Vionnet in New York, 1924
(See dress on p. 67)

Vionnet's Philosophy of Fashion. Vionnet was a great dressmaker, whereas the trend setters, Poiret and Chanel, who were her contemporaries, were great stylists. They wanted to dress all women and had great understanding of the value of publicity as a fashion force. Vionnet completely lacked a sense of publicity, made war on style piracy, refused to sell to the trade, and apparently had no desire to be a trend setter. In later years she developed such a fear of being copied that it was virtually impossible for the fashion magazines to borrow her clothes for photographs and thus give her collections the coverage that they deserved. Vionnet's philosophy, quoted by Anny Latour in her delightful book, *Kings of Fashion,* is that "Any season's models are suited only to a few women, others look ridiculous and thus must be dressed individually. Ideal dress brings the body and its movements into harmony. Harmony is possible only when one obeys the rhythm peculiar to the fabric, whether the weave is straight or on the bias. Fashion is an empty word to a real dressmaker. With each new alteration of the feminine ideal of beauty, I strive to find new harmonic variations of a given theme."

Vionnet's Influence. Vionnet, a square, sturdily built woman whose physical appearance gives little hint of the grace and charm that she puts into her designing, nonetheless has the spirit of a true artist. She has been responsible more than any other single designer for the simplified architectural structure of modern fashion. In 1960 six of her protégés or assistants were recognized members of the haute couture, Balmain and Griffe perhaps the most illustrious. When the German army occupied Paris at the beginning of the Second World War, the 60-year-old Vionnet closed her salon. Since that time she has lived in quiet retirement, respected by the entire couture. She is seldom seen in public except at the openings of her protégés, where a place of honor is always reserved for her. Vionnet worked out her designs in fabric on a half-size dress form, rather than making sketches, as is the more common couture practice. Her cuts were usually so intricate that it was impossible to copy them without ripping apart the garments. Her complete understanding of bias enabled her to fit her clothes so subtly that the suggestion of the hip or the shadow of the bust was implied, but never accentuated. Her bias cuts did not cling anywhere. There was a beautiful understated swing to her daytime clothes and an equally beautiful and statuesquely sculptured drape to her magnificent evening gowns. Her influence was apparent in all the other collections for the 20 years that she was a member of the haute couture.

Vionnet's philosophy of fashion, like Balenciaga's who was to follow her, lacked the ingredient of showmanship necessary for a trend setter. She designed from within herself, and then the other more worldly designers took her ideas and from them distilled their exciting new looks, adding that dash of daring that new fashion requires.

A new look in fashion generally arrives when the silhouette has shifted away from the look that established its designer in his position of dominance. At this critical moment some other member of the haute couture, who has greater sensitivity to the newly evolving silhouette than the originator of its prototype, is able to present a "new look" with greater validity and stronger appeal. An example of this turn of events occurred in 1921. Chanel lengthened the skirt but could not change the proportion of her silhouette to go with it. Patou understood the new proportion and displaced her as trend setter.

JEAN PATOU. After an apprenticeship in his father's leather business, Jean Patou switched to the dress business, opening his own couture salon in 1914. He was forced to close after a few months because he, like Poiret, was called to fight in the First World War, where he served with gallantry in the Near East. Like Vionnet, he reopened his salon in 1919. He had already made something of a reputation before the war and he continued to build on that success, soon becoming one of the most financially successful of the Paris couture. He alone was able to afford to have his own fabrics woven especially for him. His collections were always well received particularly by the American buyers who loved his chic, softly tailored look. He had a fine sense of design and also understood the value of publicity. He is credited with having done more to encourage American apparel manufacturers then getting started on Seventh Avenue than any other member of the French couture. It was Patou who in 1921 initiated the custom of inviting the press to a preview on the evening before he officially opened his collection to the buyers. Showing to the press has since become the established custom in Paris and elsewhere, although in recent years buyers, wholesalers, and the press all attend the same showings.

Patou's Flapper Look. Patou was tall, handsome, and gracious. He was also considered the best-dressed man in Europe in the 1920's. His brilliant gesture of inviting the press to preview his collection brought him rich rewards in the way of fashion publicity. Like the trend setters before him, he lived in the spirit of his time and designed clothes that captured it in a vital and exciting way. Skirts were lengthened in 1921. Patou relocated the waistline in 1922, and strengthened the silhouette with sharp accents and straighter lines. In 1924 he forecast his fa-

mous flapper look by accentuating the hipline in a still stronger way and showing shorter skirts with uneven hemlines. In 1925 he made his fashion forecast a reality by raising the hemline to an unheard-of, astronomical 18 inches. The new look of the flaming flapper had arrived. Chanel's look of boyish simplicity was superseded by the excitement of exaggeration that Patou was able to give to the Vionnet-inspired dress that slipped on over the head.

Patou and American Mannequins
(Trend designs on pp. 70–71)

Patou Brings American Mannequins to Paris. Patou visited the United States in 1924 on a trip that produced one of the most brilliant publicity stunts ever executed. In New York, with the expert help of *Vogue* editor Edna Woolman Chase, he selected six American society girls, trained them as mannequins, and took them back to Paris to show his clothes. Until this time all mannequins had been from the working class, having neither social background nor familiarity with the type of women who made up the clientele of the Paris couture. The American girls created a sensation in Paris. Their natural grace and charm, vitality and lack of self-consciousness were a complete contrast to the studied mannerisms of the undistinguished,

42

middle-class girls who modeled in the French salons. The American girls were not only chic and beautiful, they were socially presentable. They made such a social success and married so rapidly that two years later a second group was imported from America to act as replacements. This was the beginning of modeling as the glamorous career it is today, supplanting as it has the glamor of the chorus girl of the pre-Patou era.

In 1927 Patou began to lengthen skirts, employing the standard device of the uneven hemline to accustom the eye to a longer look. The handkerchief-point skirt of Vionnet served this purpose beautifully and by 1929 skirts were down to 8 inches off the floor. When Premet had raised skirts to this height in 1914, she scandalized the world. Now 15 years later, women complained that skirts were too long and declared that they would never go back to that "old style." Within six months however, the short skirt was definitely out. In the process of naturally evolving fashion change, Patou raised the waistline to its normal position, and a new silhouette began to emerge. Patou understood the long-waisted look so well that while it was in fashion no other designer had been able to replace him as trend setter. The normal waistline, however, required a different sensitivity to fashion, a sensitivity that Patou lacked. The designer who best represented it was Schiaparelli.

SCHIAPARELLI. Much more is known about this great personage of the fashion world than about either Chanel or Vionnet, because Schiaparelli has written a delightful account of her rise to fame, called *Shocking Life,* in which she comes alive as a truly fascinating personality. The "shocking" of the title is taken, of course, from one of her great contributions to fashion, the color shocking pink, which she named and popularized. She then used "Shocking" as a name for her most famous perfume. It is perhaps the word that best symbolizes her era, when to be shocking was to be smart.

Schiaparelli's Early Life. Elsa Schiaparelli was born in Rome. Her family were reasonably well-to-do professional people. Her father was a scholarly man, her uncle a great astronomer, her antecedents rather international, with relatives in other parts of Europe and in Egypt. From her own account she was always individualistic and irrepressible. At 14 she wrote a book of love poems that was published and received enough publicity to embarrass her conservative family. She studied painting and sculpture and was well-enough accomplished in these fine arts that Chanel once referred to her as "that Italian artist who makes dresses." On a trip to London in 1917, when she was in her early twenties, Schiaparelli met and married, in rapid succession, an attractive young man whom she heard lecturing on theosophy. They came to the United States on a honeymoon. Their finances soon dwindled and the husband, who was attractive to women generally, drifted away. In June of 1919, when their daughter was born, Schiaparelli was alone in New York and so poor that she lived in one small room in Greenwich Village and used an orange crate for the baby's crib. She became friends with some well-to-do people who helped her financially so that when the child, whom she named Gogo, developed infantile paralysis she was able to return to Paris and to get the necessary medical aid for little Gogo.

Her Taste Leads Her to a Fashion Career. In Paris Schiaparelli gravitated to the group of creative artists always associated with the "Left Bank." She worked briefly with some of them who were antique dealers, where her fine background in Italian art and her exquisite taste were at once apparent. One of her well-to-do friends who was a client of Poiret took her along to one of her fittings there, and she was greatly impressed with his exotic evening gowns. He in turn was so impressed with Schiap—as she became known—that he gave her an evening coat that she particularly admired, saying, "With your supreme style sensitivity, you could wear anything, anywhere." In dressing herself she expressed the epitome of fashion for her era and, like Chanel, she was always her own best model. Her fashion sensitivity launched her in the dress business.

Schiaparelli's First Great Success—A Sweater. A friend whom she had met in the United States came to visit her one day wearing an interesting sweater, hand-knitted with an unusual "steady" look. Schiap immediately went to the Armenian peasant woman who had created it, taking an original design that she had sketched to get a sweater made for herself. Her sketch showed a large white bow on the front of the sweater, as if a scarf had been tied around the neck. The first attempt at developing this design was dreadful, the second sweater turned out to be so small that it would have fit Gogo, but the third try was a complete success, and when Schiap wore it to a smart luncheon she was mobbed. From an admiring American buyer she took an order for 40 sweaters with coordinated skirts, promising delivery within 10 days. It took all of Schiap's persuasive powers, business know-how, and inborn impudence to get the order completed on time, but when she delivered it she was launched into the apparel-design business, with more orders than she could possibly fill. She made only black sweaters with white motifs her first season and fostered a fad that swept the fashion world. Anita Loos, whose *Gentlemen Prefer Blondes* had made her world famous

the preceding year (1926), became the first of a succession of celebrities to wear Schiap's audacious improvisations, through which both they and she profited. Of Anita Loos she says generously, "I was tossed to fame with her help."

Schiaparelli's Fashion Philosophy. Dadaism and futurism were the art movements then in their heyday. Schiap's sweater designs fitted in perfectly with these surrealistic expressions, one of which, for example, looked like an x-ray view of the chest, with white ribs outlined on black background. Schiap was much influenced by surrealism. Dali became one of her close friends, as were the artists Vertes and Berard. Their influence is apparent throughout her career in fashion. When she first opened her salon in 1927, she called it "Pour Le Sport," and she specialized in what came to be classified as spectator sportswear. Three years later, in 1930, she became the trend setter, truly typifying the spirit of her time. Suits were always the backbone of her collections, beautifully and simply cut, with strong bold accents of color and mad surrealistic buttons that were made for her by Jean Schlumberger, who later became famous as a designer of fine jewelry in fantastic settings. Schiap started the fad for gadgets. Her daring nonsense—fish buttons, fox-head gloves, newspaper-print scarves, a hat shaped like an upsidedown shoe with a shocking-pink velvet heel—these and a thousand other mad amusing ideas were just right for those last, frivolously extravagant, decadent years before the Second World War. She launched more novelties than any other designer. She was first to use zippers and first to use synthetic fabrics and rough-textured fabrics for dresses. She originated the "tailored" evening dress with its own jacket, which she considers the most successful dress of her career. Her genius for publicity was unrivaled in her day, and perhaps has been matched by no one except Dior. Her philosophy was exactly opposite that of Vionnet. As stated in her own words, "All the laws about protection from copyists are useless. The moment people stop copying you, it means you are no good and have ceased to be news. The restrictions defeat themselves." She was a complete realist, believing that "To live successfully in the modern world, one is obliged to recognize mediocrity."

Schiaparelli and Gogo, 1939
(Trend designs on pp. 71–72)

Schiaparelli's New Look. When Schiap entered the fashion world, shoulders were natural and had been so since the early years of the century when Poiret introduced the kimono sleeve. Schiap set about widening shoulders as soon as she was established. With the waistline at its normal position the wider shoulder was acceptable, and by using bold, contrasting scarves and bows at the neck, she moved the center of interest from the hipline to shoulder level. She broke shoulder width with the contrasting color of her ever-present scarf, and thus gradually forced a broadening of the shoulder line. By 1930 the fashion press was reporting a trend toward wider shoulders. Schiaparelli became the trend setter, and, in 1933 when the new look officially came in, most of the Paris couture showed broad shoulders in their collections. Schiaparelli's were the most spectacular. She used gathers, cartridge pleats, padding, braid, aigrettes—anything decorative—to accentuate shoulder width.

Schiaparelli's Influence. Chanel understood the boyish look best; Patou understood the flapper look best; and Schiaparelli understood the hard chic of the mannish look best. She made provocative original clothes for the woman who wanted to look smart rather than pretty. One press report in 1933 expressed her dominance thus: "The hard, highly individual chic of her clothes stands out like a beacon, making the rest of the couture look pretty and characterless." A study of the fashion magazines of that era shows the statement to be entirely correct. She changed the outline of fashion from soft to hard, from vague to definite. Her clothes were so photogenic, because of their sureness of line and boldness of design, that they were always in the forefront of the fashion magazines, often to the dismay of the other members of the haute couture. One lead line, for example, illustrates the excitement of her collections, "Schiap's collection is enough to cause a crisis in the vocabulary."

Her Contribution to Fashion. Schiaparelli traveled adventurously and was inspired by all of the places she visited, collecting unusual ideas and mementos which she translated into smart fashion without any of their native artiness. She inspired the artisans of Paris to make for her the most original bags, costume jewelry, belts, and scarves, and she established the first "boutique," where they were so madly and extravagantly displayed that it became one of the tourist attractions of Paris. She invented the dinner suit, the evening sweater, dinner slacks, and separates in general which she sold in her boutique. She writes that her inspiration in design came more often from the working classes than from more fashionable sources because, as she explains it, "their clothes are dictated by comfort and necessity." She believed that to be well dressed a woman's appearance should be suited to her way of life, her occupation, her loves, her pocketbook. She tried to help each woman find her type, always meeting her clientele personally and studying them at first hand, and on occasion turning them away because she felt her clothes did not suit them. She returned to the United States during the Second World War, lectured on fashion and tried to keep the spirit of the French couture from being extinguished by the war. She had remained an important member of the couture up to that time, although her dominance as a trend setter waned in the mid-1930's. After the war she was unable to compete with the new look that Dior brought to women and finally went out of business, her boutique closing in 1950.

New Leaders of Fashion. THE INTERNATIONAL SET.

Between the two world wars, a new breed replaced actresses as fashion leaders. They formed the small socially elite international set who had excellent taste as a rule and unlimited incomes with which to exercise it. They became dictators of a luxurious and capricious way of life. Their headquarters was Paris and their leadership was dependent on their ability to make other women follow the way they dressed, entertained, and talked, and to make the places and the people they preferred fashionable. The antithesis of the women of wealth and fashion in the Victorian Era, they enjoyed being photographed in the clothes of the haute couture and thus acted as willing advertisements for their favorites. The new status symbol of society came to be a place on the annual list of the ten best-dressed women in international society, of which they were the charter members.

In the mid-1930's the two leading male designers in Paris were Molyneux and Mainbocher, neither of whom was French. Captain Edward Molyneux was an Englishman who followed in the successful footsteps of Worth and Redfern by opening a salon in Paris. From his first collection in 1919, he was successful. He made smart, rather tailored clothes that looked and were very expensive. His American counterpart, Mainbocher, made the same type of chic, understated clothes. Both men were immensely popular with the American buyers, although Molyneux was better established, having been in business 10 years longer than Mainbocher. It was inevitable that Schiaparelli should be superseded by another trend setter. It could have been either of these two who took her place, and in 1936 Mrs. Wallis Simpson made the choice when she named Mainbocher as her favorite designer. Thus he designed the trousseau for the most noteworthy wedding of the century, when Mrs. Simpson married Edward VIII, the erstwhile British monarch who told the entire world over radio that he was giving up his throne "for the woman I love." The Duchess of Windsor, or "Wallie" as she became known to readers of the tabloids, chose Mainbocher as her designer simply because she believed that his clothes had the fashion-right look for her. Fashion leaders, of whom she is an excellent example, do not submissively accept a fashion. Their fashion sensitivity gives them an instinctive feeling for the fashion that is right for them and their times, and other women willingly accept their leadership. Fashion followers make fashion by their acceptance of it. Because of Wallis Simpson's fashion sensitivity, Mainbocher became the trend setter and the wedding dress that he designed for her was the most copied dress of the era.

The Duke and Duchess of Windsor
married in France, 1937

MAINBOCHER. James Main Bocher (his true name) is an American, born in 1891. He grew up and attended public school in Chicago. He showed talent in both music and art as a child, and for some years seemed undecided as to which career to follow. He first attended the Chicago Academy of Fine Arts and then he went to the Art Students League in New York City. Switching to music at the age of 20, he studied for three years in Paris and Munich. When the war broke out in 1914, he returned to New

York and worked again at fashion drawing until the United States entered the war in 1917. He returned to France with an American ambulance unit, and later worked there in the Secret Service until the war ended. Again he went back to his music and continued his studies abroad. On the night of his debut as a singer in 1921, his voice failed. Finally, he turned once more to fashion sketching after his singing career thus ended before it began. He worked first as an illustrator on the Paris edition of *Harper's Bazaar,* then on Paris *Vogue* where he advanced rapidly to become the brilliant editor of the Paris edition, a position he held for six years. In 1929 he left the magazine and devoted a year to teaching himself how to cut and drape and pin and fit, according to his own account.

Mainbocher as a Paris Designer. In 1930 Mainbocher opened his salon in Paris, financed by a group of distinguished ladies. From the first he was successful, being especially well liked by Americans who were happy to accept his look of quiet, expensive, ladylike elegance and who were of course proud that an American had joined the Paris haute couture. Mainbocher, because of his long years inside the fashion magazine world, understood the value of publicity. He was promotion-minded as well as literate, and he was always able to express his fashion philosophy in quotable form as well as to prepare a collection of fashion-right models. He had an acute fashion sense and a brilliant fashion mind. His wit was razor sharp and delightful, as illustrated by such quotations as "I have never tried to make a woman look like anything but a woman since I have a hunch that sex is here to stay," or "I veer away from exaggeration which always tends to be tiresome and dates very quickly. Subtlety is another and more lasting message," or "I am not interested in new looks or copies of old ones."

Mainbocher as a New York Designer. Mainbocher's membership in the Paris haute couture was cut short by the Second World War, when in 1939 he was forced to close his Paris salon. He returned to New York, opening a custom salon on 57th Street, and he continues to design the most expensive made-to-order clothes in New York for the most important fashion leaders who treasure the clothes he creates for them and are proud to wear them for five or even ten years because they are always smart—never dated. In the interviews that Mainbocher has given to the press over the years his fashion philosophy is clearly stated. "The well-dressed woman does not wear anything she does not understand." "The well-dressed woman always appears to have forgotten what she is wearing." "I try to design clothes that are related to life and to the body, believing as I do that my job is to establish a liaison between designing and living." At a party given for Mainbocher by the Paris couture, Dior toasted the honored guest thus, "We are all of us equals, but Mainbocher is in advance of us all for he does it in America."

Mainbocher and a Selection of His Clothes, 1961
(Trend designs on p. 72)

BALENCIAGA. When Vionnet closed her salon in 1939, this greatest of all dressmakers was replaced on the pedestal of fashion by Balenciaga, the greatest of all tailors, who had opened his salon in Paris in 1937. The life story of Cristobal Balenciaga is the story of a poor boy who rose to fame, the Horatio Alger story of the couture. Balenciaga was born in the Spanish seacoast town of San Sebastian in 1895. His mother became a seamstress after his father, a fishing-boat captain, was lost at sea, and she taught Balenciaga to sew. In his early teens Balenciaga attracted the patronage of the wealthy Torres family by admiring a beautifully made suit that one of the women of the family was wearing as he saw her leaving the cathedral on a Sunday. The woman was so intrigued when the boy told her that he could make a copy of the suit—a Paris model—if he had the fabric that she provided the fabric and allowed him to try. The result was so astonishingly good that she found him an apprentice position in a couture shop in Madrid where he learned the fundamentals of fine dressmaking and tailoring. Of course, he did not remain as an assistant for long. As early as the mid-1920's he had three shops of his own—in Madrid, in Barcelona, and in his home town of San Sebastian. (Under the name Eisa, these salons still dominate the Spanish couture.) Balenciaga made regular trips to Paris for fine fabrics and models to be copied in his salons, and Chanel was his favorite Paris source of models. The Spanish Civil War, which began in 1936, so curtailed business in Spain that he went to Paris and, operating on very limited capital, established his headquarters there.

Balenciaga Joins the Paris Couture. Balenciaga was forced to borrow money to bring out his first Paris collection in 1937. He worked fanatically to make it a success for he realized his future in Paris depended on its acceptance. His capacity for hard work has been one of the dominant qualities of his entire life. He worships perfection, shuns publicity, has never had time for casual relationships or for superficialities. He is a master tailor and the only member of the postwar couture who can actually make every model he shows, were that necessary. He never sees any of his private customers, who include the most elegant women of international society, and he avoids galas and other big social events. His life is his work. His standards are meticulous and he hates cheapness in any form, which he calls *"cursi,"* a Spanish word meaning vulgar and clumsy. He believes that "no designer can make an unchic woman chic," and he disapproves of customers who order clothes that are not right for them or who order more clothes than they need.

Balenciaga's Fashion Influence. Balenciaga has never followed any fashion trend but his own. He designs from within himself, according to his own sensitivity to fashion. He gradually changes his silhouette and, from studying his collections over the seasons, it appears that about every seven years his silhouette changes —at the same rhythmic pace as fashion generally. The difference is that Balenciaga is always ahead of the other designers. In 1945, for example, he was making suits that hugged the rib cage and curved in a stiffened form over the hips. They were the forerunners of the suits that Dior brought out as the New Look in 1947, and became the standard formula for suits until, in 1949, Balenciaga showed jackets mildly fitted in front and loose in back, a silhouette that Dior popularized as the A-line in 1954. When Balenciaga showed his first Paris collection in 1937, Carmel Snow, then editor of *Harper's Bazaar,* immediately recognized his great genius and over the following years she always tried to give him the critical acclaim that he deserved. She describes him as "a gentle-voiced Spaniard, with a quick intimate smile that he has never used to express anything but true pleasure. He has inspired devotion from everyone who knew or worked for him through the years." His reticence, so unsuited to trend setting, never permitted him to cooperate fully with the fashion press. Few of his models are ever shown in fashion magazines because he does not allow more than two garments to be photographed for any magazine issue, and those are always of his choosing. In later years he has recognized the importance of models for export and has permitted line-for-line copying by American manufacturers. His designs are always among the most popular of all that are thus produced.

Cristobal Balenciaga, 1952

Balenciaga's Fashion Philosophy. Like Chanel, Balenciaga makes clothes in which women can be comfortable, move in, and get on and off with a minimum of effort. Always a student of art, he understands the use of source material and reflects it in sound and unified design. He uses as few seams as possible and adds as little trimming as possible. He likes black —black with white, black with beige, black with yellow, black with black. He also loves the colors native to his own country of Spain—the brownish red of Spanish earth, the grayish green of the olive trees, the vivid red of the bull ring. He uses lace and ribbon bows often and always with the greatest sophistication. His clothes are never "pretty." He prefers plain necklines, unpadded bosoms, a look of ease. His dresses differ little season to season but never seem to go out of fashion. He is such a master of "proportioned cut," as he calls it, that his garments fit a woman either a size or two larger or smaller than the one for whom they are made.

Balenciaga's Personality. The House of Balenciaga had been open but two years when the war began and the Germans occupied Paris. Because he was a Spaniard, he was less harassed by the German occupation than the French houses. Since the world had never been of great importance to him, he was really not much affected by the war, and he continued to design with complete self-sufficiency and self-motivation. He has always been deaf to praise, never satisfied and never elated by success. After a collection he is wrung out and depressed and generally goes to Switzerland where he eats simple food and enjoys the sun, protected from the public by dark glasses and by a doctor friend of long standing who generally accompanies him. Balenciaga is exceedingly restless when not lost in work, and he moves from place to place, making impromptu decisions, seemingly unable to find peace or pleasure in relaxation. His one hobby is antique collecting and his houses in Spain and France are filled to overflowing. Carmel Snow, in her own interesting life story, takes credit for introducing young Givenchy to Balenciaga who became his friend and advisor, recognizing in the brilliantly creative Frenchman a kindred spirit. When Givenchy opened his own salon in 1952, he chose a location almost across the street from Balenciaga on avenue George-V. Balenciaga generally is given credit for helping Givenchy to achieve the great success that he has enjoyed, and Givenchy in turn has supported his mentor in his refusal to join the Paris Couture Syndicale and to hold their seasonal openings at times set by this governing body. Givenchy's acceptance of Balenciaga's philosophy of withdrawal undoubtedly contributed to his exclusion from the trend-setting position he might have achieved at the death of Dior.

The War Curtails Fashion. When Mainbocher became trend setter in the mid-1930's, he brought a more feminine look to fashion, with a tight midriff and fuller hemline that called for shorter skirts. How this trend might have developed cannot be known because the Second World War cut short his trend-setting influence in the same way that the First World War had forced Poiret out of his position of fashion leadership. The Second World War began in August 1939 and the German army invaded France the following spring. Paris, choosing to be occupied rather than leveled by bombs, escaped war damage but was occupied by the Germans from 1940 until the Americans marched in victoriously to end the occupation in 1944. During this long grim period, the French couture banded together under the leadership of Lucien Lelong, who was then President of the Paris Couture Syndicale, to prevent being broken up and sent to Berlin as Hitler desired in his effort to make Berlin

rather than Paris the cultural center of the world. Americans were not able to go to Paris during the "occupation," but many of the Paris couture houses remained open and did business with Germany and its allies and with the neutral countries of Europe, recognizing that the only way to survive the war was to keep their workers together and stay in business. The spirit of resistance in Paris was magnificent and the workers in the couture endured great privation and suffering. There were practically no fabrics to work with, no trimmings, no heat in winter, and miserable food the year around.

Although the United States did not enter the war until December 1941, the lack of communication with Paris and the lack of imported fabrics and models was felt immediately. In 1940 *Vogue* began reporting fashion "straight from the New York Openings," a practice that was continued throughout the war years. It was not until 1946 that buyers and the press were able to go again to Paris for the great biannual openings held in February and September. During this war period, New York was the fashion capital of America, and fashion magazines and retail stores, such as Lord and Taylor, began to promote American designers. Claire McCardle emerged as one of the greatest of these. Another was Norman Norell, who has gone on to match the Paris couture in the elegance he brings to fashion and to the acceptance accorded his clothes by fashion leaders. But no American was able, during the war years, to become a trend setter. At the end of the war the silhouette was just about where it was at the beginning of the war—the same exaggerated shoulders, perhaps a bit more grotesquely padded, the same cinched-in waist, and the same short, skimpy skirt, now a bit shorter.

The war had brought regulations to the apparel industry, limiting the amount of fabric in a garment to 3½ yards and the width of a skirt to 64 inches, for example. Because of restrictions on the mills, fabrics that were available were neither inspired nor inspiring. But perhaps the greatest restriction on fashion was the general lack of interest in it. Most women were doing war work of one type or another and wearing uniforms, or were working in factories and wearing work clothes. All were more interested in war news than in fashion news. Fashion came to a virtual standstill because the millions of average women who make fashion by accepting fashion changes that are right for the times were temporarily uninterested in this normally most fascinating of topics. The war years in Paris, like the war years in America, were unproductive of significant fashion change. The designers there were curtailed in every way and were barely able to remain in business, and of course many were forced to close. The mills were unable to supply fabric, the artisans upon whom the French couture relied for their wonderfully creative trimmings were unable to get materials to work with, and finally the couture houses were unable to get publicity because the fashion press was able to function only in a very feeble way. A world at war is not attuned to the esthetic pleasures of life. Survival comes first.

The Paris Couture Reopens. When in 1946 it was possible for the American reporters and buyers to return to Paris, there was doubt in both Paris and America whether Paris could regain her position of fashion supremacy. Many of the couture houses were unable to reopen, others were barely in operation. Workers had been forced into other jobs and fabric houses were as yet unable to supply the luxury fabrics so important to the haute couture. Momentum was far from its prewar standard and the first showings were, on the whole, disappointing. Lelong had the most exciting collection and he

proudly introduced his designer to the American press. His name was Christian Dior, "an unknown, pink-cheeked man with an air of extreme shyness," as described by Bettina Ballard, *Vogue* fashion editor.

ENTER DIOR. The success of Dior's collection brought him to the attention of Marcel Boussac, one of the wealthiest industrialists in France, who had gotten his start toward success in the cotton-textile business. Pierre Balmain, who had been a friend and associate of Dior at Lelong, had opened his own salon with good success the previous year, and when Boussac offered to back the venture with practically unlimited funds, Dior was encouraged to follow his example. Dior was 42 years old when he purchased his salon on the avenue Montaigne, and nothing he had done in his previous life forecast the astonishing organizational ability that he displayed from that moment forward. He gathered an impressive staff of assistants and workers, collected and trained mannequins, decorated the salon, and designed a magnificent first collection, all within less than a year's time.

Dior's Early Life. Christian Dior was born in 1905 and was brought up in the way that was considered proper for the upper-middle class of Paris to which his family belonged. In the 1920's he became a partner in a small modern-art gallery and thus became acquainted with many of the leading French artists of the day, such as Vertes and Berard, who in later years were proud to claim his acquaintance. His family lost their money in the great depression of the early 1930's and Dior, forced to earn his living, took up fashion sketching. The editors of both Paris *Vogue* and *Harper's Bazaar* encouraged him. At one time he did a page of fashion sketches for *Weekly Figaro, Illustrated.* From 1937 to 1939 he worked as a sketcher for Piguet, a member of the haute couture, and has always given

Piguet credit for teaching him the fundamental "art of suppression" of unnecessary detail. When the war began he was called into the army, but poor health forced him back into civilian life, and he spent two years at the home of his family in the country. He returned to Paris in 1942, called back by Piguet, but was so slow in arriving in Paris that Piguet, unable to delay indefinitely, hired someone else—the young Robert Givenchy who was later to become the protégé of Balenciaga. Dior found work almost at once, however, at the House of Lelong where Pierre Balmain, the former protégé of Vionnet, was the

designer. Lelong was devoting his entire effort to keeping the French couture from dwindling to nothing or, equally unbearable, being broken up and sent to Berlin. Thus it was that at the end of the war Dior was designing for Lelong, and Lelong, being the great public-spirited person that he was, and more interested in promoting the French fashion industry as a whole than his own House of Lelong, encouraged Dior to take the opportunity offered by Boussac.

Dior and the New Look. The life blood of Paris has always been the great French fashion industry, and all of Paris had high hopes for the new House of Dior, financed as it was by the immensely wealthy Boussac. At the opening there was a near riot. *Vogue* reported, "It was a polished theatrical performance such as we had never seen in a couture house before." The stage was set for a smashing success and Dior outdid all expectations as the New Look came in. The collection contained one stunning success after another, modeled by mannequins who even showed the clothes in a new and exciting theatrical way. And only at Dior could the New Look be found. The inner construction of the clothes gave a completely new contour to the figure. How he achieved it was a mystery. Regardless of the shape of the individual, the shaping that Dior built into his New Look collection prevailed. Even on a hanger the New Look maintained its superiority and the garment its firm shape. Entire new industries sprang into existence to furnish the interlining materials upon which the New Look depended. Dior's dream of "saving women from nature" was realized. Meanwhile his name became a household word, synonymous with the Paris couture and high fashion. Within a few seasons Dior was doing one and a half times as much business as all the rest of the couture put together, with 25 workrooms or ateliers and 1600 employees,

The "New Look" of Dior, 1947
(Other trend designs on pp. 73–75)

and with branches in New York and other great cities around the world.

Dior—Designer, Businessman, and Diplomat. As a person Dior was a seemingly gentle soul, a good man who did not smoke, swear, or gossip. He was kind to animals and to his employees. As his fame and his business grew, he provided well for his workers with insurance, good food, comforts, and conveniences. Beneath so mild an exterior it was surprising to find such a sharply witty mind, such a subtly acute business sense, and such publicity-wise diplomacy. The House of Dior was presided over by four astute women assistants: Madame Raymonde who ran the studio and was in charge of fabrics and trimming supplies; Madame Marguerite who supervised the workrooms; Mitza Bricard who supervised the hats and jewels and was the arbiter of taste for accessories in the collections; and Suzanne Luling who directed the salon and supervised customer relations. Every collection was designed with great taste, planned with consummate care, and executed with attention to every detail. Every collection was a smash success, with everything and everyone provided for: private clientele; commerical retail customers who bought for resale; and wholesale trade who bought models to copy. A Dior collection was never built around a single idea. As he expressed it, "A collection is made up of a few ideas, twelve at most." When all of them are truly creative, in wonderful taste, and express the spirit of the time, it is little wonder that Dior's name became synonymous with Paris fashion. His position as trend setter was never threatened throughout the ten years that he headed the House of Dior.

Dior's Fashion Philosophy. Dior's philosophy was frequently expressed in marvelously quotable quotes. "I am not an enemy of the female bosom, but I hate a sweater that looks as if a pair of balloons are floating inside." "Women are the most fascinating after they reach 35. A woman needs chic after the animal has lost some of its spring and the mind begins to prowl." "Fashion is basically emotion. To manufacture emotion, a man must have a working agreement with madness." In a more serious vein, Dior expressed his philosophy of fashion in these words, "Each age seeks its image in the mirror of truth. Today we reaffirm human values in feminine dress. A dressmaker tries to interpret, through the personal prism of himself, the mass taste of the moment, to anticipate this taste before it even takes form. For inspiration the designer travels, retreats to his house in the country, or just feels fabric." Surely no one has ever expressed the philosophy of fashion more clearly.

Why the New Look Succeeded. The orderly, rhythmic evolution of fashion change had been temporarily halted by the war, as a stream is dammed up by a tree that falls across it. Dior's first collection released the stoppage and permitted the pent-up changes to flow freely again. A change in silhouette was long overdue and, although the average woman was not quite prepared to accept so drastic a change as the New Look brought, the long unanswered desire for a new look enabled her to rise to meet it. The struggle continued in America for a long time, however, with fashion-magazine advertising showing padded shoulders as late as 1950, while the New Look was argued in the regular press, in churches, and on radio programs. Of course, it was accepted eventually and, in the next 15 years, American manufacturers sold millions of bouffant petticoats because every female from 5 to 75 adopted the New Look which required the support of at least one bouffant half-slip of frothy lace, nylon, stiffened net, or even horsehair braid.

Dior as Trend Setter. With the New Look, Dior reestablished Paris in its former position of fashion leadership, and he was never at a loss for trend-setting innovations. He understood how women wanted to look and was able to produce the look they wanted at the first moment they were ready to accept it. Dior expressed his thoughts about trend setting very clearly, "No one person can change fashion—a big fashion change imposes itself. It was because women longed to look like women again that they adopted the New Look, with longer and fuller skirts, and smooth rounded sloping shoulders and tiny fitted waists. The change was due to a universal change of feeling, of atmosphere. Fashions are not put over on women." Dior was always generous in giving credit to other designers. "Nothing is ever invented, you always start from something. It was Molyneux's style that has most influenced me, and I admire Chanel who revolutionized fashion in the twenties with a black jersey sweater and ten rows of pearls, and no one has ever carried the art of dressmaking farther than Vionnet."

When Dior died suddenly of a heart attack in October 1957, the fashion world was stunned and, as happens when any monarch dies, the question of who would succeed him as the ruling influence in the House of Dior was uppermost in all minds. Three likely successors were mentioned: Givenchy, Laroche, and Cardin, who was most frequently suggested since he had been a protégé of Dior before he had started his own salon the preceding season. All three were exciting young designers whose collections were highly successful. But none of the three was picked. Instead, Yves Saint-Laurent, Dior's young assistant who had received no previous publicity, was given the overwhelming challenge of becoming the head of the House of Dior.

YVES SAINT-LAURENT. Saint-Laurent was born in Oran, Algeria, in 1936. His family was French and fairly well to do. The career that young Yves was destined to follow became evident early, when at the age of 9 he began to design his sister's clothes. After finishing secondary school at the age of 18, he went to Paris to study art and within a few months had won first prize in an International Wool Society Competition for apparel design. Dior, one of the judges, hired him on the spot and Saint-Laurent entered the House of Dior as a protégé or assistant. Four years later, at the age of 22, he was appointed head of the house.

Christian Dior

55

Saint-Laurent and His Mother, 1960
(Trend designs on p. 76)

Saint-Laurent as Dior's Successor. Saint-Laurent's first collection at Dior was a sensational success and, of course, everyone was happy. World sympathy was with this shy youth, suddenly thrust into such a demanding position without adequate years of experience for assuming the management of the worldwide organization that the House of Dior had become. Probably no one could have followed in the founder's footsteps, and Saint-Laurent's second collection did not live up to the promise of the first one or to the perfection expected. He traveled to the United States to gain firsthand knowledge of Dior's good customers, the Americans, and to explain to them his fashion philosophy. He was overworked and overwrought. When asked to name his favorite pastime, his answer was

"sleeping." Certainly he was unable to delight the press with the epigrams for which Dior was famous, nor did he ever attempt to preempt Dior's image. When a reporter interviewed him in Paris, he did not sit behind Dior's great desk but in front of it, saying that he would never presume to occupy the position of the master. In 1960, after three deferments, he left Dior to do his service in the army. Of course, the House of Dior had to have a designer, and Marc Bohan, then designing for the House of Dior in London, was brought to the Paris atelier. Bohan's first line was a great success and more realistic than the last efforts of Saint-Laurent had been, and he was retained on a permanent basis. When Saint-Laurent was released from the army because of poor health at the end of a year, instead of returning to the House of Dior to whom he was still under contract, he sued the house for 120,000 francs—two years salary and grievances.

Saint-Laurent in His Own House. Within a year Saint-Laurent, financed by an American investor, opened his own salon and Victoire, Dior's famous mannequin, left Bohan to become his directress. Again the fashion world was anxious for his success and he lived up to their hopes and expectations magnificently. In his own house he seemed to be more able to express his own individual sensitivity to fashion, and the mannered, exaggerated variations on the basic and fashion-sound trapeze silhouette that he had introduced at Dior gave way to more wearable and at the same time more truly elegant clothes. His collections have been characterized by a look of less formality and more ease than Dior's clothes had, a look that seems perfectly suited to the era of young elegance symbolized by Jacqueline Kennedy. His clothes seem to illustrate a famous epigram of Oscar Wilde: "Simplicity is the last refuge of a complex people."

Chapter Four

Historical View of Fashion Trends

THE UNDERLYING causes of change in fashion are mirrored in the development of civilization. They are inherent in history, economics, and sociology, as well as in art, and we must trace the forces that have combined to shape Western civilization if we are to understand fashion today and anticipate its changes for tomorrow. The two factors on which fashion depends are the level of technological development of an era and the identity of the ideal female or "goddess" whom the average women of the era wish to imitate.

This chapter begins with a brief look at fashion history. As we approach the present our pace slows to compensate for the momentum that technology has brought to the rhythm of history. For our twentieth century the events that have influenced fashion are viewed at close range and a typical dress from each year has been chosen to illustrate how the fashion of any year not only reflects the fashion of the year before but also has within it the seeds of the year to follow.

The trend toward functionalism in dress was motivated by the dancer Irene Castle, shown here with her husband in 1915.

Technology as a Fashion Influence. The history of fashion is interrelated with and dependent on the development of methods for adapting the materials at hand to the purpose of clothing the body, for modesty or for allure, as protection from cold or as insulation from heat, reflecting the cultural pattern of the people as well as the climate of the country.

In ancient Egypt, for example, where the weaving of sheer fabrics was developed in a very early era, large rectangular strips of cloth were merely wrapped around the body and tied on one shoulder to furnish the only clothing that was needed. In the colder climates of middle Asia, however, the skins of animals were cut and sewn into clumsy garments with legs and sleeves, put together with needles made from slim, sharp bones and thread made from thin strips of hide. The crude garments of these barely civilized people were suitable for the rugged climate and their nomadic way of life, much of it spent on horseback.

Goddess Worship as a Fashion Influence. As soon as civilization advanced beyond the survival stage, the desire to be socially acceptable became a strong incentive in clothing development and joined technology as the second great force in fashion. We know that the ancient Greeks developed clothing that was beautiful as well as functional for it is comparatively easy to find examples of the classic chiton that they wore. Many exquisite pieces of sculpture have been preserved from this long-ago era (900–500 B.C.) during which the Greeks passed from barbarism to the peak of civilization.

CLASSIC GREEK GODDESSES. In this classical period the ideal female—whom the average woman wished to emulate—was a goddess: Juno, the virtuous wife of the king of the gods; Diana, the daughter associated with hunting; or Venus, the daughter associated with love. Sculptors depicted all three goddesses garbed in the same idealized way for centuries. The classic Athenian dress, a thing of beauty, mirrored the technology of the day and was suited to the lives of the women who wore it.

After the Romans conquered Greece and rose to world dominance, the high level of civilization of the classic Greeks declined, but most aspects of Greek culture, including their dress, were adopted by the Romans. The climate of Italy, of course, is sufficiently similar to the climate of Greece that the same type of draped garments were comfortable.

Classic Greek Influence
(Doric chiton)

BARBARIAN GODDESSES. The barbarians from northern Europe and central Asia, who for the first five centuries A.D. overran the Roman Empire, had a generally degrading effect on Roman culture, and this influence, of course, affected dress. Barbarian goddesses were huntresses who needed warm clothing for their cold northern winters. Their taste was a reflection of their less-advanced culture, and their fashions for this reason lacked classic sophistication. In place of the restrained, stylized motifs used as borders on the Greek chiton, they preferred gaudy, naturalistic patterns, and they wore a great variety of primitive jewelry. Hair styles too showed a lack of culture, with hair loose and long rather than arranged in the more sophisticated manner of the Greeks and Romans.

âge fashion with its rather monastic styling in which the dress of the barbarian goddess became blended with the beautiful classic fashions of the Greeks.

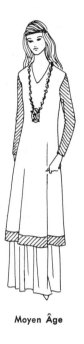

Moyen Âge

Germanic Barbarian Influence

THE TRANSITIONAL PERIOD OF THE MIDDLE AGES. The high culture of the Greco-Roman civilization blended with the less-civilized cultures of the barbarians during this period (A.D. 500–1000) when the Church was slowly strengthening its dominance and bringing culture back to the Roman level that western Europe enjoyed before the barbarian invasions. The art forms from this period are much less informative as to costume than the sculpture of the Classical Period. Mosaics perhaps furnish the best picture of the costume of the time. The dominance of the Church seems to be reflected in women's *moyen*

THE MADONNA AS FASHION GODDESS. As the influence of the Church crystallized and survival was no longer the most important influence on clothing, more varied and elaborate garments began to be worn. The development of a wider range of woolen and silk fabrics gave impetus to the diversification of styles. During this period mosaic art was superseded by painting in which the actual appearance of a garment could be much more clearly delineated, and great painters, like the classical sculptors before them, became creators of fashion by idealizing the apparel of the women used as models. Since the Madonna was almost always the subject of these paintings, she became the fashion symbol or "goddess" whose appearance the average woman wished most to imitate and thereby to become, by association, more socially acceptable. Although the pace of fashion began to gain momentum during the Middle Ages, styles changed very slowly indeed, as illustrated by the fact that the hennin (peaked hat in the illustration) was in fashion for more than a hundred years. The Madonna concept of fashion is credited with introducing both dieting and corsets, for artists consistently portrayed the Madonna with a high, tight-fitting belt to show that she was a young virgin.

Pre-Renaissance

Pre-Renaissance Fashion Developments. As early as the thirteenth century people began to look for ways to make garments fit better, and a good many of the fashions that developed in the following centuries were crude attempts in this direction. Although the shaped sleevecap and armhole introduced at this time were a revolutionary step in the right direction, the difficult problem of making a close-fitting sleeve that would permit free arm movement required several centuries of trial and error before it was finally perfected. One of the early attempts at making a sleeve that was somewhat fitted but still allowed the elbow to be bent was the slashed sleeve. In this styling, which was popular for two centuries, the outer sleeve was slashed—often with many gashes—to permit free arm movement, and a loose-fitting sleeve was worn underneath.

Another attempt at making garments that would fit produced the grotesquely padded men's tunic, or "pourpoint," that was worn above long, knitted hose. A loosely fitted garment was worn under the pourpoint, with padding stuffed between, so that a tight, unwrinkled appearance was presented while allowing a certain amount of comfort. The huge farthingale that first developed at about the same time as the pourpoint was probably an attempt at brother-and-sister styling, for these broad hoops gave to the lady a silhouette that was as imposing as her lord in his inflated pourpoint. The hinged metal case that constituted the first corset, however, was not comfortable by any standard, and men never

Pourpoint and Farthingale

permitted this constricting device to become fashionable for menswear.

Spanish fashion throughout the pre-Renaissance period was elegant and distinctive. It is not surprising, therefore, that the hoop or farthingale originated in Spain as did the corset, the ruff, silk stockings, and the fashion for wearing black in rich fabrics. Spain lost her position of fashion dominance at the time of the Renaissance, when Italian city-states rose to become the most powerful influence in western Europe.

Spanish Influence

At the same time "society" as such began to develop. The rapidity of its development is indicated by the passage of strict sumptuary laws in the latter part of the fifteenth century. These laws, which placed restrictions on the rank of an individual permitted to wear "brocade, embroidered velvet, satins, and pearl-sewn cloth of gold," are testimony to the inborn desire of the average person to become identified with high-ranking members of society.

During this very productive period in history, techniques were developed and improved for making different types of rich fabrics and inevitably their development brought new uses for them. Embroideries had been used on the garments of royalty and the priesthood for many centuries. Embroidered garments were prized both for their beauty and for the long, expensive process involved in making them, techniques that were improved greatly after the steel needle was introduced into Italy from Spain in the fifteenth century. A great new fashion for embroidery followed and, from the greater delicacy of workmanship that the steel needle made possible, the making of lace evolved.

French Fashion Dominance. Catherine de' Medici, a daughter of the celebrated Duke of Florence, became the Queen of France in the sixteenth century, bringing with her the new sophistication of the Italian Renaissance and a strong personal sense of fashion. From that time onward, France became the meeting ground of Italian and Spanish culture, synthesizing them with her own secular point of view, and upon them building her own dominance of Western fashion. Long before this time Paris had begun to have considerable fashion influence. As early as 1400 a small, waxen mannequin attired in the latest Paris fashion was sent each year to Venice, and in return rich fabrics that reached Venice from the Orient were imported into France, inspiring the fabric industries that were being established there under royal patronage. England's famous East India companies were also introducing to the West many exciting cotton fabrics named for their exotic homelands: madras from Madras; calico from Calcutta; muslin from Mosul; gingham, meaning "striped," from Malaya; and chintz, meaning "spotted," from India. Soon in France these imported cottons came to rival the domestic silks and brocades as fashion fabrics because of their scarcity and luxury prices.

LOUIS XIV. In the seventeenth century France became the dominant political power in Europe as well as the leader of fashion. Louis XIV came to the throne as a small boy in the year 1643, and his long, strong rule until 1715 was a major factor in bringing France to this position of eminence. Louis married the sister of the King of Spain and their brilliant court set the cultural pattern for European society. Under the sponsorship of this strong ruler, the manufacture of luxury fabrics was protected from competition with foreign imports. The lace-making industry prospered greatly under government sponsorship, and the Cavalier style, with its magnificent lace-trimmed collars, so beautifully depicted by the artist Van Dyck, supplanted the established Spanish fashions of ruff and farthingale.

Louis XIV Influence

Cavalier Style

Wigs, which had gone out of fashion when Louis came to the throne, remained out of fashion until he began to grow bald. When he then adopted a wig, his entire court followed his lead and as a result wigs returned to fashion. Imitation pearls were developed in this century and added to the extravagant gold and silver passementeries, laces, ribbons, striped and watered silks and gauzes that were fashionable at Versailles, where Louis had built his exquisitely beautiful palace. The philosophy of this "Grand Monarque" was succinctly expressed in his famous phrase, "L'état, c'est moi" ("I am the state"). Although he represented the absolutist monarchial point of view, he allowed his subjects considerably more personal freedom than was customary in that era, and fashionable clothes were first worn by the middle classes while Louis XIV reigned.

LOUIS XV AND LOUIS XVI. Louis XV, who came to the throne as a child of 5 at his great-grandfather's death in 1715, lacked the genius of the Grand Monarque, but the ladies of his court—Madame Du Barry and Madame de Pompadour were among them—maintained French fashion supremacy. Watteau, who is considered one of the greatest artists of all time, lived during this era (1684–1721), and the gown that he designed and used often in his paintings is considered by writers on historic costume to be in the finest taste of the entire period during which queens dictated fashion. The Watteau gown, called a "contouche," remained popular for two-thirds of a century in various modified versions.

Watteau Gown
(contouche)

About the middle of the eighteenth century, the fashion for stiff and heavy brocades of Spanish and Italian ancestry declined and crisp taffetas and dainty flowered lawns and dimities replaced them as domestic manufacturers learned the secrets of the sheer and beautiful cottons imported from the Orient. As fashion became more simple, hair styles became extreme and unbelievably complex. In 1769 there were 1200 hairdressers working in Paris alone. From the middle of the century, men's fashions began to take on a more masculine look and to differ more and more from women's fashions with which, up to that time, they had always run parallel. Tailors kept pace with the new trend in menswear, and no doubt gladly relinquished their female trade to dressmakers and modistes (milliners). During this century fashion dolls were sent from Paris to all leading European cities, disseminating fashion to all who could afford it. During this century, too, English tailors perfected modern trousers, and perhaps for this reason London was able to wrest leadership in men's fashion from Paris about 1780 and since that time has remained as dominant an influence in men's fashion as Paris has been in women's fashion.

ROSE BERTIN. Great dressmakers probably held positions of importance before this time, but the first great dressmaker to achieve lasting fame was Rose Bertin, dressmaker to Marie Antoinette, the ill-fated queen of Louis XVI from 1774 until she was trundled off to the guillotine in 1793.

Marie Antoinette
(in 1783)

The French writer Rousseau who is generally considered to have exerted the greatest literary influence of the century (the forerunner of romanticism and the recognition of the subconscious) wrote a novel *Emile*, which was hysterically admired. After reading *Emile*, Marie Antoinette built a village (the petite Trianon) in the gardens at Versailles where in fanciful shepherdess costumes she pretended to be a milkmaid in a misguided attempt to express her belief in the equality of all people.

FASHION IN THE EMPIRE PERIOD OF NAPOLEON. Although Napoleon was emperor of France for only 11 years, his influence on the arts was deep and lasting. His taste was reflected in the classic lines of the Church of the Madeleine and the Arch of Triumph, both begun in his era, and in the massive Empire style in furniture and the classic Empire style in fashion. The bold simplicity of the painter David symbolized this era, just as the cream-puff style of Fragonard mirrored the extravagant fashions of the French court of Versailles.

During the French Revolution, social life in Paris ceased, fashion journals stopped publication, and fashionable ladies and gentlemen masqueraded in the garb of common working folk in the hope of escaping the guillotine. Elaborate dress, as evidence of social distinction, was abolished by law. Ready-made clothes had come on the market in Paris as early as 1791, and by 1795, with the restoration of orderly government in France, luxuries and fashion journals reappeared.

Rose Bertin, who escaped to England during the Revolution, is credited with starting the Empire fashion on her return to Paris, borrowing it from the chemise undergarment worn by English women, which had drawstrings at the neck and at the high waistline. Its simple Directoire silhouette was right for the times, mirroring the classic Greco-Roman dress of an earlier period at a time when Napoleon was attempting to establish an empire on the classic Roman pattern. Sheer white fabrics that could be draped in imitation of the ancient statues became fashionable. The sheath and chemise, worn without petticoats and with bare legs visible to the knee, were made of such thin fabrics that tuberculosis and influenza (called the "muslin disease") reached epidemic proportions. Classic coiffures and wind-blown "Titus" bobs were popular hair styles. Pantalettes made an appearance, perhaps in the interest of modesty. They were never popular in Paris, but continued long in the less-sophisticated United States. The "spencer" or bolero, designed by Lord Spencer who simply cut the tails off his coat as a prank, became very fashionable, probably because it added warmth to the skimpy chemise. Shawls woven on the new power looms at Paisley, Scotland, also became high fashion, doubtless for the same reason.

Empire Gown and Spencer Jacket

FASHION IN THE VICTORIAN ERA. Queen Victoria ascended the British throne in 1837 and her long reign—until her death in 1901—made her the symbol of this era. Her husband, Prince Albert, died prematurely, leaving her for many years a widow. She mourned him so deeply that she never took an intense interest in fashion. Worth never claimed her as a client, always a source of chagrin to him, but perhaps a factor that kept women's fashion securely based on the dictates of French royalty.

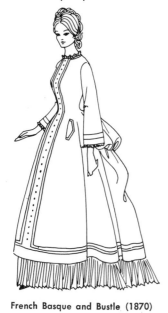

French Basque and Bustle (1870)

In France, after the Paris Revolution of 1848, a nephew of the now-revered Napoleon I was elected to head the French government. He shortly proclaimed himself Napoleon III, with the Spanish beauty Eugénie as his empress. Their court at the Tuilleries was brilliant and luxurious beyond equal in the Western hemisphere. It came to an inglorious end in 1871 when the Prussians under Bismarck defeated France in war. Napoleon III abdicated, and a republican form of government was established in France to mark the end of fashion dominance by royalty.

Fashion Direction in Our Twentieth Century.

NEW FASHION GODDESSES REPLACE ROYALTY. After the French court disintegrated, royalty of course continued to dress fashionably but no longer was able to dictate fashion. The clientele of the French couture at that time included wealthy society women of Europe and the Americas, the demimondaine, and many great and famous actresses, as well as the members of royal families. The actresses picked up the mantle dropped by the fashion leaders of the French court and became the goddess ideals and fashion leaders of their era. They were willing to have their apparel publicized in fashion magazines because they realized that their popularity would be enhanced by this excellent publicity. In the 1920's screen actresses supplanted these stage actresses as fashion ideals because they played to far greater audiences. Movie houses had sprung up in every town across the entire country and actresses who appeared in the films of that period were idolized to an extreme degree. Their mannerisms, hair styles, and fashions in apparel were copied by their adoring public. In the 1930's the wealthy international set who congregated in prewar Paris assumed the role of fashion goddess by giving more sophisticated fashion leadership in that era of hypersophistication. The annual list of ten best-dressed women which they inspired and in which their leaders were always included had by midcentury become a reliable guide to the direction in which fashion was heading.

COMMUNICATIONS ACCELERATE FASHION CHANGE. At the turn of the century, communication was accelerated tremendously by the invention of the airplane, the automobile, and the moving picture, and later by the development of radio, talking pictures, and television. The desire for new fashion was similarly quickened by the swift dissemination of fashion news in the new fashion magazines and the new neighborhood movie houses which brought fashion sensitivity to the average woman. Again, as always, the desire for fashion was fostered by its increased availability.

SPORTS FOR WOMEN INFLUENCE FASHION. The drive for equality of the sexes began during the Victorian Era when women joined men in such sports as tennis and bicycling. This daring revolt from age-old custom was a harbinger of the new functionalism in fashion. Louise Boulanger, Cheruit's great designer, correctly summed up the situation when she quipped, "When tennis came in, the demimondaine went out and fashion elegance with her." A tennis dress in the 1890's swept the ground, and a bathing costume included stockings, a corset, and knee-length bloomers, but when functional sportswear began to be created in the 1920's, the average woman was ready and willing to accept it and make it fashionable. In turn, functional sports clothes helped to popularize tennis, golf, swimming, and the winter sports.

The American Gibson Girl

Victorian Sportswear
(croquet costume)

THE SEWING MACHINE BROADENS THE BASE OF FASHION. Although the supply of fabric at a price within reach of the average woman had been one of the important effects of the industrial revolution, the processes of garment construction lagged because any garment, regardless of its intricacy, could be made by hand. (It is interesting to note in this connection that all but the last two garments illustrated thus far in this chapter were made by hand.) Elias Howe invented the sewing machine in 1846, but it was not widely used until the Civil War (1861–1865) when the government provided machines for women volunteers to use in making and repairing soldiers' uniforms. After the war the sewing machine rapidly became standard equipment in homes everywhere, and commercial patterns that followed Paris fashion became more generally available also, enabling American housewives to make their own copies of Worth's elaborate creations. The initial effect of the sewing machine was to increase the amount of lace and braid used on dresses since these trimmings could be applied so easily and quickly by machine.

In the 1880's garment factories began to appear. Cloaks and the separate shirtwaists and skirts that constituted the standard costume of the Gibson Girl era of the Gay Nineties were the first outer garments to be factory made because they did not present the insurmountable "fitting" problems inherent in the complex dresses of that era.

The wholesale apparel industry did not make extensive growth until garment construction was simplified by Poiret, Chanel, and Vionnet, since individual fitting was not important with their straight chemise dresses. At this time the garment industry took quarters around Seventh Avenue and grew and prospered. Functionalism in dress styling made the wholesale manufacture of women's outer apparel practical, and the dress industry, in turn, carried functionalism to its position of dominance as the fashion trend of the century.

Vionnet's Simplified Structure

The Twentieth Century at Close Range.

The death of Queen Victoria in 1901 officially closed her era, during which Lillian Russell's "perfect" 36-inch bust and 18-inch waist were considered to be ideal measurements. During the first decade of the new century, fashion underwent an extreme change similar to the one that occurred a century earlier, following the French Revolution.

In the pages to follow, year-by-year sketches will trace the rhythmic movements of fashion occurring during the first sixty years of this century.

1905–1911. During this period of transition, the Wright brothers flew the first airplane; the Titanic struck an iceberg and sank on its maiden voyage from London to New York; Caruso was the attraction at the Metropolitan Opera; and Irving Berlin began his illustrious career by writing "Alexander's Ragtime Band." Mary Pickford, with dimples and golden curls, was the good little darling of the young movie industry, and Theda Bara, for whom the word "vamp" was coined, personified the oriental-harem concept of woman sponsored by sophisticated Poiret. Billie Burke was in her glamorous heyday—the sketch for 1908 was copied from a photograph of her that appeared in *Vogue* magazine.

A New Look Is Forecast. Cigarette smoking by women began to be accepted in smart Parisian restaurants. Earrings with screw fasteners were invented and the rather barbaric practice of piercing ears soon became passé. Maturity, so long the keynote of feminine beauty, began to go out of fashion. Corsets forecast this change in silhouette by replacing their established hourglass shape with a straightline front which required garters to hold it in place. Soon the exaggerated silhouette of the Gay Nineties was outmoded as the new natural lines of the shift were forecast by the Empire or Directoire fashion. In 1908 *Vogue* reported from Paris, "the Directoire line is in, styles are simpler, shoulders are quite normal as the princess semi-fit is worn by the smartest women at the smartest places. Skirts are shorter. The correct walking length is absolutely to clear the ground."

Russian Ballet as a Fashion Influence. The greatest cultural event of the decade took place in 1909 when the Russian Ballet arrived in Paris for the first time, with Diaghelev as director, Nijinsky as leading dancer, and Bakst as scenic designer, introducing fashion-conscious Parisians to the rich color and oriental flavor of its costumes and settings that Poiret was to make into high fashion.

1912–1918. In this period Irene Castle exerted great influence on fashion. She and her husband, Vernon, arrived in Paris from New York in 1911 and they immediately became "the rage." Dance styles changed from the minuet and waltz to the new fox trot and Castle Walk. Meanwhile Irene Castle captivated fashionable

Paris with her exquisite grace and boyish youthfulness. She epitomized the new era of chic through simplicity and functionalism that was replacing the era of elegance. When she bobbed her hair in 1915 she started a fashion that the entire Western world followed. Close behind the Castles came Valentino, who as "The Sheik" became the first great lover of the films, and who introduced the tango and the gigolo to the movie-going public. In 1913 emerging feminists called "suffragettes" began their campaign for political equality by marching on Parliament in London to demand votes for women, many of them "smartly" attired in the new hobble skirt of Poiret.

The First World War Begins. In 1914 the First World War began in Europe. The United States was in the conflict only from the summer of 1917 until the Armistice on November 11, 1918, but the impact of the war on the American way of life was tremendous. Great numbers of American soldiers and war workers saw Paris for the first time, and interest in French fashion was stimulated proportionately. This war did not close Paris or place insurmountable restrictions on the Paris couture. Collections

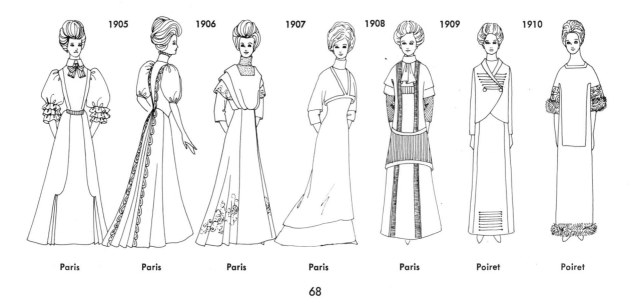

| 1905 | 1906 | 1907 | 1908 | 1909 | 1910 |
| Paris | Paris | Paris | Paris | Paris | Poiret | Poiret |

were shown regularly to the same foreign clientele as in peace time, although French women were less fashion-minded than usual. Many were working at jobs previously performed by men. They ran trolley cars, delivered packages, operated taxis, and in this way introduced the concept of women dressed in simple working clothes. This new look was reflected in the couture collections. As *Vogue* reported in 1918, "Now that women work, working clothes have acquired a new social status and a new chic."

Fashion. The first permanent-wave machine reached New York in 1915 to help the Castle bob revolutionize hair styles. Bobbie pins replaced hairpins and hennaed hair became the rage. Lipstick was invented. In 1916 *Vogue* reported, "The oriental look is out; the 'garçonne' look is in, and Chanel with it. Colors are somber, garments are untrimmed, but in spite of the war, the openings go on as usual." Silk jersey and crepe de chine "scanties" and "teddies" came in to replace the voluminous petticoats and armorlike corsets that had been essential to the bust-and-bustle silhouette of the Gibson Girl. A new stance, the "debutante slouch," requiring women to be flat-chested, was a necessary adjunct to the boyish "garçonne" silhouette.

1919–1925. Chanel, an emancipated spirit who shocked even shock-proof Paris, was the proper leader of the new trend of chic simplicity that was apparent throughout the couture. Vionnet, Molyneux, and Patou opened salons in 1919, all three destined to become famous. Only Poiret, out of step with the times, was holding fancy-dress fêtes of oriental splendor as his influence steadily dwindled. The fashion world began at this time to recognize the power of publicity. Patou in 1921 was the first member of the haute couture to hold a preview of his collection for the press. Four years later, when a Fashion Exposition was held in Grand Central Palace, the houses of Beer, Callot, Cheruit, Drecol, Jenny, Lanvin, Paquin, Vionnet, Redfern, and Worth, who were the most influential members of the couture at that time, all sent models to be shown. Both the French fashion industries and the growing wholesale-apparel industry in America benefited because the style consciousness of the thousands of women who visited the Exposition was stimulated by the French models.

1912	1913	1914	1915	1916	1917
Poiret	Poiret	Premet	Premet	Chanel	Chanel	Chanel

Influence of Art. The ultramodern schools of painting then flourishing in Paris supplanted the dance as the most important cultural influence in this postwar period. Picasso, Gris, Bracque had considerable though indirect influence on fashion. The delicate, muted colors of this ultramodern school of artists—Marcel Duchamp's "Nude Descending a Staircase" is a representative example—replaced the clashing scarlet, cerise, and vivid emerald of Bakst. Greige and biege became the rage for daytime wear. Referring to these muted colors in retrospect, Vertes, a significant artist of the 1930's, characterized the preceding decade as the "cream-cheese era of fashion."

Fashion. During this epoch the shingle and the wind-blown bob arrived. In 1925 long earrings dangled while dresses became almost sleeveless and skirts rose almost to the knee. High shoes and black stockings were replaced by black oxfords and flesh-color stockings for daytime wear. Much make-up was in fashion, including the newly developed eye shadow, and young women were arrested at public beaches because of too-scanty bathing attire. In the movies Clara Bow made history as the "It" girl.

1926–1932. In 1927 an unknown young man named Charles Lindbergh opened the era of world travel by solo-flying his "Spirit of St. Louis" from New York to Paris. Helen Wills accelerated American interest in sports and sportswear by becoming the first American to capture the tennis cup at Wimbledon. Women who had been given the ballot in 1920 and thus had helped to elect Calvin Coolidge to the presidency appeared in public in pants for the first time. In home furnishings the graceless modernistic era reached its height. In music Toscanini, Gershwin, and Louis Armstrong won acclaim, and in literature, fiction writers were busily exploring sex, while Freud and his uncomfortable theories on that subject were slowly gaining acceptance. Anita Loos wrote the definitive book of the era, *Gentlemen Prefer Blondes,* proving that the Roaring Twenties were as colorful in their way as the Gay Nineties had been.

The Era of Movie Influence. By the end of the war in 1918 the movies had become the great American pastime, and outstanding film personalities such as Greta Garbo, Gloria Swanson, and Clara Bow became fashion leaders. In the mid-1920's silent pictures were replaced by

| 1919 | 1920 | 1921 | 1922 | 1923 | 1924 |
| Chanel | Chanel | Chanel | Patou | Patou | Patou | Patou |

70

the "talkies," and Clara Bow went out with them because her girlish Brooklyn voice was at variance with her "It" image. Garbo, on the other hand, made the transition successfully with "Anna Christie," a picture that allowed her to use her natural Scandinavian accent. "Garbo Talks" was spread on billboards across America as she became queen of the silver screen. Her influence on fashion was phenomenal. The knitted pullover that she wore as Anna Christie developed the sweater into a national institution, just as her page-boy bob changed the hair style of an entire generation of young women. The Ziegfeld Follies, long a top attraction of the New York stage, had their counterpart in the new screen singing and dancing extravaganzas such as "Broadway Melody" and "Our Dancing Daughters," in which Joan Crawford danced the Charleston and the Black Bottom attired in assorted versions of Jenny's little knee-length chemise covered with beads, sequins, or swinging fringe. The great Chanel, whose costume jewelry and long ropes of fake pearls gave the proper accent to Patou's chic little flapper dresses, was invited to Hollywood in the late 1920's to design her timeless clothes

for a film. The native Hollywood designers tended to such an extravagant interpretation of fashion that pictures sometimes had to be shelved because the clothes were outmoded before the film could reach the movie theaters. "Period" or costume pictures avoided this calamity, and Mae West undulated into spectacular popularity in films as an American version of the French demimondaine of the Gay Nineties.

The Wall Street Crash of October 1929 ended the Roaring Twenties, but fashion showed little effect of the great depression that followed, continuing its customary evolutionary rhythm of slow change.

1933–1939. Schiaparelli became the interpreter of this new era. *Vogue* called her "A terse figure—the epitome of the mode." Every season Schiap's latest audacity was top fashion news. War again was just beyond the horizon, and hypersophistication in fashion seems to accompany such eras. The realist and surrealist movements in art were at their height, with Dali and his half-melted watches and other grotesquely symbolic forms a mad and disturbing leader.

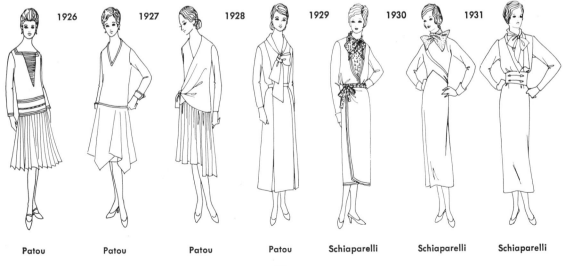

1926   1927   1928   1929   1930   1931

Patou   Patou   Patou   Patou   Schiaparelli   Schiaparelli   Schiaparelli

Mickey Mouse, an animated film character, and Charlie McCarthy, a ventriloquist's dummy, became national heroes. Schiaparelli dressed the leading actresses—Ina Claire popularized her famous "madcap," Marlene Dietrich, who wore pants and the new mannish attire with great style, found in Schiap her ideal designer, and Katherine Hepburn credited Schiap with transforming her from an angular ugly duckling into a glamorous actress.

Fashion. New synthetic fabrics furnished fashion excitement, and the zipper replaced hooks and eyes and buttons. The one-piece shirtwaist dress made its appearance. Colored nail polish was introduced. A fad for silver-fox jackets developed. Nylon stockings appeared on the scene in 1938 and superseded the more fragile silk stockings almost at once. Two-way stretch foundation garments replaced corsets while padded bras now accentuated the bosom that had been deemphasized in the 1920's. A new color, "suntan," reflected the increasing importance of sports, with sunsuits and wedgies contributing to the new outdoor fashions. The rising interest in sports encouraged greater specialization in apparel. Retail stores, alive to the trend, began to set up separate departments for beach wear and ski clothes as well as for town and country clothes, cocktail dresses, and hostess gowns. The functional idea in apparel was "in."

The International Set. In this highly sophisticated era, members of a new international set of socially elite women replaced actresses as fashion leaders. The Honorable Mrs. Reginald Fellowes—Daisy to her friends—was a representative example. She was an extremely wealthy American woman with great fashion sensitivity who worked for *Vogue* as Paris fashion editor. Obviously she did not need to work, but she enjoyed her position as fashion arbiter and her ability to make fashion headlines. According to Carmel Snow, who was then editor-in-chief of *Vogue,* "Whatever Daisy wore, she wore conspicuously." Another American member of the international set was the twice-divorced Wallis Simpson, with whom the King of England was infatuated. He lost his throne by his double defiance of divorce and royal marriage with a commoner. Their marriage in 1937 was the most newsworthy event of the era, and the Duchess of Windsor replaced Daisy Fellowes as fashion leader.

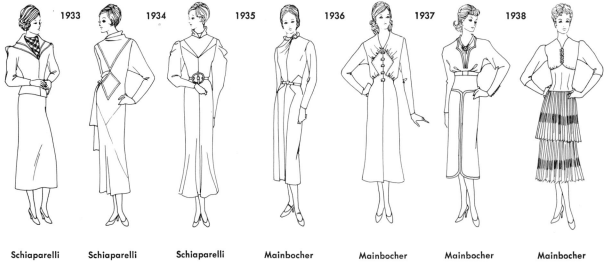

1933	1934	1935	1936	1937	1938
Schiaparelli	Schiaparelli	Schiaparelli	Mainbocher	Mainbocher	Mainbocher	Mainbocher

1940–1946. With the outbreak of the Second World War in 1939, communication with the fashion world of Paris was cut off. The United States did not actively participate in the conflict until after the Japanese attacked Pearl Harbor on December 7, 1941, but Paris fashion influence was dead throughout the entire period. The dearth of fashion news and the lack of interest in any news except war news combined to make this an uneventful period in fashion. Let us at this point discuss the trends of fashion that have developed since the beginning of the century, and examine the way in which each year's fashion reflects the previous fashion while adding something new.

Trend Analysis. The first recognizable trend setter of the century was Poiret, whose 1910 dress followed the Directoire silhouette then in fashion while expressing also a strong, individualized simplicity. In the following year Poiret shifted the center of interest to the midsection of the body, and in 1912, while retaining the silhouette, he began to forecast his famous lampshade silhouette of 1913 with the flowing ends of the long sash and the daring slit at the skirt bottom.

Following the same pattern, Chanel in 1916 began her fashion dominance by improving the fashion content of her predecessor without altering the silhouette she used. Over the four years that followed Chanel gradually changed her fashion look until in 1920 she had evolved an overskirt reminiscent of Poiret's lampshade. In the following year the natural evolutionary change in her silhouette brought it to the unchic end of a cycle.

Patou gained dominance in 1922 simply by lowering the waistline more definitely and replacing Chanel's soft lines with crisp ones. Over the next four years Patou gradually developed his distinctive flapper silhouette that reached its zenith in 1926, after which he began to lengthen skirts again, sending down the streamers that are a standard harbinger of both lengthening and shortening skirts.

By 1929 the fashion look had become similar to that of 1914 and 1921, indicating that a change was due because the silhouette had lost its smartness. At this time Schiaparelli began to set the trend. Without changing the silhouette, she subtly moved the interest to the upper third of the figure, introducing a higher waistline and

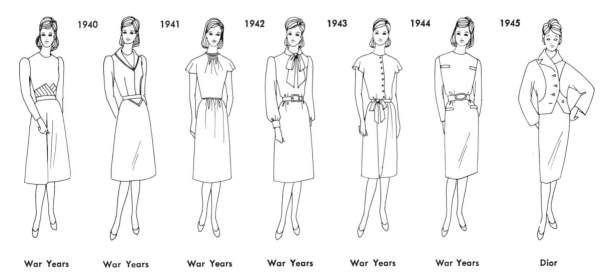

1940	1941	1942	1943	1944	1945
War Years	War Years	War Years	War Years	War Years	War Years	Dior

snug midriff. In the following year she began to widen the shoulders, continuing to develop this silhouette and forecasting the new look that swept the couture in 1933. By 1935 she had softened her silhouette until it was no longer chic, and she was then superseded by Mainbocher who understood the new soft line.

Mainbocher's 1936 dress used the same silhouette that had been evolved by Schiaparelli, but gave it a new, softened fashion look. The war interrupted the normal evolutionary rhythm of fashion change, and during the six years that it continued, fashion stood still.

In 1946 Dior took the same silhouette that had carried through the war years and gave it high fashion significance. He then reversed the emphasis, making tiny waists and great full skirts, introducing perhaps the most turbulent fashion change of the century. Once this change had been accomplished Dior then followed the accustomed pattern of trend setting, in which each year's fashion change was a natural evolutionary development of the year before. To quote *Vogue,* "The passing of one mode to another is always a gradual process, a series of subtle changes in detail and line that make up the silhouette. It is never a radical change."

From this analysis of fashion development it can be seen that the trend setter is the designer who expresses the essence of an era with the greatest fashion awareness. Trend setting seems to require such acute sensitivity to a particular era that it is not possible for a designer to continue in his position of leadership indefinitely. 1947–1960. The unprecedented success of Dior was due to the unbeatable combination of taste and talent and an infinite capacity for detail. Although he had everything, he took nothing for granted. A review of fashion magazines of the Dior years reveals that in each collection he presented several elegant fashion variations, each worthy to become a new trend setter. His sense of timing seemed to synchronize perfectly with what women were willing to accept in fashion. Most of the other members of the haute couture showed the shift at least a year before Dior decided that the moment to unveil it had come. Balenciaga was always a year or two ahead of Dior, but Dior seemed to wait instinctively until the time was exactly right to launch a new fashion, and when he introduced it, it was geared to the times as well as being

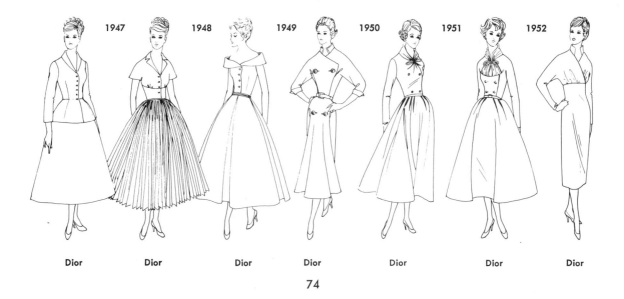

1947   1948   1949   1950   1951   1952

Dior   Dior   Dior   Dior   Dior   Dior   Dior

excitingly presented and in perfect taste. Dior put the seal of approval on the trend toward functional suitability, which had been initiated by Poiret as a battle against the "glittering atrocities" of the era of elegance.

An Era of Exaggeration. As always, an era of exaggeration was the aftermath of war. In this new postwar period, the speed of jet planes exceeded the speed of sound. Atomic energy, with its frightening implications, became commonplace. Russia put the first man-made satellite into orbit. Henry Ford II gave five-hundred-million dollars to be distributed among colleges and hospitals to improve their facilities—the largest donation on record. In 1956 a boy of 14 won $100,000 in a quiz show; a champion steer was sold in Chicago for the unrealistic price of $20,000; and Billy Graham made 56,000 conversions in one series of revival meetings. The great social spectacles of the era were as near as the television set as Grace Kelly became the Princess of Monaco and Elizabeth II was crowned Queen of the British Empire before a packed house at Westminster Abbey.

Effects of the War on Fashion. ADVANCES IN TECHNOLOGY. When the technological skills developed under the pressure of wartime urgency were released to peacetime uses, synthetic fabrics and easy-care processes came on the market in increasing abundance, temporarily overwhelming the rayon and acetate fabrics developed early in the century and in common use before the war. Nylon, orlon, and dacron became immensely popular because they were "drip-dry" and would retain heat-set pleats after washing. Other synthetic fabrics and other processes that were rapidly developed added to the easy care of clothing, particularly underthings and less expensive every-day outerwear, and had considerable effect on fashion. Wash-and-wear fabrics at first caused difficulty in design and production because they had to be styled to accommodate such fabric peculiarities as tendency to pucker and excessive stiffness or softness in texture. The new low-cost synthetic fabrics imitated wool, silk, and linen so successfully that designers in high-price houses turned to rich brocades, exotic beaded effects, and difficult bias cuts that could not be copied-down in the less-expensive lines in which synthetic fabrics were used in an effort to compete successfully with them.

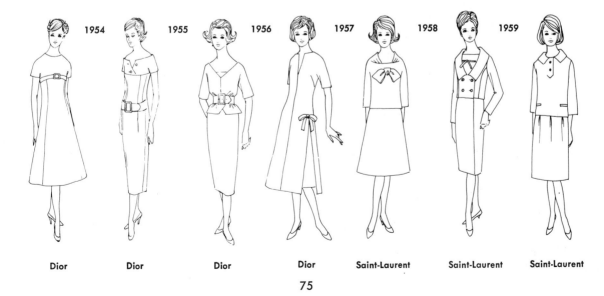

1954 Dior   1955 Dior   1956 Dior   1957 Dior   Saint-Laurent   1958 Saint-Laurent   1959 Saint-Laurent

SOCIOECONOMIC INFLUENCES. Influences stemming from the war to a great extent were responsible for the casual trend in fashion that came into full blossom in the postwar period. One of these influences was wartime gasoline rationing, which affected the relationship of people to their home environment by immobilizing families in suburbia. They learned to shop in local stores and to find entertainment in the simple pleasures of outdoor living by day and home television by night.

Another important influence was the GI bill, which provided modest stipends for returning service men and women to finish their education. It thus enabled thousands of young adults, whose education had been cut short when they joined the armed forces, to go back to college. An entirely new type of college life developed as a result of the GI bill, as service men, many of whom by the end of the war had acquired a wife and perhaps a child or two, flooded campuses across the country, often living in abandoned quonset huts that offered little more comfort and convenience than camping out. The GI allotments were barely adequate for food and simple necessities. Wives also often attended classes while husbands took turns with them at baby-sitting. The clothes that this generation of young adults wore were unpretentious and functional. The overall of blue denim, formerly the badge of the farmhand, was widely adopted, and it made its way into the wardrobe of fashion. Once college days were over for these young people and they settled down in suburbia, they found that jeans, shirts, and pullovers were ideally suited for housework and general informal wear.

Suburbanites bought station wagons to transport their families to playgrounds and beaches and built patios and recreation rooms at home. Informal living made comfortable, functional clothes potentially fashionable, and designers caught the spirit of the times and supplied the need. Saint-Laurent became the successor to Dior because he understood this new spirit superlatively well. When the casual phase that he has so sensitively interpreted has passed, as is inevitable in the relentless flow of time, some other designer, who can more sensitively catch and distill the spirit of his time, will replace him as trend setter.

The Unique Role of Paris in Fashion. How can Paris continue her dominance of fashion when there are so many qualified designers elsewhere? Italian designers, for example, have come into prominence since 1950 because their exuberant feeling for color and design is so well suited to the spirit of the times. Apparel collections shown in Florence and Rome attract a considerable number of buyers, and Pucci has carved a niche for himself that is as stable, in its way, as Chanel's. In London the English couture group has banded together officially, and with considerable success, to attract foreign buyers. American designers on the West Coast have originated much of our casual sportswear, including blue jeans, T-shirts, and other functional playclothes. Nor do all successful designers look to Paris for fashion guidance, but create to suit their own tastes for a distinguished clientele of fashion-conscious women who recognize their great fashion talent. In all these groups there are undoubtedly potential trend setters, but without a "summit" from which to be effectively publicized, their promise in this direction cannot be realized. Paris is able to furnish the requisite showcase, and in addition has several other fashion advantages.

THE SOPHISTICATION OF PARIS. Fashion design does not thrive in an ivory tower. It needs an atmosphere vibrant with the life of its time, a condition that is offered supremely well in Paris. Designers are acutely sensitive individuals who are affected by art exhibitions, the theater, concerts, and by the great and famous who are attracted to Paris because of its sophistication. This concentration of stimuli, in fact, often causes a fashion trend to develop simultaneously in several couture houses. Designers do not copy one another in such a case, but with the same stimuli it is inevitable that several of these designers, who are so closely associated with all that is going on in their world, who see the same magnificent fabric collections, who read the same fashion publications, and who meet the same celebrities, should express their fashion awareness in the same way.

PRIVATE CLIENTELE IN PARIS. In 1960 there were 34 haute couture houses in Paris, each with an average of 12,000 private or made-to-order customers. At least half the business of any couture house is its made-to-order trade. (Other enterprises of the couture include their wholesale export business, their ready-to-wear, "pay and take" boutique trade, and often a very lucrative perfume business.) The large made-to-order business is conducive to an amount of experimentation not possible in a strictly wholesale operation. In the United States the made-to-order business has rarely been successful, Mainbocher being a notable exception. Instead, the success of the apparel industry in the United States, as is typified by Seventh Avenue, has been in the wholesale ready-to-wear field, with garments that fit well and are made in a range of sizes for a range of figure groups. This dis-tinct difference in type of business operation furnishes an important clue to the continued dominance by Paris of the trend-setting function in women's fashion.

ACCESSORY AND FABRIC MARKETS IN PARIS. Another factor that must be included is that Paris offers a particularly stimulating supply market for fashion. Its concentration of skilled craftsmen supply a wealth of trimming and accessory ideas, and its great fabric market offers the latest and finest fabrics. Several excellent Italian designers have moved to Paris in the last decade to compete better with the French couture by having this fund of inspirational material available. American designers who have no interest in the Paris couture collections as a rule go to Paris earlier in each season to see the fabric showings and buy fabrics.

AN ESTABLISHED SUMMIT IN PARIS. Paris began setting trends more than six hundred years ago, and because of her established position furnishes a meeting place and a sorting ground. Even in medieval days the genius of Paris was not her originality, but rather her ability to blend the original ideas developed by others into exciting fashion, as a review of this chapter will amply illustrate. And so long as fashion writers and prospective buyers by the thousands converge on Paris from all parts of the world in January-February and July-August of each year, this concentration of interest and its attendant publicity will no doubt remain the indispensable factor in Paris's position at the "summit."

Chapter Five

Application of Fine-Arts Principles

Empress Eugénie and Her Court
Painted by Winterhalter

Tʜᴇ ARTISTIC ASPECT of apparel design is its most important as well as its most demanding consideration, requiring as great adherence to the principles of composition, as much sound artistic judgment, and as acute sensitivity to the inherent factors of taste as other branches of art. In this chapter these art principles are explained and garments are sketched that illustrate their specific applications to apparel. Chapter 11, which deals with the effective use of trimmings, is in effect a sequel to this chapter since the principles of art that are explained here furnish to the designer an indispensable guide in the selection and use of trimmings.

The Progression of Fashion Change

THE GARMENTS in the spiral arrangement on the facing page illustrate the constant, rhythmic change in fashion. The fashion pendulum swung from the hourglass silhouette of 1900 to the "new look" of the shift in 1910, and back again to the wide shoulders of the hourglass in 1933. And when that cycle had run its course after twenty years, the silhouette swung back again to the rectangular silhouette of the shift when Dior introduced the A-line in 1954.

Garments in every era follow the principles of good basic design by which it is always possible to create artistically sound, beautiful, and exciting variations on the natural shape of the human figure, fashions that are well proportioned, flattering to the wearer, and in good taste. The design element that changes is the silhouette and, with each of its variations in the slow but constant movement of fashion, interesting and effective ways must be developed to solve the problems of its new shape. Each season the subtle change in the silhouette offers the designer a new challenge to find exciting ways in which to express its particular fashion significance, while looking ahead and anticipating the subtle changes that the next season will inevitably have in store.

In this chapter the principles of fine arts are divided into three groups: *artistic composition, flattering style,* and *good taste*. It must be understood at the outset, however, that the division is merely for convenience in presentation since all fine-arts principles depend on one another and thus all of them are simultaneously applicable.

1900

1906

1907

1908

1911

1917

1919

1927

1930

1931

1934

1939

1945

1948

1951

1953

1954

1958

FASHION CHANGES
1900–1960

HOURGLASS

SHIFT

EMPIRE LINE

81

Fine-Arts Principles in Fashion Design

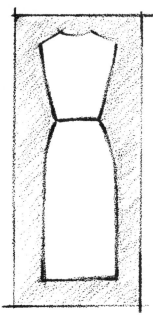

THREE DIFFERENT FACETS of the fine-arts approach to fashion design are presented in this chapter. A dress is considered first as a two-dimensional composition on the sketch pad, next it is considered as a three-dimensional composition on the body, and finally it is considered as a measure of the taste of both the person who designs it and the person who buys it. The chapter is divided into three sections, as previewed on these two pages, with descriptions and specific examples of these principles of fine arts.

An Artistic Composition. A dress on the sketch pad must be considered as a rectangular "composition" with space to be filled artistically, in the same way as a drawing or a painting is considered, dependent for its form on the same principles of proportion that govern good composition in all plastic arts.

The eye is the medium through which all plastic arts are judged and enjoyed. Compositional relationships can only be considered good or bad according to the instinctive evaluation the eye puts on them. Some people are more sensitive to good composition than others, just as some people are more sensitive to tone in music than others. Everyone's ear does not instinctively recognize perfect pitch nor does everyone's eye instinctively recognize perfect composition. Practice improves if it does not perfect, however, and principles can be formulated for good composition that help establish confidence. The first part of this chapter describes and illustrates the principles of composition that are particularly important in apparel design:

Pleasing horizontal space divisions can be planned through the Golden-Mean formula, and through divisions of space into segments that have a recurrent spacing or rhythm.

Balanced space divisions are achieved either by using the natural bisymmetry of the body as their basis or by the artistic-weight method commonly used in fine arts, in which unequal weights are balanced against the distance that they are placed from the center of the composition.

Properly scaled combinations of elements in the composition in apparel include the structure, the fabric, and the trimmings used in design, all of which require as careful selection and combination as do the elements in a painting.

A Flattering Style. In addition to being an artistic composition, a garment has the unique necessity for making its wearer more attractive by supplying attributes of beauty that nature neglected. All great designers recognize that their mission is "the creation of interesting plastic forms that subtly improve upon and thus save women from nature," as Dior expressed it. The average woman wants to look more tall and slender, with a slimmer waistline and a more attractive face than she possesses. Fortunately lines can fool the eye. Architectural design uses eye trickery as the basis for making buildings attractive, hiding with optical illusion the ugliness that is a prerequisite for their essential strength. A garment must also be considered as a dimensional architectural form upon which the deception of optical illusion is practiced. The middle section of this chapter is devoted to a description of the optical illusions that are applicable to apparel design, divided according to the effects that they can produce:

Ways to lengthen the figure
Ways to slim the waistline
Ways to frame the face attractively

The Elements of Good Taste. Good taste is the most difficult of all fine-arts principles to explain because it is intangible, easier to sense than to see. Nonetheless four of these indispensable elements of good design are defined and illustrated in the final section of this chapter:

Unity of design exists when all elements in a composition work together for one purpose.

Economy in design exists when all elements in a composition fulfill a necessary function that is related to the one central purpose.

A single strong focal point or center of interest exists when one design element dominates all other elements which in turn support it.

A means of transfer of interest exists when a track is provided for the eye, enabling it to travel easily and naturally from the focal point of the dress to the face of the wearer. For a dress is in poor taste when it rather than the wearer remains the ultimate center of interest.

The Golden Mean

THE RECTANGULAR SHAPE that represents a dress on the drawing board is usually divided into a waist and skirt at the normal waistline. This standard relationship of the two parts of a dress is satisfying to the eye, although it seldom has the 5-to-8 proportion that is known as the "Golden Mean." The eye accepts the normal, fitted waistline because the body indentation at that position produces a pleasing outline or silhouette. In addition, the imperfect proportional relationship of the two parts is usually camouflaged by trimming or other design details. When a dress is cut with a lowered or a raised waistline, however, the proportional relationship of the two parts to one another must be arbitrarily decided on, and the Golden-Mean Equation will establish eye-satisfying horizontal divisions. This equation is useful in many ways, as illustrated in the sketches and accompanying proportional scales on the two following pages.

The Golden Mean (or golden section), which enables one to divide a composition into balanced segments by measurement rather than by eye, was developed by taking actual measurements of eye-satisfying pieces of ancient sculpture where it was found that a 5-to-8 proportional relationship usually existed between the sections of which these figures were composed. When this 5-to-8 proportion is used in apparel design, or in any of the visual arts, pleasing, eye-satisfying proportions also are obtained.

The diagrams shown on the facing page illustrate the Golden-Mean Equation. In A, a simple garment shows a lowered waistline positioned according to the equation. In B, the ideal 5-to-8 proportion is compared with the 4-to-8 and 6-to-8 proportions. Here the eye can readily see that in 4-to-8 there is too much difference between the two sections, and that in 6-to-8 there is too little difference to be attractive or satisfying. The 5-to-8 proportion has been designated the Golden Mean because the product of the two outside numbers in the equation (extremes) is practically identical with the product of the two inside numbers (means). This unique interrelationship in which the smaller segment of the rectangle in A is proportioned to the larger segment as the larger segment is proportioned to the whole figure makes the proportion ideal and therefore satisfying to the eye.

$$5:8 \text{ as } 8:13$$
$$5 \times 13 = 65 \text{ (extremes)}$$
$$8 \times 8 = 64 \text{ (means)}$$

In this equation the two outside numbers are called "extremes"; the two inside numbers are called "means." The equation is perfect because the product of the means (64) is equal (almost) to the product of the extremes (65).

A. GOLDEN-MEAN PROPORTION SATISFIES THE EYE

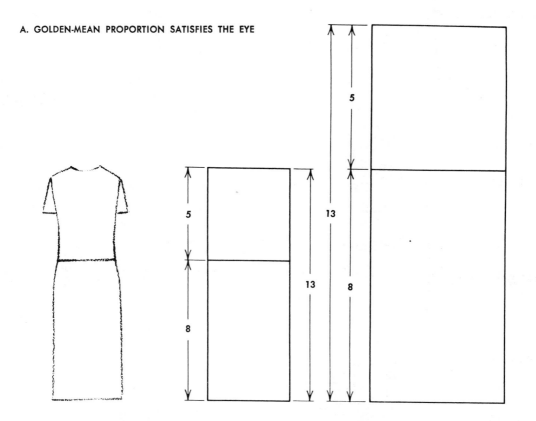

B. GOLDEN-MEAN IS NEITHER TOO LITTLE NOR TOO MUCH

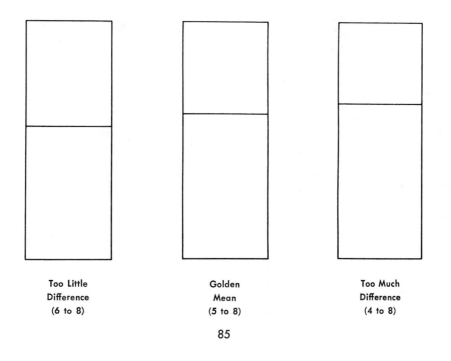

Too Little
Difference
(6 to 8)

Golden
Mean
(5 to 8)

Too Much
Difference
(4 to 8)

Practical Applications of

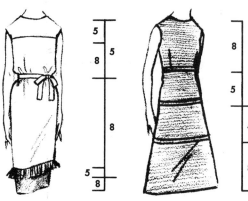

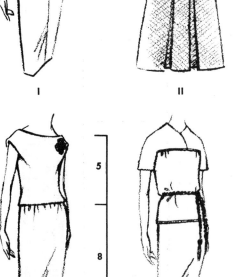

PROPORTIONAL RELATIONSHIPS IN CUT-IN-ONE DRESS

I. In this extremely complex interrelationship of proportions, the eye is willing to accept the bottom of an overskirt as the bottom of the garment.

II. An A-line shift in which the middle sections of the garment are in 5-to-8 proportion to both upper and lower sections.

GOLDEN MEAN AS A GUIDE FOR SIZE OF TRIMMING

I. Companion widths of Cluny lace are used as trim, with the width on the sleeve in 5-to-8 proportion to the width on the collar.

II. Here pockets on the waist of the dress are in 5-to-8 proportion to pockets on the skirt, and the pocket flaps are proportioned to the pockets in the same way.

SIMPLE PROPORTIONS IN THE OVERBLOUSE ILLUSTRATE USES OF GOLDEN MEAN

I. A shell overblouse illustrates Golden-Mean proportion. The bottom of the overblouse cuts the figure into two segments with the upper segment in 5-to-8 proportion to the lower segment.

II. A belted overblouse exemplifies Golden-Mean proportion. The section below the belt has 5-to-8 proportion to the section above it.

the Golden-Mean Principle

USES OF GOLDEN MEAN WITH THE WAIST-AND-SKIRT DRESS

I.   A popular type of dress in which the midriff section forms a pleasing 5-to-8 proportion to the waist section above it.

II.   A dress in which the collar furnishes an eye-satisfying 5-to-8 proportion to its waist.

I   II

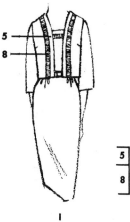

GOLDEN MEAN AS A GUIDE IN SPACING OF TRIMMING

I.   Here a costume trimmed with self-puffing uses 8-to-5 proportion for trimming width to plain fabric width that serves as its border.

II.   A dress trimmed with a triple row of tucks in the skirt uses an arrangement in which the tucks are in 5-to-8 proportion to the hem.

I   II

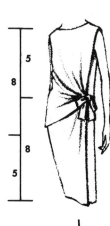

GOLDEN MEAN IN INTERRELATED PROPORTIONS IN THE OVERBLOUSE

I.   In this asymmetrically draped overblouse, the skirt has 5-to-8 proportion to the overblouse on the right side, and the overblouse is draped up so that the proportion on the left side is 8-to-5.

II.   The skirt has 5-to-8 proportion to the overblouse and the overblouse and its scarf are proportioned to one another in the same way.

I   II

The Principle of Rhythm

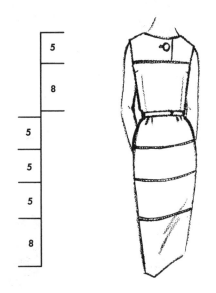

THE IMPORTANCE OF CUTTING a garment horizontally into artistically satisfying segments has been discussed, and various 5-to-8 proportional arrangements by which this can be accomplished have been illustrated on the preceding pages. In many of the illustrations, it will be noted, the garments were cut into more than two segments, anticipating the topic here under analysis: the use of orderly repetition, or rhythm, as a design tool.

Rhythm in design delights the eye for the same reason that rhythm in music delights the ear, inducing a sense of excitement through the recurrence of the beat. Rhythm in design results from lines or masses that act as accents because they are repeated in an orderly, predictable pattern. Rhythm patterns are inherent in the repetition of pleats and tiers, in rows of banding, in spaced pockets and buttons. The pattern may be dignified or gay, crisp or gentle, stately or demure. The one purpose of rhythm, regardless of its form or mood, is to lead the eye—as on stepping stones across a brook—from the periphery of the garment to its center of interest.

Rhythm is of two types: *uniform rhythm,* with beats of equal intensity that are repeated often enough to form a distinctive pattern; and *diminishing rhythm,* with beats of successively weakened intensity, like the widening ripples in the disturbed stillness of a pond. The dress shown on this page, which is cut into six horizontal sections by bands of fagoting and a belt, illustrates both the uniform and the diminishing types of rhythm. The three evenly spaced rows of fagoting in the skirt illustrate uniform rhythm. The button that forms the center of interest is the "stone dropped into the pond." The row of fagoting at the bottom of the yoke is the initial strong ripple, while the belt and the three rows of fagoting in the skirt act as diminishing ripples, with the bottom of the skirt forming the final ripple, weaker because it is at a still greater distance from the center of interest.

The dresses on the facing page illustrate several practical uses of rhythm, with their rhythm patterns explained by the small diagrams.

UNIFORM RHYTHM

DIMINISHING RHYTHM

UNIFORM AND DIMINISHING RHYTHM COMBINED

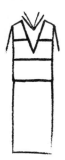   

The Principle of Balance

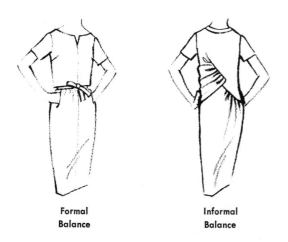

Formal
Balance

Informal
Balance

A GARMENT ACHIEVES its balance from the relative volume and impact of the details of line and trimming used in its design, and it satisfies the eye as an artistic composition only when the "artistic weights" of its details are in balance. Artistic balance is of two types: *formal or symmetrical balance,* which is achieved when two masses of equal size (volume) or strength (impact) are placed at equal and opposite distances from the center; and *informal or asymmetrical balance,* which can be achieved in the three different ways illustrated in the diagram on this page.

When only two elements are to be balanced, a satisfying arrangement is easy to establish, but as the number of elements increases, so does difficulty in establishing balance among them. The wonderful mobiles of Alexander Calder illustrate asymmetrical balance in which many elements take part. In these works of art, actual weight is the balancing factor, whereas in design the eye measures the impact received from every detail in the composition and assigns a "weight

value" to it, and finds a composition satisfying only when the weight values balance.

Informal balance is used almost entirely in the fine arts, whereas formal balance is more frequently used in apparel design because of the natural bisymmetry of the body. Formal balance presents fewer problems, but informal balance is more appealing to the eye, and often more flattering to the figure as well. In formal, symmetrical balance, the detail forming the center of interest (the bow on the dress at the top of this page, for example) is generally thrown slightly off balance to add impact and interest to the composition. Six dresses in which balance is used in interesting ways are shown in the sketches on the facing page and explained by the accompanying diagrams.

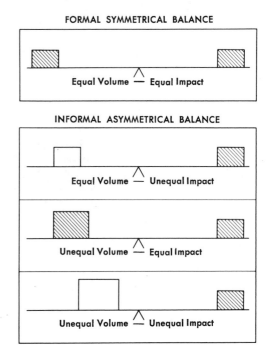

FORMAL SYMMETRICAL BALANCE

Equal Volume — Equal Impact

INFORMAL ASYMMETRICAL BALANCE

Equal Volume — Unequal Impact

Unequal Volume — Equal Impact

Unequal Volume — Unequal Impact

DRESSES THAT ILLUSTRATE THE PRINCIPLE OF BALANCE

Symmetrical

The eye accepts both sides as being alike.

Asymmetrical

Brown   Yellow

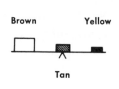

Tan

Light, bright color has the heaviest weight because it has the strongest impact.

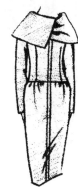

Large, plain side of the collar is balanced by the smaller, draped side.

Asymmetrical

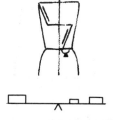

As a weight is placed farther from center it requires a heavier weight for balance.

Heavier weights are balanced by greater volume in this extremely complex design.

The Principle of Scale

SCALE IS THE TERM used to express the impact relationship between a garment and its design details. Thus "in scale" means that a satisfying relationship exists, whereas "out of scale" indicates that certain design elements are too heavy or too light, too large or too small to harmonize with the feeling of the fabric and silhouette of the garment. Perhaps the concept of scale can be clarified by an illustration from interior design, where the furnishings of a room must be scaled or proportioned to the room in which they are used for a pleasing effect. When the room is too small for its furnishings, it looks crowded and the furnishings appear too large,

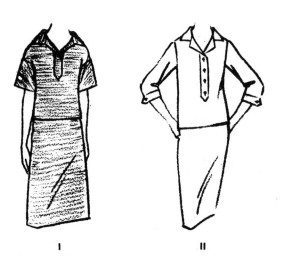

I   II

The costume worn by Twin I is made of crinkly tree-bark crepe, whereas its scaled-down twin is of smooth wool jersey. The excellent styling of these two garments results from their structure and trimming details being scaled to coordinate properly with the fabric used.

I   II

The exaggerated trapeze silhouette of the suit worn by Twin I, in bold black and white mohair fabric, is in scale with the trimming of stunning black patent-leather bow belt and immense buttons. The scaled-down copy beside it, of pastel silk linen with grosgrain trim, has a more wearable A-line silhouette which is in scale with the general restraint of its fabric and trimming.

heavy, or ornate. When the room is too large for its furnishings, it appears cold and bare, and the furnishings look small and cheap. The same furnishings can look large in one room and small in another because the eye measures their size only in relation to the room in which they are used. Transferring this illustration from home furnishings to apparel, the silhouette and the fabric of a garment represent the "room," and the structure and trimming of the garment become its "furnishings." Scale identifies their relationship to one another. Twin I is bolder or more exaggerated, whereas Twin II has a more restrained or delicate scale.

I   II

Exaggeration in scale—full chiffon sleeves, tightly fitted sheath silhouette, and stark open neckline are properly combined in the dress worn by Twin I. The sedately young taffeta dress beside it is equally well designed, with its dirndl skirt, puff sleeves, and ingénue bows all expressing the same scaled-down feeling.

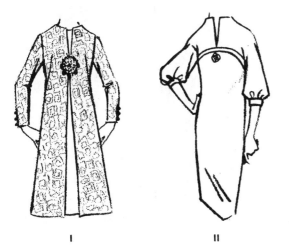

I   II

Twin I wears Saint-Laurent's famous rajah costume of heavy, off-white brocade with very slim sleeves and a huge jeweled brooch. It is the obvious inspiration for the scaled-down dress beside it, in which all details are reduced in impact to produce a sedate and wearable garment. The fabric of this dress is smooth flannel, and the properly scaled ornament is a gold filigree button.

Eye-Fooling Lines

THE AVERAGE WOMAN is shorter and is inclined to have narrower shoulders and a thicker midsection than is ideal. Dress manufacturers nonetheless must produce garments that are proportioned to fit average women, and designers therefore must employ the deceptive device of optical illusion in order to "fool the eye" into believing that average women are more attractively proportioned than nature made them. These everyday miracles of optical illusion are possible because the eye is a sense organ without reasoning power, believing anything that it sees.

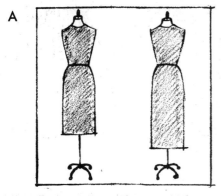

Short vs Long (A). The eye judges any measurement of length or width in relation to other length and width measurements in the same composition, as was explained in the analysis of scale. The long skirt on the right tends to increase the apparent height of its wearer simply because its length measurement is proportionally greater than its width measurement as compared with the shorter skirt beside it. The wearer also appears slimmer in the longer skirt because the width appears to be decreased in proportion to the length. But skirt length must follow fashion trends, and, except when long skirts are in fashion, designers use more subtle forms of optical illusion to make women look taller and slimmer than they actually are.

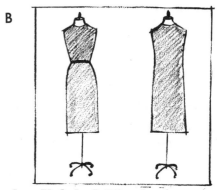

Belted vs Unbelted (B). In the waist-and-skirt dress on the left, a belt cuts the figure horizontally. This standard styling is contrasted with the unbelted shift beside it. The effect of a belt is to shorten the figure because it cuts the garment into two sections, each of which is shorter and wider than the original unbelted garment. The eye judges the length-to-width proportion of the sections in evaluating height.

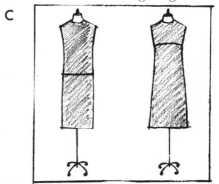

Low vs High Waistline (C). Waistline placement is used by the eye for judging height since it defines the length of each section of the garment. The high-waisted dress gives an illusion of greater height than the low-waisted garment because the eye automatically takes the longer of two sections as its yardstick, ignoring the shorter section. The low-waisted dress, with its relatively equal and thus shorter sections, therefore looks broader and shorter than the high-waisted dress.

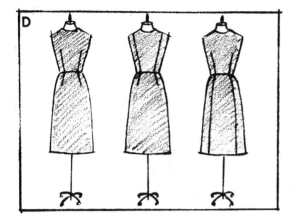

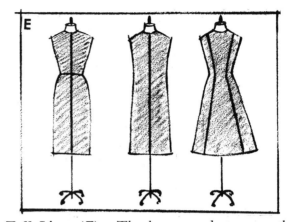

Slim Lines (*D*). All three garments are shown with dartlines drawn in both above and below the waistline. A waistline segmented by vertical lines looks slimmer because the eye uses the center panel formed by the lines in judging waistline width. The slimming effect is increased when the panel is extended to the shoulder as shown in the middle sketch, because the longer, stronger track carries the eye upward and outward. For this reason the lines emphasize shoulder width and by comparison make the waistline appear more slender. When panel lines extend down to the hemline, as shown by the figure on the right, the torso is slimmed and lengthened.

Tall Lines (*E*). The longer and stronger the line, the more effective it becomes in producing the illusion of height. Long, strong lines from neckline to hemline are so effective that the button-down sheath shown at the left has extreme popularity in women's and half-sizes. The button-down unbelted shift in the middle sketch offers the maximum illusion of length but it does not slim the waistline. The long lines of the princess dress at the right are perhaps the most effective since they not only lengthen the figure but also slim the midsection when fitted-in at the waistline as shown in the sketch.

Slim vs Tall (*F*). The tightly fitted and flared hourglass silhouette and the unbelted shift silhouette alternate in fashion. The hourglass automatically slims the midsection at the expense of shortening the figure and the shift automatically lengthens the figure at the expense of widening it at the waistline unless eye-fooling lines are introduced by the designer to counteract these often undesirable side effects. Skillful designers use the principles of optical illusion discussed here to create styles that are fashionable and flattering. On the two following pages twins again are introduced to show by comparison different tricks that can be used for creating the illusions of height and a slim waistline.

Hourglass Slims the Waistline **Shift Adds Height**

The Illusion of a Tall Slender Figure

ALTHOUGH THE LENGTH of a line can be measured in inches, its strength or impact can be measured only by the amount of time that the eye chooses to dwell on it. Strength comes from reinforcement with buttons, stitching, binding, or other trimming. Strength also comes from the absence of competing and therefore distracting elements in the composition. The combination of line length and strength produce the illusion of a tall, slender figure. As a line is strengthened it draws the eye more strongly and holds it for longer periods of time. Length and strength of line thus determine the

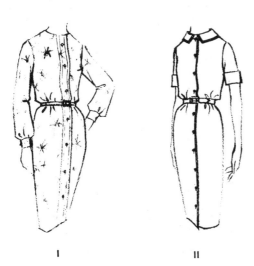

I   II

The button-down front is the styling most often used for accenting height. A strong illusion of height is induced in the plain-color dress on the right by the contrast of the vertical line and by the weak self-belt. The illusion of height is less pronounced in the print dress because the contrasting belt is a stronger line than the self-fabric tucking detail of the vertical closing.

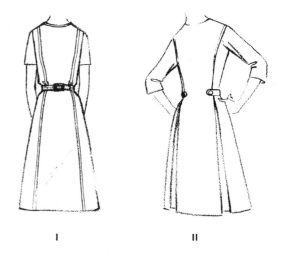

I   II

A center panel lengthens the figure as these two dresses illustrate. But a strong belt weakens the illusion of height that the long, strong seamlines produce. Twin I seems less tall than Twin II, in which a partial belt leaves the front panel free to furnish a clear track for the eye. Note how widened style lines made by the pleats at the hemline and by the flange fold at the shoulder cleverly slim the waistline.

force of the illusion to which the eye must respond. When they work together they fortify one another, but when they work at cross purposes, they tend to be confusing and displeasing. For example, as the eye travels up a line from the hem to the neckline, any other line at right angles is distracting, and the stronger the line the greater the distraction. The self-belt is used when the tall illusion is of most importance, for example, because it distracts the eye very little. The twin dresses on these two pages are examples of the use of line to give the illusion of height.

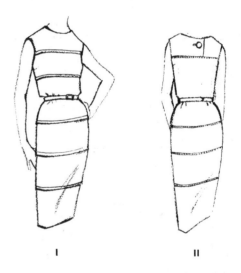

I   II

Horizontal segments with well-proportioned spacing have a ladder effect that is similar to a row of buttons and equally pleasing to the eye. The wide spacing between beltline and yoke in the dress on the right produces a taller effect than the dress on the left since the eye uses the longest segment of each dress as its yardstick in evaluating height.

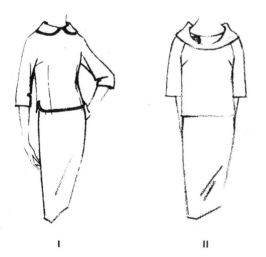

I   II

In the overblouse on the left, the binding at its hemline shortens the figure because its definite color contrast cuts across the body at its widest point. The self-hem of the overblouse on the right does not hold the eye, and the sparkling pin in the collar draws attention strongly upward because it is the only note of contrast on the garment—and a very strong one.

Adding Height and

PRINCESS LINES

LARGE COLLARS

Princess Lines. A garment that fits snugly through the midsection is very effective in giving the illusion of a slim waistline, as both twins illustrate. The twin on the right also appears taller because the long vertical lines furnish an unbroken track for the eye from the hemline to the top of the shoulder. The twin on the left appears less tall because the style line at the hip cuts across the figure to divide it into two segments. Styling of this type is often used effectively to make a tall girl look shorter. Otherwise it is best when developed in a fabric such as a spongy woolen where the style lines tend to be obliterated.

Large Collars. A large "away" collar is an effective slimming device because the width it adds at the shoulder makes an extreme contrast with width at the waistline, convincing the eye that it is smaller than it actually is. Both twins illustrate this point. In addition, both use the device of cutting the waistline into vertical segments to make it appear still slimmer. The twin on the left wears a strategically placed corsage, and the twin on the right has an asymmetrically styled collar that extends down to become a partial overskirt. The long line thus formed from hem to a point above the actual shoulderline adds height in this skillfully designed dress. The dress on the left actually shortens the figure because its white organza collar contrasts with the black crepe of the dress, cutting the figure into two relatively short, wide segments.

Slimming the Waistline

Bolero Jackets. Both twins are wearing dark dresses with white bolero jackets that are always effective in slimming the waistline. The width of the bolero hemline accentuated by color contrast convinces the eye that the waistline by comparison is narrower than it actually is. Maximum slimming effect is obtained when an exaggerated width of sleeve increases the contrast, as is here illustrated. The slimming effect in the costume on the right is less exaggerated than in the one on the left, but height is added instead. The long V-neck gives the eye the entire length of the garment from hem to shoulder to use as its yardstick for measuring height. This trick of bringing the skirt color up to the neckline is an effective device for adding height.

Wide Belts. A wide, tight, contrasting belt always slims the waistline but it also decreases the apparent height because it cuts the garment into segments that are comparatively short and wide. A belt of self-color or, more often, of self-fabric is almost always used in larger sizes to avoid shortening the figure. Here both twins wear comparable cotton dresses from the volume market. The wide, contrasting patent-leather belt worn by the twin on the left is often used in smaller sizes, whereas the inconspicuous self-belt with a self-covered buckle worn by the twin on the right is appropriately used in women's and half-sizes where designers must constantly practice all known forms of optical deception to give the illusion of a slim, young figure.

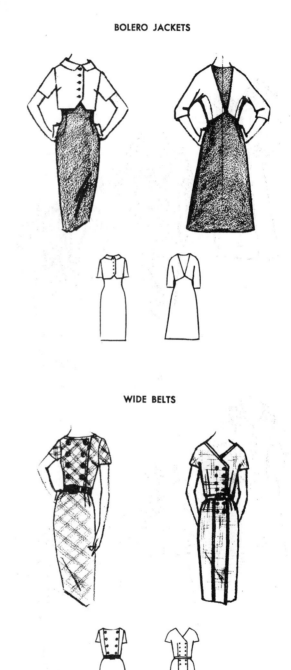

BOLERO JACKETS

WIDE BELTS

99

The Illusion of an Attractive Face

A

B

TO BE FLATTERING, a dress must draw attention to the face of the wearer. On these two pages four commonly used methods of styling are illustrated in which the dress "does something" for the wearer because the eye is led to the wearer's face. The dresses at the left generally have simple styling, relying heavily on a strong neckline for their sales appeal. On the facing page the examples show more intricate styling.

Strong Collar on a Simple Dress (A). The easiest way to draw attention upward to the neckline and the face is to make a simple basic dress with a strong collar to act as its main attraction, as shown in A. The dress on the far left has a flattering "away" collar detailed with self-tucking. The strong Chelsea collar with button accent used on the two-piece knit in the middle furnishes definite direction for the eye. The oversize Peter Pan collar with its casual grosgrain tie acts as a flattering frame for the face in the dress on the right.

Neckline Styling with an Expensive Look (B). An expensive-looking collar or scarf adds to the sales appeal of a dress and furnishes an attractive frame for the face, as shown in B. The collar of the dress on the far left is embroidered with jet beads and edged with delicate ball fringe. The two-piece flannel outfit in the middle uses a coordinated silk paisley scarf inside the casually unbuttoned neck. The dress on the right has narrow grosgrain ribbon threaded and knotted to trim its flattering portrait collar for an expensive handmade look. Here again, garment structure is so simple that neckline styling is the main attraction.

100

The dresses on this page use line in addition to trimming to produce the illusions of a slim, young figure as well as an attractive face. In expensive garments more intricate cuts are possible, and line and structure can thus play a greater part in styling, whereas in less-expensive dresses trimming plays a more definitive role.

Simple Collar Acts as Focal Point in Strong Design (C). When a dress is cut with interesting style lines, its collar can act as a focal point and give strong direction to the eye without being large or intricate as the three examples in C illustrate. The high-style dress on the left needs only a narrow ring collar to effectively frame the face since its peg skirt combined with the strong bodice design furnish adequate support. The softly draped chiffon dress in the middle furnishes sufficient design interest to lead the eye to the simple neckline that becomes the focal point of the dress. In the dress on the right, the center-front detail of band and tiny self-buttons subtly leads the eye to the effectively simple collar and the face of the wearer.

Ways to Frame the Face without a Collar (D). When the styling of a dress does not require a collar, some other way is found to frame the face. Either the design of the dress furnishes it, as shown by the sketches in D at the right, or the wearer accessorizes the garment with her own jewelry, scarf, or pin, fulfilling this need for a frame often subconsciously. The two-piece costume on the left is shown with the original patent-leather fruit trim of Cardin which furnishes a most effective eye-pulling device. The middle dress, by Galanos, relies solely on its beautiful lines, which might be augmented properly by personal jewelry. The dress on the right, like its counterpart in the same position on the facing page, uses delicate detailing, here in self-bias, as its effective face-framing device.

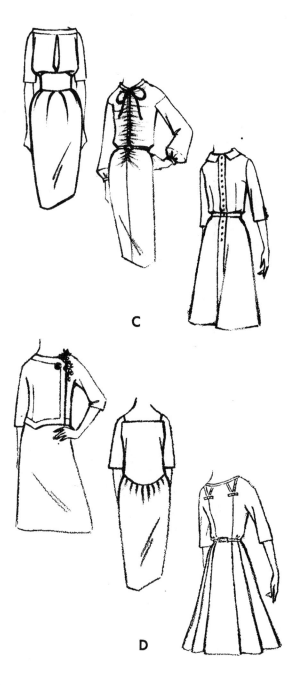

101

Unity of Design

GOOD TASTE is the instinctive recognition of "what goes with what"; the ability to discern —by eye—new combinations of fabric and styling that will be attractive and satisfying to many people and therefore have fashion appeal. Taste is the intangible factor that makes one dress look appealing and another dress look dull or busy, gaudy or cheap. The first element of good taste is *unity of design*. Fabric, silhouette, structure, and trimming must all belong together. A dress lacks unity when it seems to have been assembled from parts left over from other gar-

The classic coat dress on the right is a direct descendant of a simply styled oriental garment dating back to ancient Persia. Its collar then was the small mandarin type. The same collar is still in the best of taste, or no collar need be used, but a large dressy collar is entirely out of keeping with this dress type and produces a lack of unity.

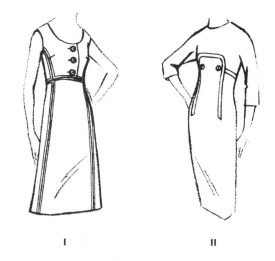

The Empire line of the dress on the right has a charming feminine look, whereas the button-down front of the dress on the left belongs on a tailored garment. The dressy Empire style lines and the tailored button-down closing have a completely opposite feeling, as if sections from two entirely different dresses had been inadvertently combined.

ments, as happens when the designer's eye is uncertain about the combination of elements. A dress lacks unity also when the original design is weak and the designer, belatedly recognizing its weakness, literally hangs trimming on it in a misguided attempt to add interest. In the illustrations on these and the following pages, Twin I shows garments lacking in good taste, whereas Twin II shows garments (which might have come from the same department in a store) in which the elements of good taste are present.

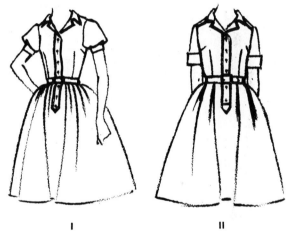

I   II

I   II

The type of shirtdress at the right has become an American classic because it is the most simple, comfortable, and thus suitable garment for casual wear—a man's shirt translated to a woman's needs without losing its style value. Attempts to improve the shirtdress with feminine touches such as "cute" sleeves and a trim midriff (Twin I) are in bad taste.

The sleeve of the classic shirtdress worn by Twin II has an easy, comfortable fit suited to its casual styling. The short, fitted sleeve on the dress worn by Twin I is not suited to the casual cut of the waist and rolling the sleeve only accentuates its inappropriateness. The wide, dressy belt is in equally bad taste, being wholly unsuited to casual wear.

Economy of Design

THE SECOND ELEMENT of good taste is *economy of design*. Every line and detail of a dress should be essential to the completeness of its design. The strength of a design is weakened by extraneous elements that do not contribute to its central, unified theme. This "busy" type of overdesign seems to result from a designer's desire to make a garment look important or expensive, but the wished-for result does not follow. Overdesign cheapens a dress. Good things come in small packages, and an unnecessary amount of detail suggests that much was used because it was not expensive. Although the eye

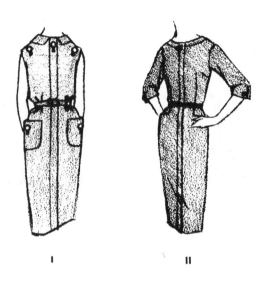

On the dress at the left the scattered, large pearl buttons with their contrasting buttonholes—particularly on the shoulder where they serve no purpose—give this dress an overtrimmed look. The dress at the right uses one large button for the neck and smaller buttons on the sleeves to furnish adequate trimming in combination with the good belt and flattering band detail at center front.

Embroidered ruffles, in quantity, overtrim the dress on the left to the point that it looks like an inexpensive, little-girl dress. The dress on the right combines full, bishop sleeves and ruffled cuffs with a simply cut bodice that uses the same eyelet embroidery of the cuffs in a restrained, waist-whittling bib effect.

is excited by strong design, it is wearied and bored by uneconomical use of design elements. How much of this detail can be used before it becomes too much? When any part of the trimming can be removed without being missed, or when any of the structural style lines can be simplified or eliminated without detriment to the design, the elements that can be deleted are too much. A beginner tends to overdesign, especially in sketching. When sketches are translated into muslin, this concept of economy must be adopted with great forthrightness if the effect is to be one of good taste.

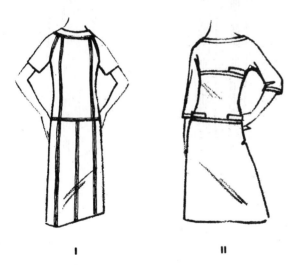

I   II

The group of tucks used as trimming on the dress on the right registers as a single impression, and the simple bodice repeats this rhythmic pattern in self-color Schiffli embroidery for a strong, uncluttered style. In the dress on the left the tiny evenly spaced groups of tucks in the waist conflict in size, direction, and spacing with the tucks in the skirt for a very busy effect.

On the dress at the left all possible seams have been accented with welt stitching, resulting in a tasteless and boring effect, whereas the dress beside it is in excellent taste. Welt stitching used in moderation accents the nicely proportioned sections of the dress and the pocket flaps that serve as its strong, well-coordinated trimming.

A Strong Focal Point

A CENTER OF INTEREST or focal point is essential to any good design. "Focus" is the term used here to express the relationship of the center of interest or dominant design feature of a garment to its other compositional elements. A design is "in focus" when one strong feature dominates and all other features support it. Focus must be considered as a taste factor since

In the dress on the left, lack of economy in trimming produces monotony because interest is scattered over too wide an area. Its "good" twin on the right shows how the design can be improved by removing the distracting bows and pockets, substituting a self-belt, and strengthening the "shirt" look by adding weight to the front-button detail.

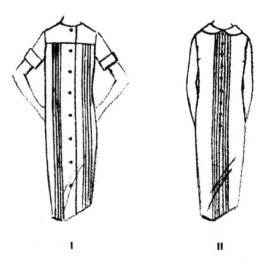

In the dress on the left the interest is scattered and weak. The buttons are too small, the cuffs too important, and the tucks too far at the sides for strong design. In the dress on the right trimming detail concentrated at center front adds to the illusion of height. Buttons are placed in the upper $\frac{5}{8}$ of the panel to draw the eye upward, and the properly scaled collar becomes the satisfying focal point of the design.

the evaluation of the relative strength of the design elements used in a garment depends on the innate taste of the designer. On these two pages Twin I illustrates garments that are boring to the eye because they have no strong center of interest, whereas Twin II shows garments of similar styling which have a strong focal point.

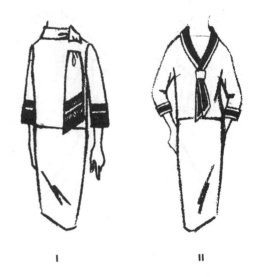

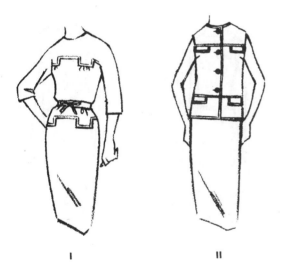

I   II

The repetition of the strong angular pattern in the one-piece dress on the left is very tiresome and lacking in taste. In the overblouse, on the other hand, the angular effect of the pocket flaps is toned down by the repetition of the welt stitching on the garment edges, and the design plays up the pearl buttons sufficiently to permit them to direct attention upward.

Unimaginative use of colorful trimming in equal amounts on scarf and cuffs in the overblouse of Twin I produces a monotonous, unaccented effect. In the overblouse worn by Twin II, the collar is strengthened and the trim on the cuffs is weakened enough to permit the collar to become the center of interest.

A Single Focal Point

WITH NO STRONG focal point the eye is bored; with two strong focal points the eye is frustrated, moving back and forth interminably from one center of interest to the other in a futile effort to find a satisfying point at which to rest. A center of interest must have more eye-pulling power than any other design element in the garment, and all other elements must

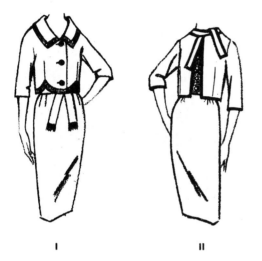

In the suit worn by Twin I the collar competes with the scallops and tie at the waistline. In the suit worn by Twin II the tie is moved up to make the neckline the strong center of interest while the braid binding acts as a simple supporting detail with no intrinsic interest of its own.

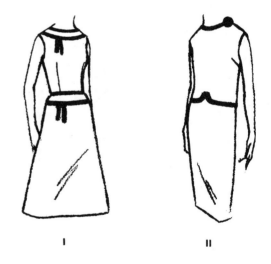

The dress on the left is nicely proportioned and well designed except for the tassels that form dual centers of interest. In the garment on the right the accent at the neckline has been strengthened to become the center of interest, and the binding at the bottom of the overblouse directs the eye upward and cleverly narrows the width of the hipline.

support it by echoing its design message with weakened impact. When all elements are of equal value, as illustrated by the bad twins on the two preceding pages, the effect is that of troops without a leader; with two focal points, as illustrated by the bad twins here, there are two equally strong leaders, one of which must be reduced to troop rank.

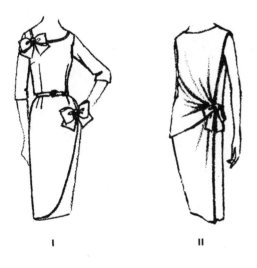

I   II

A single strong bow, supported by radiating folds, furnishes the center of interest for the dress on the right. The strong pair of bows on the dress beside it have such equal impact that they pull the eye back and forth from one to the other. Since they both serve no purpose but seem to be tacked on as an afterthought, they lack taste on two counts.

I   II

In the dress on the left the contrasting embroidery that trims the skirt is equaled in value by the trim on the midriff in combination with the full bishop sleeves. In the dress on the right, the skirt band has less impact because the contrast between fabric and self-color embroidery is less pronounced. The eye can easily move up and rest at the strong square neckline since the amount of embroidery on the waist gives it adequate support.

Transfer of Interest

A GARMENT on a rack in a store attracts potential customers because of its strong appeal through color, fabric, and interesting and expensive-looking design detail. When the garment is tried on, its "hanger appeal" is overshadowed by the need for it to be flattering and thus "do something" for the wearer. To accomplish this transfer of interest in which the focal

The focal point of the dress at the left consists of the four buttons which are placed so low that the eye cannot bridge the gap between them and the neckline. When two more buttons are added, as shown on the right, adequate track is supplied because the strong neckline furnishes additional pulling power and "does something" for the wearer.

In the dress shown at the left the skirt seams are trimmed with contrast piping to become much stronger design details than the band at the neckline, and they cause the eye to turn downward from the belt rather than upward to the face of the wearer. In the dress shown at the right the narrow, "quiet" band of self-fabric from hem to neckline leads the eye upward to the face where interest centers.

from Dress to Wearer

point shifts from the garment to the wearer's face, a track must be provided for the eye from the focal point of the garment to the face. The bad twins on these pages do not have an adequate track for the eye; the good twins illustrate techniques by which this transfer of interest can be accomplished by moving the focal point upward.

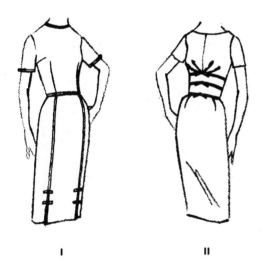

I   II

Interest in the dress worn by Twin I centers in the bow detail at the hemline. Contrast binding leads the eye up only as far as the waistline, and without a track up to the neckline the eye returns to the bows. In the dress worn by Twin II, the triple-bow detail at the midriff forms the center of interest, while a center seam and radiating folds of unstitched darts lead the eye strongly upward.

I   II

In the dress on the left the strong contrasting bands on the skirt hold the eye because there is nothing in the simple styling of the waist to compete with their powerful attraction. In the dress on the right the subtle quilted effect of self-color machine stitching that trims the skirt is carried up to accent the waist, aided by leather buttons and a leather string tie.

The Arrowhead in Design

AN ARROWHEAD so strongly influences the eye to look in the direction to which it points that it has become the standard convention used for road signs. Arrowheads are used in apparel design for the same purpose, always exerting strong influence on the eye, commanding it to look in the designated direction. This strength is due to the convergence of three lines at a single point, almost imparting to the line itself a sense of movement.

Taste is required in the use of the arrowhead in design. Its impact must be controlled, its form softened to be suitable for feminine ap-

parel, and its purpose of leading the eye to the face fulfilled.

The twin sketches here show varied applications of the arrowhead principle. They are paired on the basis of how well they fulfill the taste requirements just listed. The simplest use of the arrowhead is the pointed tab end that is standard on sleeve and skirt plackets of the shirt dress, but the arrowhead principle is used in a surprising number of less obvious ways in the style details here illustrated. The small diagrams show the pattern of eye movement which the arrowhead conformation induces.

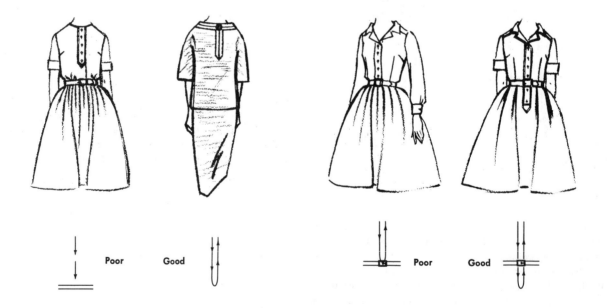

A strong design feature—here the neckline and button detail —must counteract the downward pull of a strong arrowhead and bring the eye back up to the face, as in the good twin.

The combination of the arrowhead pointing downward and the strong neckline pulling the eye upward has a noticeable lengthening effect on the silhouette of the good twin.

112

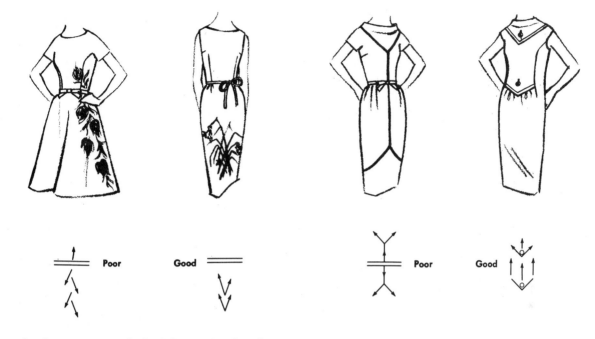

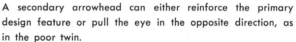

Arrowheads are present in both of these embroidery designs and each subtly leads the eye in the direction toward which it points.

A secondary arrowhead can either reinforce the primary design feature or pull the eye in the opposite direction, as in the poor twin.

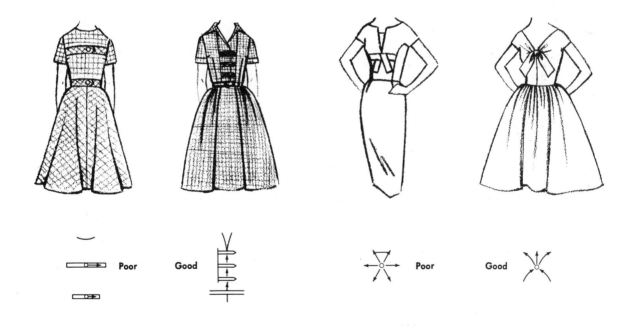

Horizontal tabs can furnish a ladder for the eye when they are well spaced, providing there is supporting pull at the neckline, as in the good twin.

An arrowhead made by the ends of a knotted tie exerts a subtle pull on the eye that is effective unless the attention is distracted by conflicting style lines, as in the poor twin.

Techniques of Apparel Design

Chapter Six

Introduction to Structure: Waist and Skirt

Production in Quantity
Layers of fabric with "marker"
on top are cut into pattern pieces

APPAREL DESIGN, of course, is first of all an art, but like any other art in which an original must be duplicated in quantity, apparel design must also be treated scientifically. Quantity production requires precision and accuracy that depend on technical knowledge and skill for profitable operation. The practical considerations that must influence a designer were discussed in Chapter 2. In these more technical chapters in this section, the interrelationship of practical and artistic factors and their application to specific design problems will be analyzed.

This chapter presents the "slopers" for waist and skirt. These blueprints of the dress form act as basic patterns from which all other patterns can be developed. In the two chapters that follow, the development of commonly used dress styles from the slopers is shown and discussed, and Chapters 9 and 10 round out the study of structure with similar presentations of sleeves and collars.

Technical Aspects of Apparel Design

A DESIGNER may make a sketch with original styling and smart lines but it is the shape of the pieces used to develop the style in fabric that gives the design its structure or cut and thus determines its fashion acceptability. Each part of a dress requires a pattern, and the structure of a garment is an expression of the interrelationships of the pattern pieces that make it. Block patterns, known as "slopers," are used to make all other patterns—the slopers for waist and skirt are shown on the facing page. Patterns are developed from these slopers by simple drafting techniques. When the slopers fit properly, patterns that are correctly developed from them also fit properly. Since slopers furnish the basis for style development, they are presented as an introduction to this "structure section" of the book.

Although the actual work of cutting and constructing a garment is usually done by an assistant, the successful designer, as a rule, has "arrived" by first being an assistant. But regardless of the road traveled to the designer's position, an understanding of the technical problems of structure and fit that are inherent in trans-forming ideas into profitable garments is of tremendous importance. Buyers and others who are interested in the merchandising of apparel find that a working knowledge of the technical aspects of apparel design is invaluable. Structure is presented more from the viewpoint of "understanding" than of "doing" at the background level of the designer and the buyer of apparel. A beginner in the field of apparel design cannot become an expert merely by reading these chapters. Intense practical application is as necessary in apparel design as in any other highly specialized field to enable the novice to overcome the uneasiness and lack of assurance that identifies the inexperienced beginner.

In presenting structure throughout this section, the sloper for waist, skirt, sleeve, or collar is first analyzed, after which standard variations and methods of styling are presented. Emphasis is always on theory. The limitations of various structures are pointed out, and the most practical uses are discussed. The medium-price misses daytime dress house that was described in Chapter 1 will remain as our example for all analyses throughout the book.

Block Patterns for Waist and Skirt

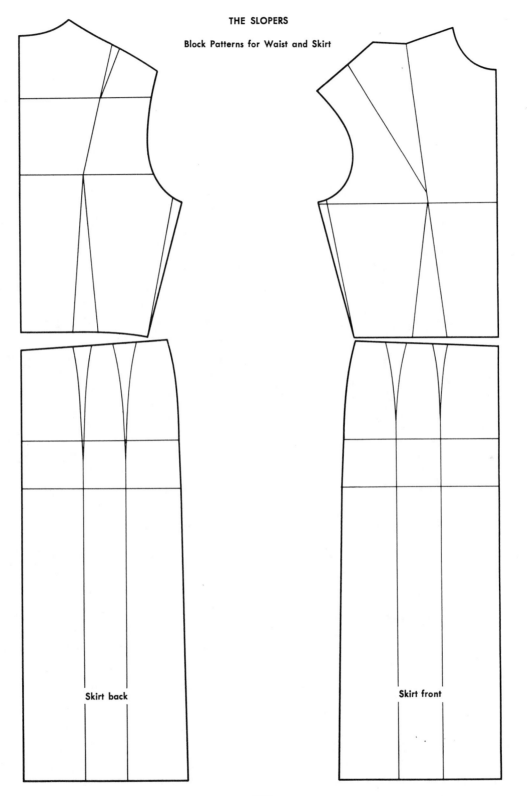

Skirt back

Skirt front

THE DRESS FORM

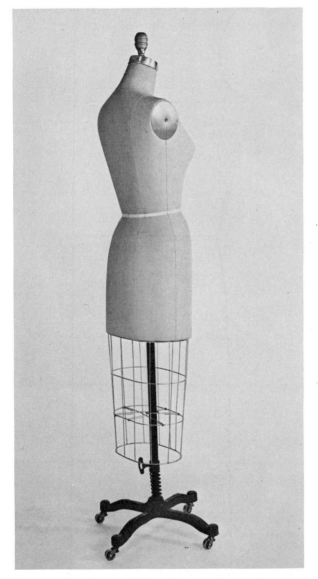

THE DRESS FORM as shown above does not represent actual body contour, but is instead an idealization of the human form as it would appear attired in a properly fitted girdle, bra, and slip. The purpose of the dress form is to furnish a stable and unyielding model on which a dress

Fitting the Dress Form

can be accurately fitted. Its canvas covering is made in eight sections, with seamlines strategically placed to act as useful demarcation lines in pattern development. Like the human form, the dress form is smaller at the waistline than at the bustline or the hipline. From a side view the bulge of the bustline at the front seems approximately equal to the bulge of the hipline at the back, while the back-waist section and the front-skirt section of the figure by comparison seem to be relatively flat. This counterbalance enables a person to maintain balance physically, but it confronts the designer with the problem of molding flat fabric around these complex curves that give the body its shape. The dress form can be made without arms and thus make it easier to fit the upper part of the figure where the curves are most troublesome. Arms are not necessary in the development of sleeves which generally are drafted from measurements. A wire cage can be used to represent the lower section of the skirt for the same reason, since no fitting is necessary below the torso.

Fitting with Darts. The slopers furnish an accurate blueprint of dress-form contour. They are made to fit around the curves of the figure by means of darts rather than by the shaped-seamline technique used for the dress-form covering. Fitting with darts is the most commonly used method for fitting dresses, since with darts a garment requires less labor in production and it is also easier to make the alterations that must often be made in fitting individual customers. Darts "take up" the excess fabric rather than requiring it to be cut away as is necessary with the curved-seamline method of fitting the figure.

THE PURPOSE OF A DART. The purpose of a dart is to eliminate the excess fabric in a pattern piece so that it can take on the curved contour of the body beneath it. The slim triangular shape common to most darts is marked on the pattern and transferred to the fabric. When the two sides of the dart are stitched closed, the fabric between its converging seamlines is eliminated from the garment surface. The figures at the right illustrate the "dart" principle. In the upper diagram the sloper for the back of the skirt is shown with the dartlines marked; and in the lower diagram a muslin skirt cut from the sloper is shown pinned up on the dress form, with the darts closed. Note how these darts take up the unavoidable excess that occurs because the pattern, of necessity, is flat, and the form that it must fit is rounded. Darts begin "from nothing" at the fullest part of the torso and become progressively wider as they approach the edge of the sloper that represents the waistline. A dart is necessary only when the fullest part of the figure is in the interior of a pattern piece, from which point the dart begins, and its size and shape are determined by the curvature of the form beneath.

DARTS AND GRAIN. Darts in the slopers are bisymmetric. In other words, the two halves are mates when measured from the center line of the dart. The center line is placed on "straight grain" (parallel with the threads of the fabric) whenever possible because a dart fits best when the "grain" of the fabric as well as its contour is balanced. Since dart seamlines attract the eye, they usually are planned as style lines in a garment, and mechanical balance, in some situa-

Basic Skirt Sloper with Darts Open

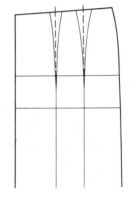

Muslin Pattern on Dress Form with Darts Closed

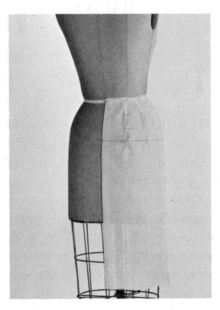

tions, must be sacrificed for eye appeal. "Sloper" darts that fit the waistline, however, are centered on straight grain, and an explanation of "grain" therefore needs to be made at this point.

Fabric Grain

GRAIN DIRECTION IN FABRIC

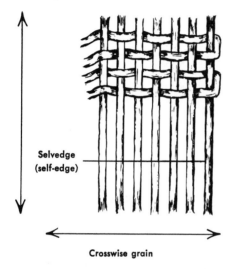

Lengthwise grain is parallel to selvedge

Selvedge (self-edge)

Crosswise grain

THREAD DIRECTION in woven fabric is called "grain." Lengthwise grain identifies the threads that run parallel with the selvedge. Crosswise grain identifies threads that run across the fabric. In the weaving and converting industries, lengthwise grain is called "warp" and crosswise grain is called "filling," from the process by which fabric is woven. In weaving, each warp thread emanates from a separate spool or cone and is held under tension in the loom while a shuttle carries the filling thread back and forth through the warp threads from one selvedge to the other again and again to produce the interlaced web of myriad threads that makes up fabric.

Importance of Grain. In all basic slopers and in most garment patterns, lengthwise grain runs up and down in order to permit crosswise grain, which has more elasticity, to run around the body and give ease across the shoulders and the chest and through the torso, so that the garment is comfortable to wear. Lengthwise grain hangs or falls more softly than crosswise grain, and garment pieces cut "on the cross" have a stiff, awkward appearance and are uncomfortable as well. The grain direction of every pattern piece has an effect on the fashion look of its garment and should be planned for most advantageous use.

Identification of Grain. Anyone who works with apparel must learn to identify lengthwise and crosswise grain by eye, without the selvedge in view to point it out unmistakably. One method of identification that usually is satisfactory is the comparative strength of warp and filling threads.

COMPARATIVE STRENGTH OF WARP AND FILLING THREADS. Warp threads are usually stronger than filling threads because they must withstand tension during the weaving process. For this reason fabric usually tears more easily lengthwise than crosswise. Filling threads often show a lack of uniformity, in which case crosswise grain can be identified by the shading of heavy and light streaks that run across the fabric.

COMPARATIVE ELASTICITY OF LENGTHWISE AND CROSSWISE GRAIN. Crosswise grain has more elasticity than lengthwise grain because the warp threads are held taut in weaving, whereas the filling thread serpentines over and under them. For this reason lengthwise grain takes and holds creases better than crosswise grain, and a fold in the fabric on the length of the fabric stays in better than a fold across it.

Straight Grain. The chief concern of the beginner "draping" with muslin is to keep the grain straight (with lengthwise grain perpendicular to the floor and crosswise grain at right angles to it, at the marked positions in the diagram). When the grain is not straight, muslin patterns do not mold to the figure properly, and garments made from them do not fit properly. Because of the precision necessary to make slopers that will fit well enough to be used as a basis for all other patterns, it is recommended that pattern paper rather than muslin be used in their preparation. The inherent elasticity in muslin becomes a handicap in sloper development rather than an advantage. Of course, slopers as well as all other patterns developed in paper must be "proved" in muslin before use.

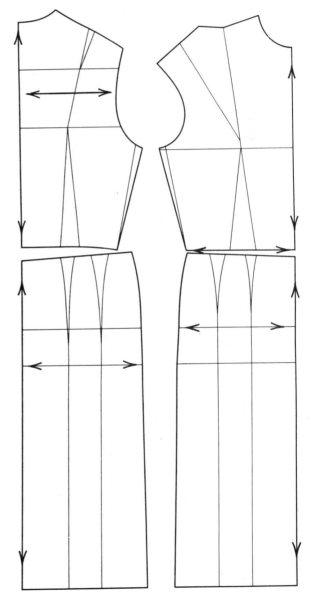

Introduction to the Skirt Sloper

A. DRESS FORM REPRESENTS BODY STRUCTURE

Waistline

Hipline

Torsoline

THE SKIRT SECTION of the dress form introduced on page 120 is compared in A with actual body structure to show the practical way in which body proportions can be encased in the rigid, idealized framework of a dress form. Equal segments make up the flattened cylindrical skirt section of the form. They are gradually squeezed in above the torsoline to form the waistline. B shows how the cross-section of a skirt at the torsoline is made up of four equal segments, whereas at the waistline the segments are not only smaller than at the torsoline but the back segments are smaller than the front segments. The waistline is normally 10 to 11½ inches smaller than the torsoline (see Table 1), and the back waistline is normally 1 inch smaller than the front waistline.

B. CROSS-SECTIONS OF WAISTLINE AND TORSOLINE

The back half of the dress form is squeezed in more than the front half at the waistline

Back

Four equal sections below the torsoline

—Torsoline—   —Waistline—

Front

Table 1.   Typical Figure-Type Measurements

Fig. Size	Waist Meas.	Typical Increments at Torsoline					
		BAUMAN		WOLF		SUPERIOR	
12	26		37		36½		36
10	25	11	36	10½	35½	10	35
8	24		35		34½		34
6	23		34		33½		33
11	25½		36½		36½		36½
9	24½	11	35½	11	35½	11	35½
7	23½		34½		34½		34½
5	22½		33½		33½		33½

C. FITTING SLOPER TO WAISTLINE

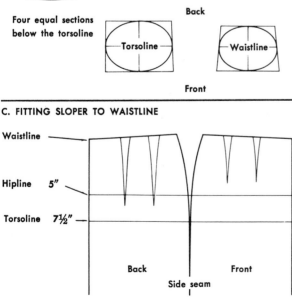

Waistline

Hipline   5″

Torsoline   7½″

Back   Front

Side seam

The Waistline Squeeze. The front and back skirt slopers are shown side by side in C to illustrate how the darts and the side seam combine to take up the amount by which the waistline is smaller than the torsoline. The side seam is actually a dart that is cut apart, both to make

124

production easier and to afford a means of alteration. The curved contour of the side seam takes up enough fabric to compensate for the curve of the figure in that area, just as the contour of the darts enables them to take up enough fabric to compensate for the curve of the figure in their areas. Since the waistline squeeze is graduated from minimum at center front and back to maximum at the side seamline, the panel dart (nearer the center) is smallest and the side-seam "dart" is the largest. And since the back waistline is ½ inch smaller than the front waistline (on the half), each back dart needs to be ¼ inch wider and automatically becomes proportionally longer than its companion front dart.

In production one large dart may replace the two darts of the sloper in order to cut down costs, especially when the long sloping hip is in fashion. In better garments, on the other hand, three darts may be used in styling the high, rounded hip contour.

Dress Forms. In this study dress forms were used from three leading manufacturers, in the junior and misses size ranges and from the years 1956–1963. Just as car manufacturers present individual body styling, so each dress-form manufacturer presents a slightly different concept of the ideal human body. Table 1 and the six skirt diagrams in D show the scope of these differences. The panel dart may be positioned either at the edge of the "panel third" of the waistline (Type I) or it may be moved ⅛ inch to the left of this position (Type II). The position of the panel dart is correlative with the position of the panel dart in the waist that it must match, and the wider lateral position of the bust apex used for some forms causes their panels to be wider than others. The waistline measurement of the front-skirt sloper can be used to define panel width precisely. Note that dart width, which varies with figure type, remains constant throughout the size range

D. TYPICAL DART ARRANGEMENTS

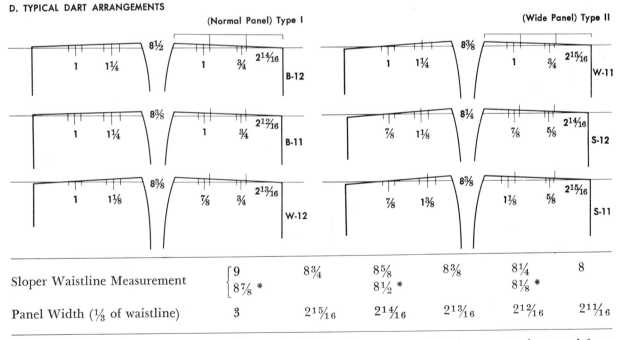

Sloper Waistline Measurement	$\begin{cases} 9 \\ 8\frac{7}{8}* \end{cases}$	8¾	8⅝ 8½ *	8⅜	8¼ 8⅛ *	8
Panel Width (⅓ of waistline)	3	2¹⁵⁄₁₆	2¹⁴⁄₁₆	2¹³⁄₁₆	2¹²⁄₁₆	2¹¹⁄₁₆

* Panel-width thirds are taken to next larger ¹⁄₁₆ inch and are measured in from center front and from side seam, allowing the discrepancy to occur in inner third of waistline.

Introduction to the Waist Sloper

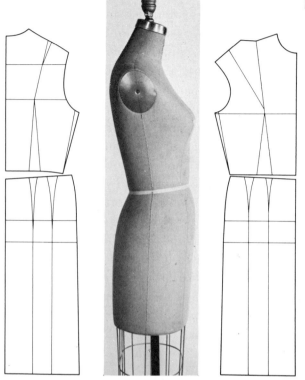

A. SLOPERS AND THE DRESS FORM

der seamline with darts open and closed. Note that the front shoulderline (closed) is shorter than the back shoulderline because of the progressive narrowing of the shoulder from back to front. The excess in the back is eased in at the shoulder seam for better fit.

Dart Size, Shape, and Position. A dart always begins "from nothing" at whatever position the curvature begins on the particular dress form used. A dart is precisely as large as necessary to compensate for the difference between the larger chest or torso measurement and the smaller measurement at the waistline or shoulderline. The waistline darts and the side seamline which acts like a waistline dart all have straight seamlines because the body contour beneath them permits it. Hip darts and the side seamline of

THE RELATIONSHIP of the skirt and the waist slopers to the dress form and to one another is shown in A. The waist section of the form, like the skirt section, is squeezed in at the waistline, but although the lower part of the skirt is a simple cylinder that requires no special drafting, the upper part of the waist is a complex of curves that requires shoulder darts, a neckline, and an armhole that must be accurately defined.

Alignment of Darts. The purpose of a dart is to reduce the "working" or finished-garment width of a pattern piece to the measurement of the seamline to which it extends. B shows how the waist and skirt slopers, which are so disproportioned when the darts are open, will match at the waistline when the darts are closed. C illustrates this same point by showing the shoul-

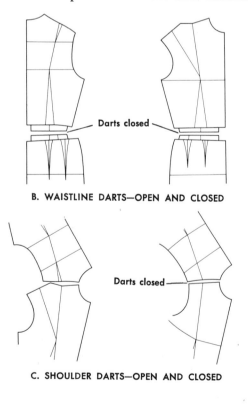

B. WAISTLINE DARTS—OPEN AND CLOSED

C. SHOULDER DARTS—OPEN AND CLOSED

126

the skirt have curved seamlines because the body contour beneath demands it. The front dart in the waist is shorter than the back dart because the bust apex where it ends is centered on a shorter front length (neckline to waistline), whereas the dart apex in the waist back is centered on a longer back length (shoulder point to waistline). Just as in the skirt, the front dart in the waist is shorter than the back dart.

Waistline Darts. The position of the front dart depends on the lateral position of the bust apex (its distance from center front), and one dart must be used, rather than two as in the skirt, because the hemispheric contour of the bust requires that the waistline dart extend precisely to its apex point and that it be centered on straight grain. One dart is used in the back-waist sloper in order to match the front. Back panel width is not critical because the back is relatively flat and it is planned therefore to permit the dartlines of back and front to meet at the shoulder, as is often desirable in drafting other patterns.

Use of Table 2. Table 2 offers a practical method for using the front-panel width to compute the width of the waistline darts and of the back panel. The waist front is normally 1 inch wider than the waist back at the underarm, but only ½ inch wider at the waistline, a discrepancy that is resolved by making the back dart ½ inch smaller than the front dart. The proportional relationship between panels and their darts shown in the table brings straight grain automatically across the front waistline and a proper matching of front- and back-panel lines at the shoulder.

Table 2. *Torso Circumference Used for Finding Panel and Waist Dart Widths* * (in inches)

a Torsoline (see Table 1)	b Sloper Torsoline (a ÷ 4)	c Sloper Waistline (b − ¾″)	A Front-Panel Width (c ÷ 3)	B Front-Dart Width (A × ⅔)	C Back-Dart Width (B − ½″)	D Back-Panel Width (C × 2)
39	9¾	9	3	2	1 8/16	3
38½	9⅝	8⅞	3	2	1 8/16	3
38	9½	8¾	2 15/16	1 15/16	1 7/16	2 15/16
37½	9⅜	8⅝	2 14/16	1 15/16	1 7/16	2 14/16
37	9¼	8½	2 14/16	1 15/16	1 7/16	2 14/16
36½	9⅛	8⅜	2 13/16	1 14/16	1 6/16	2 13/16
36	9	8¼	2 12/16	1 14/16	1 6/16	2 12/16
35½	8⅞	8⅛	2 12/16	1 14/16	1 6/16	2 12/16
35	8¾	8	2 11/16	1 13/16	1 6/16	2 11/16
34½	8⅝	7⅞	2 10/16	1 13/16	1 5/16	2 10/16
34	8½	7¾	2 10/16	1 13/16	1 5/16	2 10/16
33½	8⅜	7⅝	2 9/16	1 12/16	1 4/16	2 8/16
33	8¼	7½	2 8/16	1 11/16	1 3/16	2 7/16
32½	8⅛	7⅜	2 8/16	1 11/16	1 3/16	2 7/16
32	8	7¼	2 7/16	1 10/16	1 2/16	2 5/16
31½	7⅞	7⅛	2 6/16	1 9/16	1 2/16	2 4/16

* Type I dart plans: Read straight across.

Type II dart plans: For columns A–D, go up to the column that is ⅛ inch larger.

Pattern Paper and Muslin. Pattern paper is recommended for use in sloper development. Of course, a sloper must be put into muslin and tried on the dress form for checking before it is made in hard paper for permanent use. Particularly important check points are the shoulderline, the side seamline of the waist, and the width across the upper part of the back. It is recommended that a sleeve be set in for this purpose. When a sleeve hangs straight and fits easily, and when its center line matches the shoulder line and its underarm line matches the side seamline of the waist, the armhole and the seamlines that lead into it are correct.

E. EASE ADDED AT UNDERARM

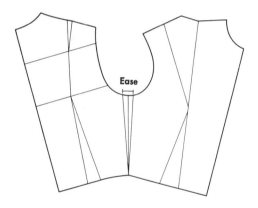

Underarm Seamline. The waist front and back with underarm seam closed are shown above. The narrow (1 inch) triangular section of ease extending from underarm to waistline is always added in drafting the sloper, since it is necessary to the proper use of the French curve in making the armhole. This ease is necessary when a sleeve is set in. For garments without sleeves, all or part of it may be cut away. (The method for finding the length of the underarm seamline, which is the reciprocal of armhole length and depends on it, is shown in Chapter 9.

Table 3. Measurements for the Armhole (in inches)

Size	Bauman (a)	(b)	Wolf (a)	(b)	Superior (a)	(b)
12	5 12/16	7 7/8	5 9/16	7 12/16	5 9/16	7 13/16
10	5 9/16	7 5/8	5 6/16	7 9/16	5 6/16	7 10/16
8	5 6/16	7 3/8	5 3/16	7 6/16	5 3/16	7 7/16
6	5 3/16	7 1/8	5	7 3/16	5	7 4/16
11	5 9/16	7 5/8	5 9/16	7 12/16	5 9/16	7 10/16
9	5 6/16	7 3/8	5 6/16	7 9/16	5 6/16	7 7/16
7	5 3/16	7 1/8	5 3/16	7 6/16	5 3/16	7 4/16
5	. . .	. . .	5	7 3/16	5	7 1/16

(a) Armhole length (sleevecap length − 5/8 inch).
(b) Typical back width at quarterline.

The French Curve. The Dietzgen 2152-17S French curve is used for making all curved (elliptical) lines that appear on the patterns shown in this book. When used in the scientific way here demonstrated, this French curve is a measuring device that is as accurate for making curved lines as the ruler is for straight lines and the compass is for circles. Wherever the curve is used, it is positioned in relation to three specific, triangulate location points (1, 2, 3) to which the curve must be precisely matched if it is used properly.

Dress-Form Measurements. Certain measurements must be taken on the particular dress form used as a preliminary step to sloper development. Measurements are taken first on the waist to check the waist-tape position (skirt measurements cannot perform this service so readily) and to correct its position if necessary. It is essential that the waist tape be centered on the crease in the dress form where its waist and skirt sections join beneath the canvas cover, since patterns for both waist and skirt are positioned at the midpoint or center of the tape which therefore must represent the waistline.

Back-waist length is measured from neck seam to center of waist tape, and since back length is graduated in quarter inches (15¾–16–16¼ inches, etc.) misalignment of the waist tape is easily detected.

Neck rise (distance from bottom of neckline up to shoulder point) can be found (only indirectly) by cutting an L-shape template, marking panel width on the lateral arm, and using the vertical arm to measure neck rise (which varies from ⁸⁄₁₆ to ¹⁴⁄₁₆ inch on the dress forms used in the study).

Front-waist length, which is also graduated in quarter inches, must be measured indirectly since it includes bust protrusion. A practical method for taking this measurement is shown, using pattern paper wide enough to cover both bust apexes, pinned at center of waist tape and folded straight across at the bottom of the neck. (On the forms used in the study it is consistently ½-inch greater than actual center-front measurement from bottom of neckline to center of waist tape.)

Side-seam length can be found by measuring from shoulder point to the center of waist tape (here in sixteenths of an inch) and subtracting the armhole length shown in Table 3.

Waistline circumference (normally in half-inch gradations) can be measured with a tape measure. Half-of-front and half-of-back waistline measurements that are needed are found by dividing the total circumference of the waistline by 4 and adding ¼ inch for the front and subtracting ¼ inch for the back.

Torso circumference and side-seam and center-back lengths can be found by first measuring 7½ inches down from center of waist tape at center front and marking this torso level with a pin. Use a long ruler to measure up from the floor to establish side-seam and center-back levels at the same distance from the floor as the center-front level. Mark each with a pin. Measure the torso circumference at the level marked. This measurement, like the waistline measurement, is graduated in half inches. Divide the total measurement by 4 to find the needed width of front torsoline. Find the length of the dress form from torsoline to waistline at the side seam and center back by comparing their measurements with the 7½-inch measurement at center front. (Side seam is consistently ⅜ inch longer than center front on forms used in study, and center back is always either slightly longer (⅛ inch) or shorter (⅛ or ¼ inch) than center front.)

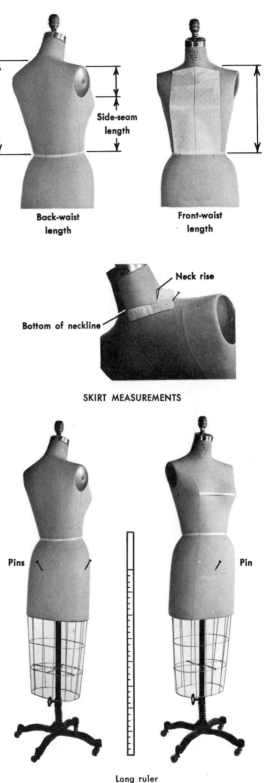

WAIST MEASUREMENTS

Side-seam length

Back-waist length

Front-waist length

Neck rise

Bottom of neckline

SKIRT MEASUREMENTS

Pins

Pin

Long ruler

129

Skirt Sloper Step by Step

STEP 1. PATTERN LAYOUT AND SIDE SEAMLINE

Draw a line to represent center front of skirt (23-inch length arbitrarily chosen). At right angles to this line, draw lines to represent the *waistline*, 1 inch below top edge of paper; the *hipline*, 5 inches below waistline; the *torsoline*, 2½ inches below hipline; and the bottom of torso, 7½ inches below torsoline.

For the *side-seam location*, measure over from center front on torsoline and mark its width (one-fourth of torso circumference). Measure the *hipline* ⅛ inch less and *bottom of torso* ⅛ inch more than torsoline. Draw in the side seamline in two steps: (a) from torsoline to bottom of skirt; (b) from torsoline to hipline, with ½ inch for overlap above hipline.

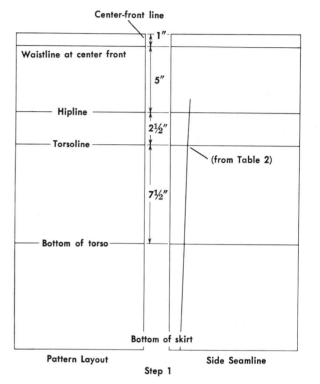

Step 1

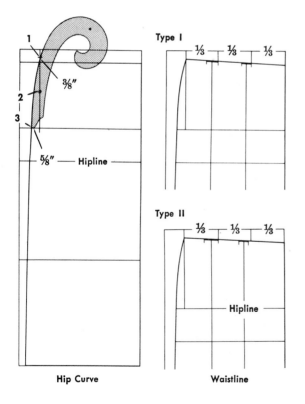

Step 2

STEP 2. WAISTLINE SQUEEZE

Hip curve: Erect a line perpendicular to the hipline, over ⅝ inch, and extend it up for the distance measured as hip rise (here 5⅜ inches) to establish the side-seam point (where waistline and side seam meet). Use a French curve for this section of the side seam, touching the side-seam point for Point 1, balance hole centering on the line for Point 2, and the end of the curve resting on the hipline and overlapping the side seam for Point 3.

Waistline: Draw in the waistline from side-seam point to center front. Divide the waistline into thirds, using Table 2. Mark dart widths and centers on pattern. The diagrams in D on page 125 can be used to determine dart width for different skirts. The points that mark the division into thirds furnish location points for both darts in Type I skirts, but in Type II skirts the panel dart is moved ⅛ inch to the left. (For off-scale waistlines that have a larger or smaller differential than is shown in Table 1, the second dart must gain or lose the amount necessary to keep the waistline at the correct size.)

130

STEP 3. CONTOUR OF THE DARTS

Shorter darts: Rounded hip contour requires shorter darts than sloping hip contour. Shorter darts end theoretically 1 inch above the hipline, although the length of the dart is proportional to its width, and the narrower panel dart ends above this level. Use the French curve touching the dart mark at the waistline for Point 1, tangent to the center line of the dart 1 inch above the hipline for Point 2, and the end of the curve resting on the hipline for Point 3.

Longer darts require an extra step. Use the ruler to mark in the dart from the hipline to 1½ inches above it, extending the lines for an additional ½ inch to furnish an overlap for the French curve. Use the French curve touching the dart mark at the waistline for Point 1, and tangent to the ½-inch overlap for Points 2–3. Note that the French curve is placed lower for the wider second dart than for the narrower panel dart.

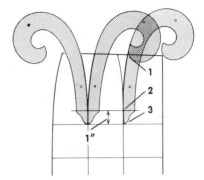

Shorter Darts (Wolf and Superior forms)

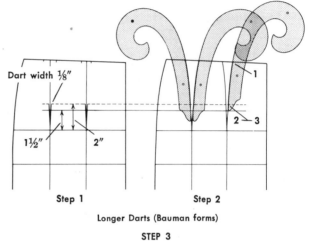

Dart width ⅛"

1½"   2"

Step 1   Step 2

Longer Darts (Bauman forms)

STEP 3

STEP 4. THE BACK OF THE SKIRT

The pattern: Trace the back from the front as shown. (The back is a duplicate of the front in size, shape, and location of the second dart center for all sizes and for all brands used in the study.)

The waistline and darts: Draw in the waistline using the center-back length found by measurement on the preceding page. Take panel width from Table 2. Mark the width of both darts on the waistline (each adds ¼ inch to the width of the companion front dart). Extend the center line of the panel dart to skirt bottom.

Dart contour: These long darts are made by the same two steps as the long front darts. Use a ruler to make the lower half of the dart and the French curve for the upper half. The darts end 1 inch below the hipline and the straight section extends up 1½ inches above hipline where its width is ¼ inch. Use the French curve to draw in the upper section of the dart, overlapping for ½ inch above the straight section.

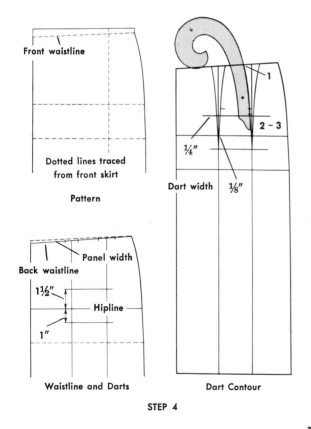

Front waistline

Dotted lines traced
from front skirt

Pattern

Panel width

Back waistline

1½"

Hipline

1"

Waistline and Darts

Dart Contour

1

2 - 3

¼"

Dart width   ⅛"

STEP 4

131

SLOPER DEVELOPMENT

Waist Front Step by Step

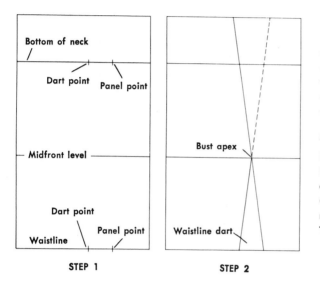

Bottom of neck

Dart point   Panel point

Midfront level

Bust apex

Dart point

Panel point

Waistline

Waistline dart

STEP 1   **STEP 2**

STEP 1. PATTERN LAYOUT

Measure up from the waistline edge of the paper on the center-front edge, mark the center-front (bottom of neckline) and midfront lengths, and draw in lines at right angles to the center front to represent these lengths. Use pattern paper approximately 2 inches wider than the dress form, measured from center front to underarm, and 3 inches longer than the center-front length, for ease in working.

STEP 2. DART LAYOUT

Mark panel width and dart width, using Table 2, at waistline and at neckline. Draw in the two dartlines from waistline to neckline, crossing at the midfront level to form the bisymmetric waistline dart and extending to the top of the paper to act as a guide for neck shape and shoulder-dart placement.

STEP 3. NECK SHAPE

Use the French curve with the balance hole centered over the extension of the center-front line (edge of paper) for Point 1, resting on the bottom of the neckline for Point 2, and tangent to the dotted extension line of the dart for Point 3. The curve does not touch the extension line but is placed $\frac{1}{8}$ inch to the right of it as shown.

STEP 4. SIDE-SEAM-WAISTLINE POINT

Pin the waistline dart closed, then pin the pattern to the dress form. Anchor it first at the shoulder-neck area, then at center front, with 4 pins as shown. The center front will seem too long because of the bust protrusion. Anchor the waistline at the dart position and then at the side seam. It will fall at the middle of the tape only to the side seam.

STEP 5. SIDE SEAMLINE

Fold the pattern back upon itself along the seamline so that it "splits" the armplate screw. Pin the pattern securely to the dress form, first at the waistline and then at the underarm. (The underarm seam on the dress form is so often out of alignment that it is not depended on to position the side seamline. The armplate screw, however, is dependable.)

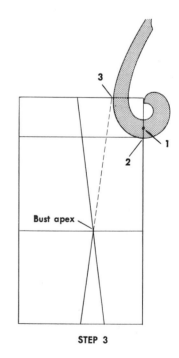

Bust apex

STEP 3

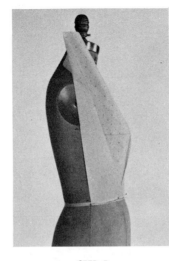

STEP 4   STEP 5   STEP 6

STEP 6. LOCATION OF SHOULDER DART AND SHOULDERLINE

Force all excess in the pattern up to the middle of the shoulder and pin it into a dart, the edge of which is the extension line of the waistline dart drawn in Step 2. Fold the dart to the left, then fold the top of the paper back on itself across the shoulderline and crease it. (The shoulderline on the dress form may be incorrect but can be corrected after a sleeve is set.)

STEP 7. COMPLETION OF SHOULDERLINE

Remove the pattern from the dress form, and fold it double on the midfront line so it will lie flat while you work on the shoulder. Crease in the dart and repin it, folded to the left. Draw in the shoulderline as a straight line, following the crease (Step 6). Measure shoulder width on the dress form and mark it on the pattern. Cut the shoulderline with the dart closed. Mark the outer edge of the dart. Open both shoulder and waistline darts and true in the shoulder dartline.

STEP 8. COMPLETION OF SIDE SEAM AND ARMHOLE

True in the side seamline on the creased line made in Step 5. Find the side-seam length as shown on page 129. (Side-seam length plus armhole length make up the total length from shoulder point to waistline.) Add the half-inch extension at the underarm, as discussed on page 128. Draw the line at right angles to the side seamline at the underarm. Taper it to nothing at the waistline. Use the French curve to make the armhole, touching the end of the shoulderline for Point 1, and balancing on the half-inch extension line for Points 2–3. The balance hole may be centered on the underarm line or between this line and the half-inch line, as shown in the alternate diagrams. Cut the side seamline and the armhole line to complete the pattern.

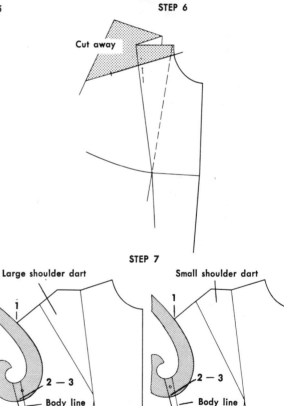

STEP 7

STEP 8   (Alternates)

133

Waist Back Step by Step

STEP 1. PATTERN LAYOUT

Use pattern paper 2 inches longer than the center-back length and 2 inches wider than the measurement from center back to underarm. Measure and mark the waistline up ½ inch from the bottom of the paper, mark the neckline as measured up from the waistline, and mark the neck rise (shoulder level) as measured up from the neckline. Draw in the waistline and the shoulderline at right angles to center-back edge of the paper.

STEP 2. DART LAYOUT

Mark the panel and dart widths (from Table 2) on the waistline and shoulderline. Measure and draw the mid-back and the upper-quarter lines at right angles to the center back. Draw in the two dartlines from waistline to shoulderline, crossing at the midback level, to form the bisymmetric waistline dart.

STEP 3. NECK SHAPE AND SHOULDER DART

Neck shape: Put in the neckline with the French curve, touching the shoulder point (and extension of dartline) for Point 1, and resting on the center neckline mark for a distance equal to the neck rise for Points 2–3.

Shoulder dart: Measure over from the shoulder point a distance equal to the panel width and mark the dart position. Make the shoulder dart the same width as the waistline dart, measured at the same distance from the dart apex.

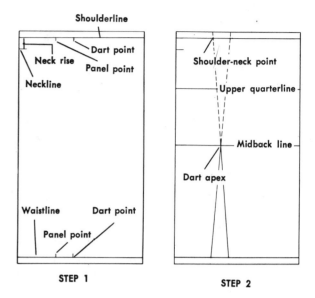

STEP 1

STEP 2

STEP 4. ON THE DRESS FORM

Pin the darts closed and anchor the pattern to the dress form, using 4 pins at the center back. Pin the midback section firmly at the armhole. Fold the paper back at the side seamline, and crease and pin, just as with the front. Mark the outer half of the shoulderline to coincide with the shoulderline on the front sloper.

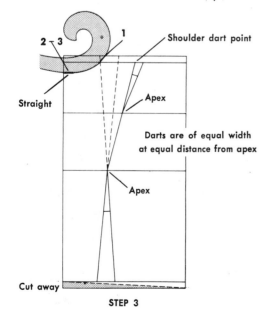

STEP 3

STEP 4

STEP 5. WAISTLINE SHAPE

Remove the pattern from the dress form and fold it double on the midback line so it will lie flat while you true in the waistline. The contour of the waistline depends on its width in proportion to the midback width and varies from dress form to dress form. A curved extension can be made with the French curve as shown.

STEP 6. SIDE SEAMLINE AND ARMHOLE-DIRECTION LINE

Side seamline: True in the creaseline of the side seam. Measure and mark it to be the same length as the side seamline of the front and add the half-inch extension in the same way. *Armhole-direction line:* Draw a line to connect the shoulder-width mark at the quarterline (Table 3) with the waistline point at the underarm to furnish a match-point on the midback line which is needed for making the armhole.

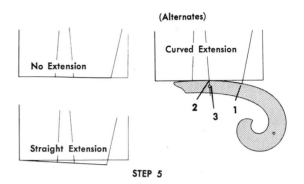

STEP 5

STEP 7. COMPLETION OF SHOULDERLINE

True in the shoulderline, placing the French curve on the shoulder point for Point 1, touching the shoulderline (dotted line) for Point 2, and the balance hole over an extension of the dartline for Point 3. For shoulder with up-curve, the shoulderline is merely extended. For shoulder with reverse curve, the French curve is reversed as shown in a second step.

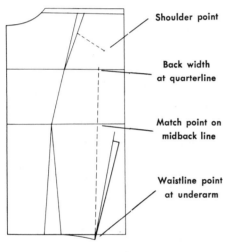

Shoulder point

Back width at quarterline

Match point on midback line

Waistline point at underarm

(Step 6)

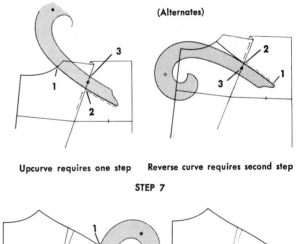

Upcurve requires one step   Reverse curve requires second step

STEP 7

STEP 8. UPPER ARMHOLE (OVERARM SECTION)

Connect the outer edge of the waistline dart with the shoulder-width point on the quarterline. The shoulderline terminates at the intersection of this line and the shoulderline. Use the French curve to true in the armhole, touching the shoulder point for Point 1, the quarterline point for Point 2, and the midback point for Point 3.

STEP 9. LOWER ARMHOLE (UNDERARM SECTION)

Since the underarm section of the back waist matches precisely with the section of the sleeve that joins it, a practical way to true it in is to place the back of the sleeve sloper so that its underarm point joins the underarm point of the waist and pivot it up until it lies tangent to the armhole in the midback area.

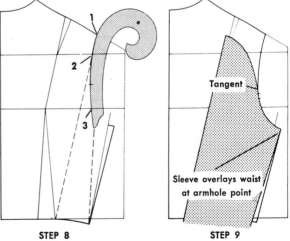

STEP 8   **STEP 9**

How Silhouette Changes Affect the Dress Form

DRESS FORMS are altered slightly each year as a continuing prelude to fashion change, which subtly swings from the rectangular silhouette of the shift to the triangular silhouette of the hourglass and back again. Changes in the contour of the dress form are made in order to furnish a proper foundation on which designers can build the varied exaggerations of silhouette that represent fashion in the different eras. The look of any fashion begins with the foundation on which it is made, for the contour of a dress form is reflected in all patterns made on it.

1952   1962

B. SILHOUETTE CHANGES

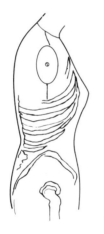

A. BODY STRUCTURE

Dress Forms Interpret Body Structure. The question is often asked, "How can dress forms change constantly and still be realistic representations of the same human body when the body contour of an adult female remains relatively stable?" The bony structure of the body is indeed stable and certain parts of it, such as the ridge of the pelvis that outlines the hip and the ball-and-socket shoulder joint, define body con-

tour in a strong, unyielding way. But the rib cage, which gives the upper part of the body its form, does not extend much below the bust and thus does not furnish a rigid framework for the flesh at the waistline, as shown in the anatomical diagram at the left. For this reason the contour of the body can be molded or compressed in this area and made to adjust to quite a range of silhouette variation. Thus the waistline is the area of the body in which changes that affect the silhouette are most frequently made. As the waistline is moved up or down and eased or compressed, the fashion look of its silhouette is changed. Over a ten-year period (1952–1962) the waistline moved downward in imperceptible steps, never more than $\frac{1}{4}$ inch in any one year. The relatively high waistline of the 1950's with its gently sloping hipline seems much longer than the long-waisted form of the 1960's with its necessarily high hipline. The lengthening of the waist gave a different proportion to the silhouette, and a different fashion look resulted from it, as the dresses sketched in B illustrate.

Slopers Interpret Dress-Form Changes. Since changes in dress forms are reflected in their slopers, an analysis of slopers from these two eras aids in understanding dress-form changes. Other differences besides the location of the waistline become apparent. A shorter waistline causes the hip section of the skirt to extend higher with a straighter side seamline. The hip darts are longer and have less curvature, too, because they begin to taper from a higher level. When the waistline is lowered the skirt has a more squarely proportioned hipline because the shorter darts have more exaggerated curvature. The longer waistline of this form requires a fuller bustline for balance. When the bust is enlarged the center front of the waist is lengthened in proportion to the amount by which the shoulder dart is increased in size. The shoulderline is squared slightly to be in-drawing with the stronger rectangular shape of the skirt.

"SIZING" MEASUREMENTS REMAIN STABLE. Some measurements remain quite stable, particularly those in areas that the bony framework of the body supports. The measurement from neck point to shoulder point (shoulder width) varies only slightly and the general contour of the waist back remains quite constant. The circumference of the body at the torsoline is not subject to change either, because women who are accustomed to buying the same size dress season after season expect it to fit as well one season as another. Measurements such as torso circumference and back width are kept stable so that the same size garments can be worn by the same people as comfortably one season as another.

C. SLOPER CHANGES

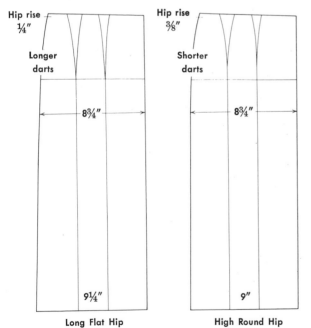

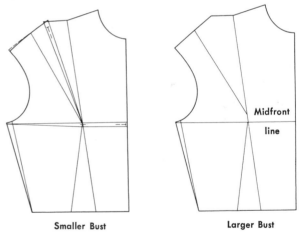

Smaller Bust   Larger Bust

The Skirt. When the high round hip is changed to the long flat hip, the amount of hip rise is reduced slightly, the darts are longer and have less curvature, and the width of the skirt is increased at the hemline. The torso and waistline circumferences can remain the same, as shown.

The Waist Front. The shoulder dart takes care of bust protrusion. The change in the sloper from a full bust to a smaller bust is shown in the diagrams above. The midfront line is slashed all the way from center front to the side seamline on the larger-bust sloper. Then the shoulder dart is slashed down to the bust apex and lapped the desired amount, after which the midfront line is lapped enough to bring the center-front line back to its normal straight-grain position. The shoulder dart is enlarged by spreading rather than lapping at the two positions. Note that the center-front length changes as the bust size changes, but the underarm length is not affected.

Chapter Seven

Styling the Waist-and-Skirt Dress

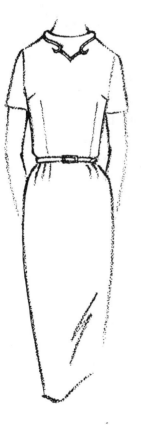

A WAIST-AND-SKIRT dress is made by combining one of many possible skirt styles with one of an equally large number of possible waist styles which become a dress when they are joined at their common, closely fitted waistline.

Most skirt types can be styled also as separate skirts, but separate waists can be used only as boleros or jackets that end above the waistline. A waist that reaches to the waistline cannot be used as the pattern for a tuck-in bodice or an overblouse merely by adding an extension below the waistline. Different patterns are required for these cut-in-one structures which form the subject matter for Chapter 8.

In this chapter commonly used skirt structures are presented first, followed by commonly used waist structures. The chapter closes with a discussion of waist-and-skirt combinations that are particularly successful. The simplest waist-and-skirt dress—the sheath shown in the sketch—is also one of the most popular styles, and for these reasons it acts as an appropriate introduction to this chapter.

The Role of the Sloper in Styling

Pattern Development. The diagrams on the facing page show the front waist-and-skirt slopers, which were developed in the preceding chapter, and the pattern for the sheath-dress front that is developed from them. Only the fronts are shown because the sloper can be used without change for the waist back and the skirt back requires the same change as the skirt front.

To make the *sheath skirt* from the sloper skirt, the only change required is the addition of ease. The sloper is shown cut apart and spread ⅛ inch at each dart position, thus increasing the circumference of the skirt by 1 inch (the minimum amount of ease that can be allowed to give room for sitting and bending). Since the darts must remain at sloper size, the waistline becomes 1 inch too large. When a garment is being constructed, the operator passes a stitch at the waistline that holds in this slight ease.

To make the *sheath waist* from the sloper waist, the only change required is the relocation of the shoulder dart at the underarm seamline. First the new dartline is sketched on the pattern at the desired position, generally with an upward tilt as shown, to give the illusion of a high young bustline. Next the new dartline is slashed from the seamline to the bust apex. Then the shoulder dart can be folded and pinned closed, as shown, which automatically opens the dartline slash at the new position. The new dart is usually shortened slightly to avoid convergence with the waistline dart.

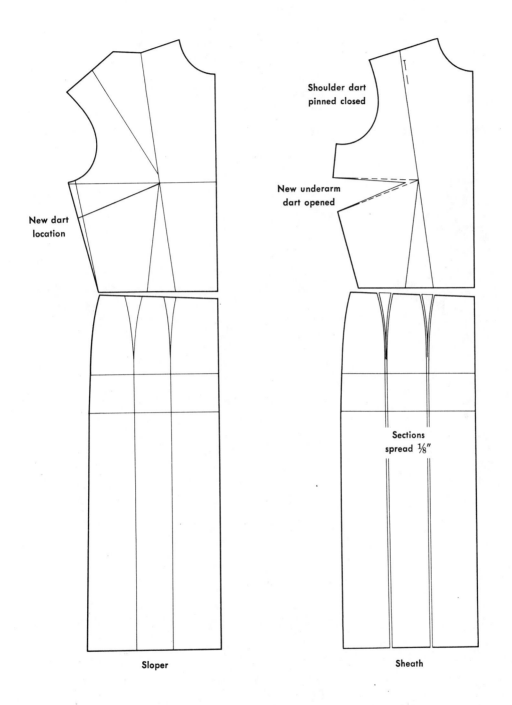

New dart
location

Shoulder dart
pinned closed

New underarm
dart opened

Sections
spread ⅛"

Sloper

Sheath

Pattern for Sheath Dress
Requires Only Simple Changes in
Basic Slopers

SKIRT STYLING

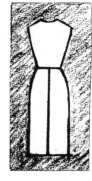

All skirt-silhouette types can be developed from this basic sloper.

FLARED SKIRTS	STRAIGHT SKIRTS	DRAPED AND PEGGED SKIRTS

Restrained Styling

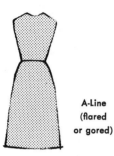

A-Line (flared or gored)

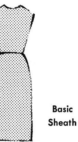

Basic Sheath

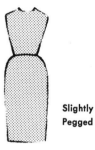

Slightly Pegged

Moderate Styling

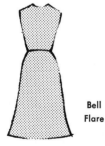

Bell Flare

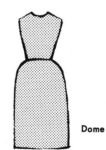

Dome

Draped and Pegged

Exaggerated Styling

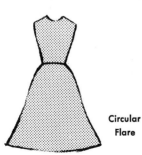

Circular Flare

Dirndl

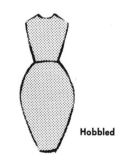

Hobbled

The Family of Skirts

Skirt-Silhouette Types. In the skirt silhouettes on the facing page the types and amounts of possible skirt variation are shown. Skirt silhouettes divide naturally into three groups: flared, straight, and draped and pegged. Skirt styling generally is accomplished by first choosing the appropriate silhouette type and then deciding on the amount of exaggeration to use. Note that the three restrained skirts, which stand closest to the sloper skirt, look much alike. As exaggeration increases each skirt type takes on an increasingly distinctive silhouette.

Triangle
(wide at bottom)

FACTORS IN SKIRT-SILHOUETTE VARIATION. A comparison of patterns for different types of skirts will aid in the understanding of skirt-silhouette variation. At the right the moderate member of each of the silhouette groups is illustrated and its pattern is shown to demonstrate the two factors responsible for silhouette differences. The *location* at which the ease is added immediately places the skirt in a specific group, and the *amount* of ease used determines the amount of exaggeration the skirt will have. The slim waistline of the flared skirt results from the triangular shape of its pattern, the hippy look of the pegged skirt from the reverse triangular shape of its pattern, and the distended hip and straight-hanging sides of the dome skirt from the rectangular shape of its pattern.

STRAIGHT SKIRTS

Rectangle

PLEATED SKIRTS. Both the flared and the straight skirts can add movement to their silhouettes through pleats. In fact, straight skirts are pleated as often as not. Pleated skirts are discussed as a separate styling technique later in the chapter since various pleat types are interchangeable with different skirt types.

DRAPED AND PEGGED SKIRTS

Triangle
(wide at top)

Straight Skirts: Sheath, Dome, and Dirndl

The Sheath Skirt. Slim and trim, the sheath skirt's hemline width generally is no more than 1½ inches greater than its circumference measured at the hipline, 5 inches below the center-front waistline. The sheath demands a good figure, and the woman with a good figure usually prefers the sheath because it shows off her trim hipline to the best advantage.

STRAIGHT SKIRTS will be presented first since one of them—the sheath skirt—has already been introduced. Examples of the sheath are illustrated at the right, along with the dome and dirndl. Block patterns for all three types are shown for comparison. Note that the average skirt width ranges from 1 yard (4 × 9 inches) for the sheath to 3 yards or more for the dirndl. Only the sheath requires a shaped side seam. The fuller skirts can be cut straight because there is no need for shaping at the hip. The type of fabric to be used is an important factor in planning any skirt since a stiff fabric produces any amount of bouffance with less actual width than does a soft fabric. Although all three skirts are members of the same straight rectangular group, each is a distinct style with a look of its own.

The Dome Skirt. This skirt style has only occasional popularity as a daytime silhouette, being much more suitable and popular for evening wear. Its "look" is smartest when it stands out stiffly at the hipline and then drops straight down, requiring stiff fabric or lining to give it enough crispness to retain this exaggerated shape. Without an exaggerated hip line, the dome tends to look like a skimpy dirndl.

The Dirndl Skirt. A practical and popular daytime style, the dirndl is usually styled with a look of exaggerated width and has a naturally rounded hipline because of the great amount of fabric that must be gathered in at the waistline. Gathers, unpressed pleats, and crystal pleating are all used to fit the skirt in to the waistline; pleats give a somewhat flatter silhouette than the more bouffant gathers.

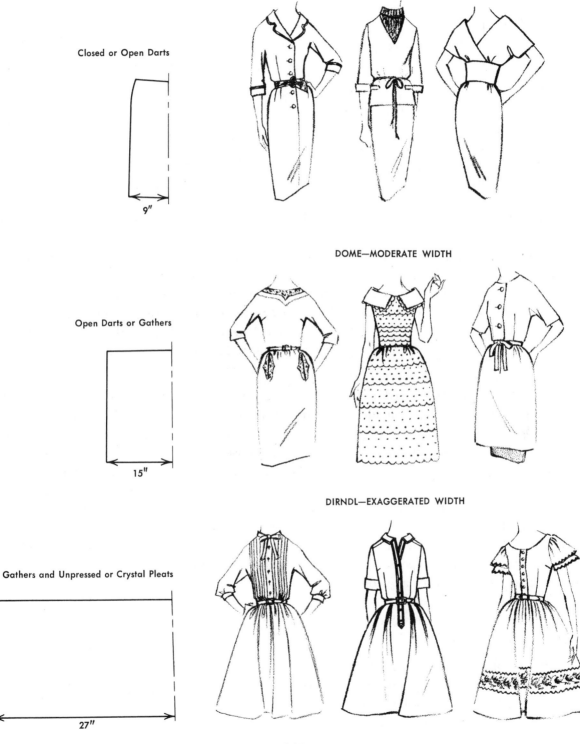

SHEATH—RESTRAINED WIDTH

Closed or Open Darts

9"

DOME—MODERATE WIDTH

Open Darts or Gathers

15"

DIRNDL—EXAGGERATED WIDTH

Gathers and Unpressed or Crystal Pleats

27"

The Flared-Skirt Sloper

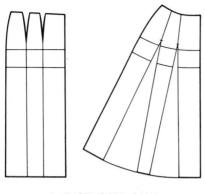

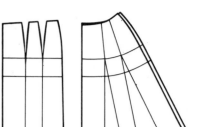

A. FLARED SKIRT FRONT

B. FLARED SKIRT BACK

Development of Skirt Front (A). Skirts can be fitted as well with darts that begin at the hemline as with the waistline darts used in the basic sloper. There is no point, of course, in closing these darts at the hemline; they remain open to become the flare in a skirt that fits smoothly at the hipline without darts.

PIVOTING THE DARTS. A dart is pivoted by swinging it around on its axis to relocate it at another seamline, a technique introduced at the beginning of the chapter where the shoulder dart in the waist sloper was pivoted to the underarm. The same pivot method is used for the flared skirt. First the dart excess of the waist dart is cut away, then the skirt is slashed up to the dart apex which always acts as the pivot point. The side sections of the skirt are pivoted to close the darts above and, as they move away from one another at the hemline, compensating darts are opened below. The width of any compensating dart that opens is always equal to the width of the dart that closes when measured at the same distance from the pivot point.

Development of Skirt Back (B). The back of the flared skirt is a replica of the front except that it is ½ inch narrower, as shown in B, where the skirt back is shown superimposed on the skirt front. The pattern for the skirt back must be checked with the front in this way and corrected if necessary. The skirt will hang properly with the side seamline falling straight down only when the front and back side seamlines are identical. Note that the pivot points of the back darts are 1 inch lower than for the front darts to compensate for their being ¼ inch wider than the front darts.

Trueing the Waistline (C). The shape of the waistline is responsible for the hang of any flared skirt. The skirt ripples evenly all around after the waistline is properly trued in. A method for using the French curve to true in the waistline is shown in C. As drafted, the flares in the skirt are concentrated at the two pivot points and trueing the waistline has the theoretical effect of substituting many small darts to produce many small flares that give the ripple effect.

C. USE OF
FRENCH CURVE

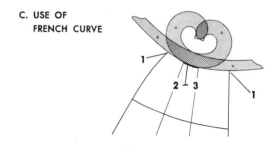

The Unique Qualities of Bias. The seamlines of the darts are shown as straight lines in A and B, for only straight lines can be pivoted. As a result the flared skirt sloper is ½ inch narrower through the hip than the basic sloper from which it was made.

D. PIVOTING
CURVED DARTS

Diagram D shows the theoretical overlap of the curved seamlines of the darts. In the diagram, ½-inch overlap is added at the side seam position to show the amount lost.

E. BIAS STRETCH
AND BIAS SAG

Diagram E shows why it is possible to reduce the width of the pattern in this way. The grain lines that have been drawn show that the grain above the hipline is virtually true bias. One of the unique qualities of bias is that it has enough inherent stretchability to compensate for the loss of width sustained in the pivot. This flared skirt is an excellent example of the reciprocal ways in which bias reacts. When used under tension to fit and mold the figure above the torsoline, it has a highly desirable mobility, stretching or contracting as necessary to give a smooth easy fit. But when bias falls free, as it does below the torsoline, it will sag in proportion to the degree to which it deviates from

straight grain. The mobility of bias here becomes instability that is the weakness of the bias flared skirt. The inherent tendency of a fabric to sag because of its weave is often the factor that determines the most practical way in which to style it.

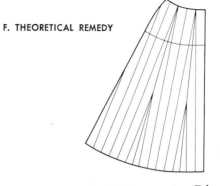

F. THEORETICAL REMEDY

MULTIPLE GORES REMEDY BIAS SAG. Diagram F shows the theoretical remedy for bias sag. Here the two-piece skirt from E has been split into 10 gores (2½ gores shown), each of which is centered on straight grain. The effect is to reduce the degree of bias at the seamlines to the point that there is no appreciable sag. But when the sag quality of bias is eliminated, the molding quality is also lost and it is necessary to redraft the gores to give back the ½ inch they lost, as shown in G. This is the theoretical development of the gored skirt. In practice, the basic skirt sloper is simply cut apart at the desired seam positions, the dart excess is cut away, and the desired amount of flare added—always an equal amount at facing seamlines.

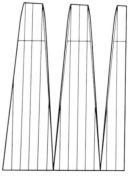

G. ACTUAL REMEDY

Restrained to Exaggerated Styling of the Flared Skirt

THE THREE PAIRS of twins on this page illustrate several factors that enter into the choice of flared-skirt styling. The twins on the left wear skirts with bias flare, whereas the twins on the right wear skirts with multiple gores. In each example both skirts have the same width and the same silhouette. The way in which each dress has been styled is the important factor in the choice of skirt type. The twins at the top of the page both illustrate the restrained A-line silhouette, the twins in the middle illustrate the moderate bell flare, and the twins at the bottom illustrate the exaggerated semicircular flare.

Drafting Techniques. THE A-LINE FLARE. This restrained flare is made by the same method used for the bell flare that was our example on the preceding page. The difference is that the darts are closed only half-way, causing the flare to be only half as full and the back of the skirt to be only ¼ inch narrower than the front of the skirt. Any desired variation can be made in this skirt silhouette, ranging all the way from the basic-skirt sloper to the flared-skirt sloper.

THE SEMICIRCULAR FLARE. The semicircular flare is made by slashing the bell flare from hemline to waistline and spreading the sections the desired amount. Here the sections are slashed at the dart positions and spread half the width of the dart at each slash to preserve balance. Note that in bias skirts a choice of the position for straight grain is possible.

GORED SKIRTS. All gored skirts are drafted by the technique shown for the 10-gore skirt on the preceding page. The basic skirt sloper is copied, but the dartlines are not drawn in. The gore positions are planned and drawn in as vertical lines. The dart excess is mathematically divided among the gore positions, keeping the original proportion of less toward the center and more toward the side seam, and dartlines are drawn in at the gore positions. The pattern is then cut into gores and the gores are pinned to pattern paper on which hemline and hipline have been drawn. Flare is added mechanically in equal amounts on facing gorelines so that the gore seamlines can fall straight down.

RESTRAINED FLARE

A-Line Flare

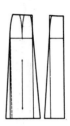

A-Line 6-Gore

MODERATE FLARE

Bell Flare

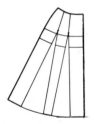

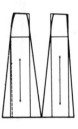

Bell 8-Gore

EXAGGERATED FLARE

Semicircular Flare

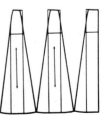

Full 10-Gore

Bias-Flare Variations

Wrap-Around Bell Flare

Overlap Follows Flare Line

Unpressed Pleats

Unpressed Pleats Follow Flare Line

Circular Flare

Graduated Flare Is Greatest
at True Bias Position

True Bias —

Multiple-Gore Variations

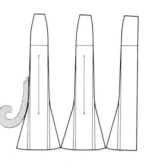

10-Gore Trumpet Flare

Exaggerated Trumpet Flare
Adds Width to 10-Gore Skirt

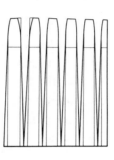

17-Gore Skirt

Differential in Dart Width
Is Disregarded in This Skirt

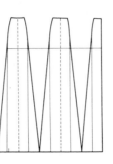

Simulated 20-Gore Skirt

10-Gore Skirt with Center
Stitching to Simulate 20 Gores

Pleated Skirts

PLEATED SKIRTS never go out of fashion because they are so comfortable and attractive. Many dresses depend almost solely on their pleated skirts for design interest, as the sketches on the facing page illustrate. For analysis, pleated skirts are divided into three groups according to the method by which they are made to fit the figure above the torsoline, since pleat styling largely depends on this mechanical factor.

Straight Pleats—Without Shaping. The pattern for the skirt with the single inverted pleat shown on the facing page is made by adding twice the amount of the desired depth or "underlay" of the pleat to the sheath pattern at the center-front position. The shallow (½ inch) all-around side pleats on the skirt next to it would be planned in a similar way. Double the underlay depth (½ inch × 2) is multiplied by 48, the number of pleats used, and this amount of underlay excess (48 inches) is added to the skirt circumference (36 inches) at the torsoline, making a total skirt width of 84 inches. Shallow pleats of ½ inch or less are gathered in to fit the waistline, causing the skirt to have a silhouette more like the dirndl than the smoothly fitted sheath, unless a fitted yoke is used at the hipline. All-around pleated skirts are usually styled with pleats that are deeper than ½ inch so that they can be "contoured-in" to a smooth, neat hipline.

Contoured Pleats—Shaped to the Waistline. Contoured pleats are planned and figured like straight pleats, the difference being that the dart excess is added to the underlay. In the skirt with three inverted pleats note how the dart excess is added to the pleat at the princess line so that it can shape-in to the figure. When pleats can be contoured in this way, the skirt fits like a sheath skirt above the torsoline. In a skirt with several pleats the dart excess is divided among them, and in an all-around pleated skirt each pleat takes its equal share.

Tapered Pleats for Flared and Gored Skirts. Pleats taper (narrow at the waistline and wider at the hemline) in gored and flared skirts. One method for making tapered pleats is shown in the pattern for the skirt with two inverted pleats, in which a separate underlay section is tapered to match the flared line of the pleat. Another method for tapering pleats, which is done on circular skirts by the commercial pleater, is known as "sun-ray" pleating.

FORMULA FOR ALL-AROUND PLEATS

Twice the underlay depth,
Times the number of pleats,
Plus the torsoline circumference,
Equals the total width required.

STRAIGHT PLEATS—WITHOUT SHAPING

Straight Inverted Pleat

CONTOURED PLEATS—SHAPED TO FIT WAISTLINE

Contoured Inverted Pleat

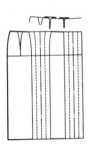

TAPERED PLEATS—FOR GORED AND FLARED SKIRTS

Tapered Inverted Pleat

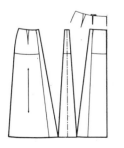

153

Draped-and-Pegged Skirts

EXAGGERATION at the hipline in draped-and-pegged skirts contrasts with the flared skirts which are kept slim through the upper section and widened at the hemline for a style that is both attractive and practical. But when the skirt sloper is pivoted the opposite way, with increased width at the hipline and decreased width at the hemline, attractive and practical skirt styling is more difficult to achieve. The skirt sloper is as narrow at the hemline as can be worn comfortably, and when it is narrowed further, a slash becomes necessary. In eras when long skirts are in fashion, the wrapped hobble skirt may become high style, as it did in 1913, but its impractical styling must be considered too extreme for general daytime wear. Exaggerated width at the hip is often accompanied by a tightly fitted midriff that preserves the illusion of a slim figure while accentuating the hipline in a way that looks like a styling exaggeration and not an anatomical fact.

Side seams are not essential to pegged skirts because the fullness at the hipline makes alteration unnecessary and, as a rule, a side seam falls off grain and therefore is not likely to hang straight. When the back and front of the skirt are cut in one, this problem is avoided.

Styling Analysis. The family of draped-and-pegged skirts is divided according to the location of the drape that produces the pegged effect: at both sides, at one side, or at center front. For each type one restrained and one exaggerated garment is shown. All types of pegged skirts can be developed from the skirt sloper, as the block patterns show. Note that the different drape locations produce different types of styling. Skirts draped at both sides are particularly suitable for eras when short skirts are in fashion. Skirts draped to the center are better adapted to eras when skirts are long. The restrained skirt that is draped at both sides is as wearable as a sheath skirt, and the side-draped skirt of the surplice dress is a popular version of the wrap-around overskirt. When handled sensitively, this type of skirt styling offers both variety and wearability as well as being subject to extreme exaggeration.

DRAPED AT BOTH SIDES

Slightly Pegged

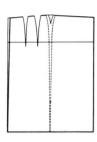

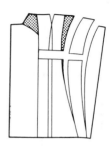

Draped and Pegged

DRAPED AT ONE SIDE

Restrained Surplice Drape

Sarong Variation

DRAPED AT CENTER

Draped Circular Flare

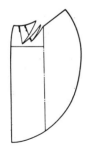

Hobble or Harem Drape

Preview of Waist Styling

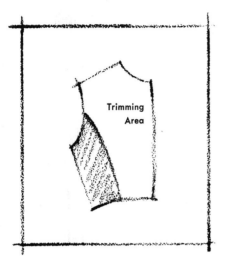

Trimming Area

Waist Styling with Darts. A great variety of silhouettes is available in skirt styling, but waists are all rather close-fitting and thus are quite similar to one another in silhouette, although the darts that give waists their characteristic shape can be moved to any number of different locations. Dart placement is always a matter of individual styling since the dartlines in a waist must harmonize with the styling of the skirt used with it. Skirt structure depends on the silhouette chosen, but waist structure depends on skirt styling. A waist not only must harmonize with its skirt, but also it must harmonize with its sleeve and its collar if either is used. Three-fourths of all waist-and-skirt dresses are styled

by the pattern for the sheath waist that was introduced on the second page of this chapter. When this standard two-dart waist is not suitable, another waist type is selected on the basis of mechanical suitability and taste. The development of different ways to style a waist forms the subject matter for the remainder of this chapter.

Standard Dart Positions. The most common types of waist styling that use darts are illustrated on the facing page. Three of the dresses have darts that are located outside the trimming area and the other three use their dart excess for trimming. The sheath waist and the sloper waist have the dart excess divided whereas the other four waists combine the dart excess into one large dart. The darts are located at a different seamline in each waist, the one similarity among them being that their focal point is always the bust apex. Note too that regardless of dart location the amount of excess contained is in every instance identical. A circle, centered on the bust apex, has been superimposed on each of the six patterns in order to dispel the common optical illusion that a short dart, as at the center front, is smaller than a long dart, as at the neckline. The dart excess of the sloper remains the same regardless of the location or the number of darts used.

THE VERSATILE DARTS

Sheath Waist

Sloper

French Dart

Waistline Dart

Neckline Dart

Center-Front Dart

Styling with the

Standard Two-Dart Styling. The popularity of the sheath waist is due to its excellent fit as well as to its unobtrusive dart pattern. A waist fits best when the dart excess is divided between two darts, one of which is at the waistline, for only in this way can the waistline be on straight grain. Not only does the grain follow body contour, but it also furnishes a stable anchorage for the skirt, since on straight grain there is equal stability at all points.

Waist Styling with a Single Dart. Styling situations arise, of course, in which a single dart is

INTRICATE STYLE LINES

STRIPES AND OTHER GEOMETRICS

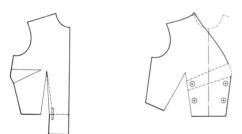

The dress on the left can use the underarm dart since it does not conflict with the style lines in any way. The style lines of the dress on the right, however, which cross the front of the waist at an angle, would not harmonize with a dart-line at the underarm. A large waistline dart is preferable because the bias grain that the dart causes at the side waist coordinates well with the angled style lines.

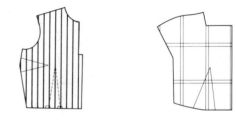

Geometric patterns present individual problems. The striped dress, for example, can use an underarm dart, and here it is centered on straight grain so that the stripes meet at its seamline while dart tucks replace the waistline dart to keep the pattern simple. In the plaid dress one large waistline dart is used because it correlates very well with the bias grain of the kimono sleeve.

Waistline Dart

preferable, either for mechanical or esthetic reasons. Four of the six sketches on the preceding page showed waists with a single dart—and the curved waistline that inevitably accompanies it. Most of the waists to be analyzed in this chapter have a type of styling that one of those four sketches represents. On these two pages twins are again used to illustrate four common styling problems that are often solved satisfactorily by the use of the waist pattern that has all of the dart excess combined in one large dart at the waistline.

LOW ARMHOLE OR UNDERARM LINE

TUCKS OR PLEATS IN WAIST FRONT

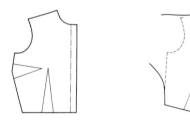

A waist with its sleeve set into the normal armhole can use the standard waist pattern. But a waist styled with a low dolman armhole often effectively uses a pattern with all excess in the single waistline dart, since the bias sleeve has the same grain direction as the bias side section of the waist.

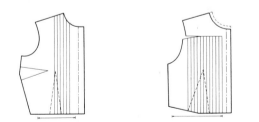

The tucked section of the waist front on the left ends at the bust apex and thus does not conflict with a dart at the underarm. But when a pleated or tucked front section of the waist continues beyond the bust apex, as shown on the right, it is usually mechanically impossible to use the underarm dart and a single waistline dart is used, often with part of the dart excess eased in.

Darts Used as Trimming

SHOULDER DART

Shoulder dart at flange position combined with waistline dart is often used in this styling in larger sizes.

Shoulder dart and waistline dart divide the excess with extra ease added to accentuate the soft effect.

Shoulder dart alone at flange position in a sophisticated dress of stiff slipper satin.

NECKLINE DART

Neckline dart alone with all excess in the one dart used as soft ease cleverly held in by a knotted tie.

Neckline dart with excess divided among three unstitched darts to act as trimming for this print dress.

Neckline dart combined with a yoke to give the effect of a draped twist.

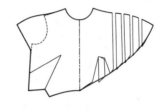

Center-front dart placed below the apex level for an interesting bias-midriff effect.

French dart on the right is balanced by waistline dart on left in asymmetrical styling.

Center-front dart with enough extra ease pivoted in to form a cowl-type neckline.

Center-front dart in a surplice effect takes up all excess on both halves of the waist front.

Center-front and underarm darts used in conjunction with the slash-and-spread technique for a draped twist.

Center-front dart used to form a surplice effect with added excess pivoted in at the shoulderline.

161

Styling the Bias-Cut Bateau Waist

A. BIAS-CUT WAIST

B. PREPARING BIAS SLOPER

Bias- and Straight-Grain
Slopers Compared

C. SPLITTING FRENCH DART

Step 1

Step 2

BIAS STYLING looks smartest when it is kept simple. The distinctive molded look that bias imparts to a garment does not require intricate design, nor are curved style lines, darts at the waistline, or set-in sleeves mechanically suited to bias styling. Raglan and kimono styling are suitable for sleeves and the bateau neckline that is cut straight across is often the most appropriate neck styling.

Adjustment for Bias. Any regular pattern (for straight grain) requires adjustment before it can be used successfully with bias grain. When true bias is used at center front as the dresses at the left illustrate, the fabric molds around the curves of the figure more closely than with straight grain so that a bias pattern is smaller than a straight-grain pattern. In B a bias pattern is shown superimposed on a straight-grain pattern. This pattern was adjusted for bias by using a waist pattern with all excess in one French dart, cutting it in muslin with the center front on a true-bias fold as shown, fitting it to the dress form, and making the necessary corrections. Both left and right sides of bias patterns must be fitted because the straight grain of the fabric crosses from one side of the pattern to the other. The pattern half that is considered better is the one in which lengthwise grain runs from the shoulder to center front.

The French Dart. Placed low on the underarm seamline, the French dart has the effect of combining the underarm dart and the waistline dart. This dart position is ideal for bias-cut waists because the dart can be centered on straight grain, a position in which it fits best and shows least. The French dart is used infrequently except for bias where it becomes the standard dart position. To reduce the amount of excess taken up by one large dart, this dart is often split as shown in the two steps in C. The split dart makes an attractive trimming feature, as shown in the dress on the right above, as well as being mechanically sound. Note that the dartlines are always slightly spread at the bust apex to give the illusion of a high, rounded bustline.

Fabric Limitations in Bias Styling. Many fabrics have either an unbalanced thread construction or a surface pattern that makes it necessary to use a seam at center front, as shown in the plaid dress on the facing page. But whether cut in one piece or with a center seam, pattern placement requires extreme precision. A one-piece pattern must have its center line on true bias. A two-piece pattern must have both left and right halves cut on duplicate grain if the garment is to set true and straight on the body. The commonly used cowl structure is generally avoided when a center seam must be used. Cowls are made most successfully from fabrics in which warp and filling are almost identical.

Bateau Development. The bateau neckline, as shown in the plaid dress on the facing page, is the simplest type of styling that can be used with bias. In addition, it is the initial development step in drafting the cowl neckline. The diagrams at the right show in simple steps how the bateau is drafted. A high neckline is illustrated but the neckline can be planned at any desired depth at center front and at any desired breadth at the shoulderline. When an extra fold or two is added to the bateau, the cowl neckline is the result. One extra "gratis" fold, as shown in the sketch, develops automatically in any of the bateau necklines as a "side effect" when the straight edge of the neckline falls free.

Step 1

Mark the desired neck point and shoulder point on the pattern. Connect these two points with a straight line.

Step 2

Measure over from center front a distance equal to the length of the line drawn in Step 1 and draw a line at that position parallel to center front.

Step 3

Pivot the armhole side of the pattern out until the shoulder point marked in Step 1 touches the vertical line drawn in Step 2.

Step 4

Draw in the new bateau line from the shoulder-point intersection to the center front at a right angle to the center front. Cut away the excess above this line.

Development of the Cowl

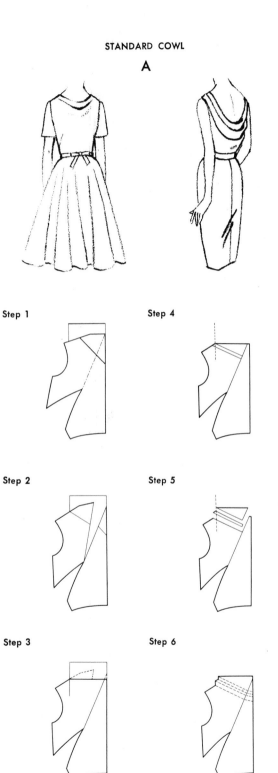

STANDARD COWL

A

Step 1

Step 2

Step 3

Step 4

Step 5

Step 6

The Cowl Neckline (A). The cowl neckline is developed by adding one or more folds to the bateau neckline. In the sketches at the left, one fold is shown in the front cowl and two folds in the back cowl. One fold is used for the step-by-step diagrams. The first three steps show how to make a bateau neckline of the desired depth and width, and the following three steps show how additional folds are added to form the cowl. A deepened neckline is usually accompanied by a widened shoulderline, and a good proportion is obtained when the shoulderline is drawn across to the line of the center front at a 45° angle, as shown. The French dart is reduced as the cowl is deepened because the cowl is formed from the dart excess that is pivoted to the neckline. When the neckline is lowered to the bust apex, the entire dart is transferred to the neckline. For a still deeper cowl, or for any cowl at the waist back, the necessary excess can be obtained by pivoting the pattern out from the center-waistline point.

The Square-Neck Cowl (B). The square-neck cowl has a practical lining section that extends from the neckline edge of the cowl to the waistline, holding the cowl in place, both on a hanger and on the wearer. Diagrams 1 and 2 show how the lining section and the neckline are planned. In all other respects, the same standard method of development is used as for the cowl at the left.

The Underarm Cowl (C). The underarm cowl is another practical development based on the cowl principle. In this case the straight-grain slopers are used and the darts are pivoted to the armhole to furnish the cowl excess. Underarm cowls are particularly well suited to sheer fabrics since their structure eliminates the underarm seam. Note that the dress with the midriff can have a higher underarm, as is often desirable.

from the Bateau Waist

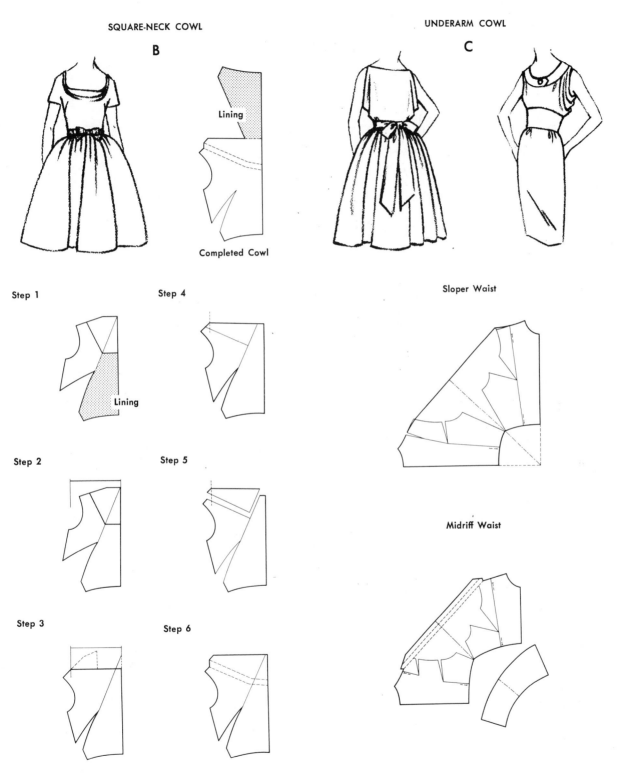

SQUARE-NECK COWL

B

Lining

Completed Cowl

UNDERARM COWL

C

Sloper Waist

Midriff Waist

Step 1

Lining

Step 2

Step 3

Step 4

Step 5

Step 6

WAIST STYLING

GORED-WAIST FRONT—STYLING VARIATIONS

Step 1. Plan style line on waist pattern with dart excess moved to a position that is not affected. (Excess here has been moved to center front.)

Step 2. Cut waist apart on the desired style line. Then pin the darts at center front closed to return the panel section to its original shape.

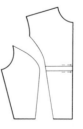

166

The Gored Waist

WAISTS, LIKE SKIRTS, can be made to fit the figure as well with gores as with darts. The sketches and their two-step diagrams demonstrate a simple technique by which commonly used types of gored waists can be developed from a waist pattern in which darts are used. Any darted waist can be used in this development, but generally a pattern is chosen with the darts in a position that will be out of the way of the planned style lines. Here a waist with two darts at center front is used since the center-front section of the waist is not affected by the drafting that is to be done.

There are excellent advantages to be gained when a waist is styled with gores instead of darts. The grain of each of the pieces can be planned individually, thus producing interesting effects with patterned fabrics, as well as a better, more sensitive fit. The straight style lines of the darts can be replaced by style lines that are curved or otherwise shaped to produce flattering and attractive effects. Gored styling is the technique most often used in the couture market where production cost is not a controlling factor and where style lines rather than trimming constitute sales appeal.

Development of Waist Front. All the waists here shown follow the same drafting technique. In every case the style line passes through the bust apex, and in every case the style line extends from one pattern edge to another, making it possible for the pattern to be cut into two separate pieces. In each case, the style line is planned and sketched on the pattern as Step 1,

then the pattern is cut apart on the style line, after which the center front darts can be pinned closed, as shown in Step 2.

Development of Waist Back. The standard sloper back can be converted to a gored back most easily by redirecting the waistline dart to form a smooth line up to the apex of the shoulder dart and then cutting the pattern apart and eliminating both darts, as shown in the diagrams below.

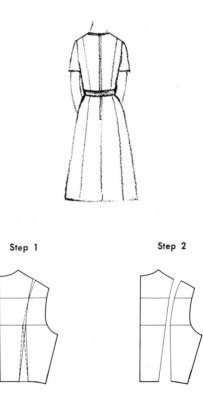

BASIC GORED-WAIST BACK

Step 1   Step 2

Gore-and-Dart Techniques

A. GORE COMBINED WITH DART

Step 1

Step 2

B. PARTIAL GORE (NOT ENTIRELY SEPARATE)

Step 1

Step 2

Gore and Dart Combined (*A*). The gore technique is not limited to style lines that cut through the bust apex. A style line can be drawn in any area that the designer wishes, but unless the bust apex is cut by a style line, the dart excess remains as a dart. Darts in the waist front cup the fabric around the curve of the bust to accommodate the pattern piece to the contour of the body. Any pattern piece that must fit over the bust requires a dart. When the style line does not cut the waist at the bust apex, the dart remains in the larger piece of the pattern; but no dart is needed in the smaller piece. This styling, as shown in A, is an extension of the gore technique shown on the preceding page. In Step 1, after the style line is sketched in, an additional line representing the dart is drawn from the bust apex to the style line at the desired angle. In Step 2, after the pattern is cut apart at the style line, the new dartline is slashed up to the bust apex, and the original dart then is pinned closed. This combination of gore and dart techniques forms the basis for both yoke and midriff styling, a discussion of which occupies the next four pages.

Partial Gore (*B*). This is another variation of the gored technique. Here the waist is slashed only as far as the bust apex rather than all the way across the pattern, and thus remains in one piece. In this example the side section of the waist is cut into strips and spread to add enough excess to form the folds through the midriff.

The techniques illustrated in A and B can be combined. Style lines not only may be drawn at a distance from the bust apex as shown in A, but in addition they may extend only part way across the pattern, as shown in B. This combination technique produces flattering partial yokes that retain the elongating illusion of a front panel which is dispelled by any line that cuts entirely across the figure. Here the waist with the center-front dart is used again since it is out of the styling area and thus enables the designer to visualize better the style lines as they will appear when the garment is on the figure.

The Partial Yoke at the Midriff (C). This yoke is developed like the gore-and-dart waist in A, except that the style line extends only part way. After it is cut the dart is slashed up to the bust apex. When the center-front dart is pinned closed, the new dart opens automatically, as shown in Step 2 of the diagram.

The Partial Yoke at the Shoulder (D). The partial shoulder yoke is developed in the same way. In addition, lines representing the dart tucks are continued all the way to bust level and a slash line is drawn from the bust apex to the armhole edge of the pattern so the excess from the dart can be divided among the dart tucks. The division of the dart excess among several "split" darts is the only difference between the single dart-tuck styling of C and the multiple dart tucks of D.

C. PARTIAL YOKE AT MIDRIFF

Step 1

Step 2

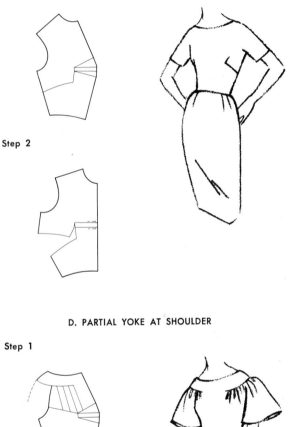

D. PARTIAL YOKE AT SHOULDER

Step 1

Step 2

The One-Piece Yoke of the Shirtdress

CASUAL VS FITTED STYLING

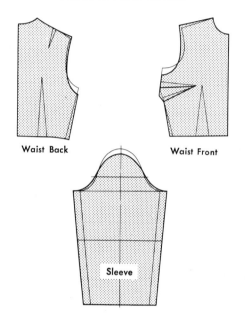

Waist Back   Waist Front

Sleeve

THE ONE-PIECE yoke is a fundamental design feature of the classic shirtdress. It is copied faithfully from the man's shirt and is a miracle of mechanical perfection. The yokeline cuts straight across the back of the waist and drops slightly over the shoulder in front. The yoke generally is styled with the lengthwise grain of the fabric running across the body to hold the shoulderline firm and square. The yoke eliminates the back-shoulder dart (as a yoke should) and permits additional ease to be introduced across the back where it is needed in the more casual activities of a woman's existence for which the classic shirtdress is so ideally suited. At the front the yoke drops over the shoulder only slightly and therefore replaces the shoulder seam to soften and broaden the shoulderline.

A. CASUAL SHIRTDRESS IN STANDARD STYLING

Back view

B. VARIATION OF CLASSIC SHIRTDRESS STYLING

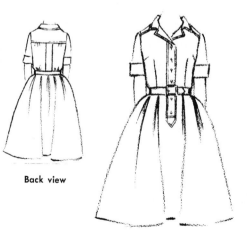

Back view

Casual vs Fitted Waist Styling. At the left the sloper patterns for the shirtwaist are superimposed on the regular waist slopers for comparison. Note that the broader shoulderline of the shirtwaist is accompanied by a lowered armhole and a broader sleeve. An explanation of the drafting procedures involved in converting the regular slopers to shirt styling must wait until Chapter 9 since the conversion of the sleeve is the initial step. The shoulderline of the shirtwaist is automatically broadened in proportion to the amount that the armhole is lowered, as it must be to accommodate the broadened shirt sleeve. The underarm seamline is also straightened to make the waistline "easier," and the back waistline dart is replaced by dart tucks that coordinate with the soft ease below the yokeline. A center "pleat" is sometimes introduced at the back, as shown in B on the facing page. It is usually stitched closed since it is not for ease but rather to counteract the broadening and shortening influence of the horizontal yokeline. The shirtwaist requires a completely redrafted pattern because proportioned amounts of ease must be introduced throughout in order to produce the characteristic look of this casual silhouette. The one-piece yoke belongs strictly to the shirtdress. Two-piece yokes with shoulder seam and a close fit are used with all other types of yoke styling.

DEVELOPMENT OF ONE-PIECE YOKE

Step 1

Step 2

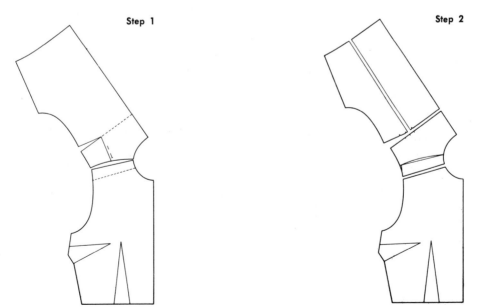

Two-Piece Yokes at Shoulder, Midriff, and Hipline

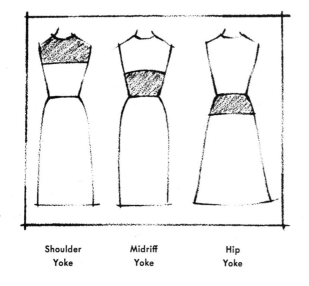

Shoulder Yoke   Midriff Yoke   Hip Yoke

THE GORE-AND-DART variations shown earlier furnish a proper introduction to the gore-and-dart techniques of yokes of the three types shown here, in which garments are cut apart horizontally to form yokes either at the shoulder or above or below the waistline. The sketches on the facing page illustrate these three yoke positions. A pattern for only one garment from each group is shown since the same principle applies to all.

Purpose of the Yoke. The purpose of all waist yokes generally is to utilize the dart excess of the waist as soft ease that is controlled by a fitted yoke section. The purpose of the hip yoke is to provide a smooth, tightly fitted hipline from which darts are eliminated, in combination with a pleated, a gathered, or a circular skirt. In a circular skirt the hip yoke is the only means available by which the hip section of the garment can be kept smooth and fitted, otherwise the flares of the skirt begin at the waistline.

Yoke Styling. The hip yoke must cut across the pattern at a level no lower than the point of the darts if it is to accomplish its express purpose of eliminating the darts from the yoke section (as discussed in the partial gore-and-dart technique). The waist, on the other hand, is seldom cut across at the point of the dart (bust apex level) because a style line at that level divides the waist into two parts that are approximately equal, and the division of space into equal horizontal segments is unattractive to the eye. Horizontal lines in good design divide a composition into proportioned segments, as discussed in Chapter 5. When waist yokes are used in styling, proportion is the most important consideration. The advantage of both partial and complete shoulder yokes is that they provide for the introduction of ease, while keeping the neckline and shoulderline of the garment trim and smooth, as is necessary when a collar is to be added or a sleeve set in. Yokes above and below the waistline keep the midsection of the figure smooth and trim while permitting the introduction of ease in the bust section above or in the skirt section below.

FITTED SHOULDER YOKES

Step 1
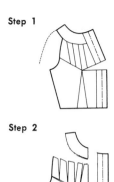

Step 2

FITTED MIDRIFF YOKES

FITTED HIP YOKES

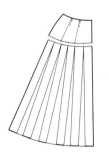

173

Short Jackets, Peplums, Flounces, and Overskirts

THE RECTANGLE that a garment represents can be cut interestingly into sections that fall free, but styling of this type, to be pleasing to the eye, must divide the composition into well-proportioned segments. The three groups of garments shown on these two pages illustrate common uses of this type of styling: short, separate jackets and jacket effects, overskirts and overskirt effects (from short to long), and flounces.

Short Jackets. Short jackets are practical and popular. They slim the waistline and add desirable versatility to an outfit, making it possible to wear the same costume comfortably from 9 to 5, and then to be properly dressed for an informal evening occasion by simply removing the jacket. Any jacket that is no longer than the standard waist pattern can be cut from it, but jackets of hipbone or longer length require the so-called "torso" pattern that will be discussed in the following chapter.

BOLERO VARIATIONS

Peplums, Flounces, and Overskirts. Peplums and overskirts are actually skirts that are cut shorter than full length. Flounces are relatively short skirt sections below extremely long hip yokes (the skirt beneath the flounce may or may not be cut away). The horizontal divisions of the figure made by overskirts and flounces are not easy to handle artistically. This fact probably accounts for their relatively infrequent use, except in custom designing where the proportional divisions of the design can be adjusted to the individual customer. Unless a skirt is proportioned properly, the effect is often one of shortening the apparent height, and for this reason all overskirts and flounces are commonly assumed to be suited only to tall women who want to look shorter. Overskirts require extra fabric and labor, and frequently the benefit in sales appeal from an overskirt cannot be justified. The average customer often is more responsive to styling detail and trimming above the waistline than below it.

OVERSKIRTS

175

Waist-and-Skirt Styling in Classic Combinations

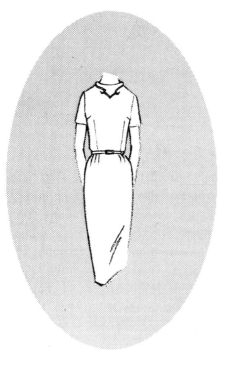

THE SHEATH DRESS presented at the beginning of this chapter, as an introduction to waist-and-skirt styling, is, of course, a classic style. A sheath waist, however, is often combined with other skirts and a sheath skirt is often combined with other waists. In fact, the many waist-and-skirt combinations that are mechanically possible have made it necessary to present skirts and waists separately in this chapter. Good taste imposes many restrictions on styling, causing some combinations of waist and skirt to be much more successful than others, and accounting for the popularity of the six "classic styles" illustrated on the facing page as well as for the popularity of the sheath dress.

What Makes a Style Classic? Good taste decrees that a dress must look as if its waist and skirt are "mates." Darts or style lines in the skirt that match darts or style lines in the waist contribute to this unified effect. When waist and skirt are well mated, they often remain favorites in spite of fashion change. Combinations like those on the facing page fall in this category. All have this well-mated or coordinated styling usually found **in** a classic. Such dresses are the "bread-and-butter" dresses of the industry, requiring only a change of belt each season or a different fabric to enable them to retain their popularity. Classic styles make little concession to high fashion, reflecting its current trend only in mildly longer or shorter skirts and mildly wider or narrower shoulders, while the waistline remains at its normal position, fitting the figure in a normal way. All these dresses have the same good points:

MECHANICAL BALANCE. Their well-mated styling above and below the waistline gives a look of unity and balance to the design.

FLATTERING LINES. Their flattering lines contribute to the illusions of youth or of a tall, attractive figure.

ARTISTIC EXCELLENCE. Their styling is uncluttered, their proportions are excellent, the mood or feeling of the garment is unified, and the total impact is unobtrusively effective. They offer an undated type of styling in which the average woman feels well dressed.

Tailored Button-Down Sheath

Classic Shirtdress with Dirndl Skirt

Belted Princess-Line Dress

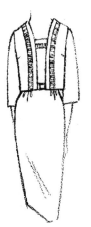

Basic Sheath with Matching Jacket

Soft Cowl Neck and Full Flared Skirt

Draped Wrap-Around Surplice Dress

Chapter Eight

Styling the Cut-in-One Dress

Saint-Laurent

THE CONSIDERABLE limitations that exist in cut-in-one styling (all dresses are cut-in-one if they are not made from waist and skirt joined at a normal fitted waistline) and the great possibilities that develop once the limitations are comprehended and observed are explained in this chapter.

The styling possibilities of cut-in-one structures are broad and exciting, but mechanical limitations confront the designer every step of the way. The waist-and-skirt dress is much easier to work with because waist and skirt can be cut as separate units in which differences can be reconciled at the waistline seam. It is comparatively easy to achieve a good fit with the waist-and-skirt dress because the dress form acts as a firm foundation on which to adjust it. But cut-in-one structures, which must combine a smart silhouette with excellent fit, are more difficult to develop, particularly in styles that stand away from the body as most cut-in-one styles do. The couture relies heavily on cut-in-one techniques, whereas inexpensive lines use the waist-and-skirt techniques almost exclusively.

179

EMPIRE-LINE AND TORSOLINE STYLING VARIATIONS

Skirt Types Used in Empire-Line and Torsoline Styling

Sheath   Pleated   Gathered   Flared   Gored   Pegged

Empire-Line Styling Possibilities

Gathered more often than pleated

Flare usually does not begin above the normal waistline

Pegged effect usually does not begin above the normal waistline in daytime dresses

One-Piece Torsoline Styling Possibilities

Two-Piece Torsoline Styling Possibilities

Cut-in-One Styling

Limitations on Cut-in-One Structure (A). Three cut-in-one dress types with the normal silhouette are shown in A at the right. One dress is cut across at the torsoline, one is cut across at the Empire line, and the fitted sheath that is dimly seen between them is not cut across at any level. It is not used as a dress but the dresses on either side of it use it for their pattern.

Possibilities in Cut-in-One Styling (B). In addition to the two replacements for the fitted shift that are shown in A, there are five ways in which cut-in-one dresses can be developed. The only one of these structures that can be tightly fitted is the princess dress. Only one structure is practical for the unfitted shift, but the demifitted silhouette can be made as a straight-cut (2-gore) or a bias-cut (4-gore) shift or as a multigore princess dress.

Chapter Preview. The chapter begins with the development of the basic patterns for these varied cut-in-one structures: the torsoline and Empire line slopers, the unfitted and demifitted shifts, the fitted and demifitted princess dresses, and finally the bias-cut shift. The second half of the chapter analyzes the styling of the cut-in-one dress types: the straight and bias-cut shifts, the princess dresses, the two-piece jacket and overblouse costumes, the low-waisted (torsoline) dresses, and the high-waisted (Empire line) dresses. The most important consideration in learning to use cut-in-one styling effectively is the necessity both to understand the mechanical limitations of the different structures and to appreciate the remarkable styling possibilities they offer once their limitations are accepted. The chart on the facing page illustrates the wide range of skirt styling possible with Empire and torsoline structures.

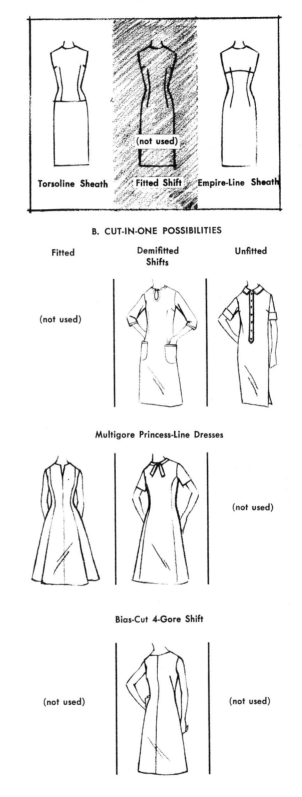

A. CUT-IN-ONE LIMITATIONS

(not used)

Torsoline Sheath   Fitted Shift   Empire-Line Sheath

B. CUT-IN-ONE POSSIBILITIES

Fitted   Demifitted Shifts   Unfitted

(not used)

Multigore Princess-Line Dresses

(not used)

Bias-Cut 4-Gore Shift

(not used)   (not used)

Torsoline and Empire-Line Slopers

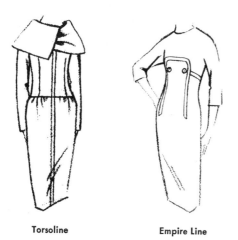

Torsoline   Empire Line

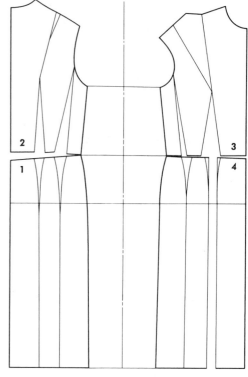

FITTED-SHIFT SLOPER (THEORY)

THE NECESSITY for the side seamline to balance from underarm to hemline places limitations on the development of all cut-in-one structures. In the waist-and-skirt dress the waistline seam holds the garment in position so it is not essential for the underarm seam of the waist to balance in order for the side seamline of the garment to hang straight, but in cut-in-one structures the only control on the side seamline is its bisymmetry. The sheath dress poses a greater balance problem than the gored dress which has additional seamlines at which fitting can be adjusted. The fitted princess dress is a mechanically sound structure for this reason, whereas the fitted shift is not, a fact that becomes apparent as its development is delineated. Nevertheless, the fitted shift is the first cut-in-one structure to be developed in this chapter. Although it cannot be used as a dress, the fitted shift becomes the very successful torso sloper when the skirt section is cut away, and it is the framework on which the fitted Empire-line sloper is based. Torsoline and Empire-line structures are also applicable to demifitted and unfitted silhouettes. They are developed simply by

planning their style lines on the desired structure. Only the fitted Empire-line styling requires extra drafting.

The fitted shift can be developed in four steps:

Skirt Back. Position the skirt back on pattern paper, with hemline and 5-inch line drawn in at right angles to center-back line. At the side-seam point erect a balance line perpendicular to the hemline.

Waist Back. Position the waist back to match skirt at side-seam point after slashing the sloper up to the breakpoint of the armhole and opening a second dart of sufficient width to enlarge the waistline of the waist to match the waistline of the skirt.

Waist Front. Position the waist front the same distance from the balance line as the waist back at both underarm and waistline points. Open the second dart wide enough to bring the center front to straight grain (parallel with balance line).

Skirt Front. Split the sloper on the panel dartline. Position the front section to line up with the center front of waist. Position the side section at the same distance from balance line as skirt back at waistline, hipline, and hemline.

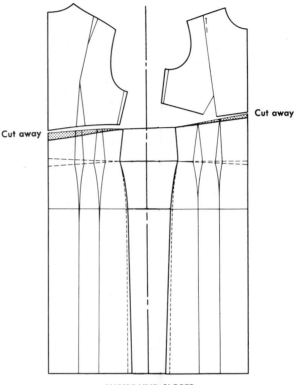

TORSOLINE SLOPER

EMPIRE-LINE SLOPER

The fitted *torsoline* sloper, which is standard for fitted jackets and long-waisted dresses, is made when the skirt section of the fitted shift is cut away at any desired level below the normal waistline. The torso sloper cuts away the skirt with its unwieldy darts extending to the hemline. The excessive width of these darts is not apparent or objectionable in the torso sloper, but darts that extend to the bottom of a skirt are unthinkable. Another defect of the fitted sheath is the transverse wrinkle across the waistline which results from the body being longer at the curved side-seam area than at the relatively straight center front and back areas. In the torso sloper this defect is improved when the waistline is allowed to drop at center back, as it can if additional ease is introduced (an impossibility in a full-length shift).

The fitted *Empire-line* structure can elimi-

nate the large front darts and push up the waistline wrinkle to the Empire line where it can be cut away. For these reasons the Empire line is the most popular style for a sleekly fitted dress without a waistline seam. Note in the torsoline sloper that the amount added to the front darts is shown as a straight column that reaches up to a position below the bustline. The point at which this column crosses the slanting seamlines of the darts is the highest point at which the Empire line can be drawn to eliminate this excess. When the Empire line is placed at this level, the sheath skirt can be substituted since the excess can be lapped out. It is necessary, however, to use the torso sloper to plan the midriff section of the skirt above the normal waistline. Once the midriff has been planned, the upper sections of the waist can be replaced by the waist slopers cut off at the Empire line.

Unfitted and Demifitted Shift Slopers

Demifitted   Unfitted

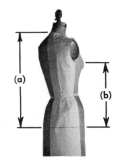

Measurements from Dress Form

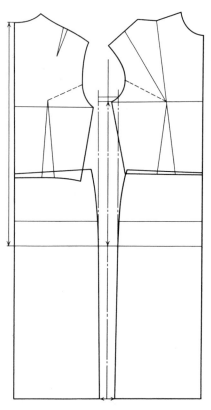

A. SLOPER DEVELOPMENT

A NEW DRAFTING principle is used in the development of these free-hanging unfitted and demifitted shifts. To compensate for the lack of indentation at the waistline, the slopers must be lapped enough at the waistline to maintain straight grain at the torsoline and thus cause the skirt to hang evenly at the hemline. Two measurements made directly on the dress form furnish necessary information: (a) the amount to lap the back slopers is found by measuring from the back of the neck to the torsoline; (b) the amount to lap the front slopers is found by measuring from the underarm sloper position to the torsoline. (The back laps more than front.)

Diagram A shows the slopers positioned on the pattern paper with the correct amount lapped at the waistline. The skirt slopers are positioned first because the torsoline is the reference point from which the measurements made on the dress form are transferred to the pattern. As always, the side seamline must be balanced. Back and front skirt slopers are positioned at least 1½ inches apart with the balance line midway between them (on pattern paper that is prepared as for the torso slopers).

Diagram B shows the side sections of the waist cut away for clarity. Lines are now drawn from the torsoline up to the underarm level parallel with the balance line in order to furnish the framework for the new side seamlines. The

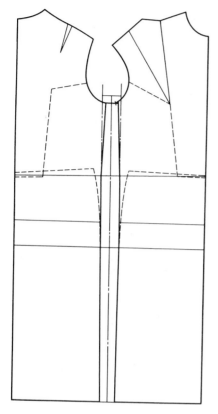

B. UNFITTED SHIFT

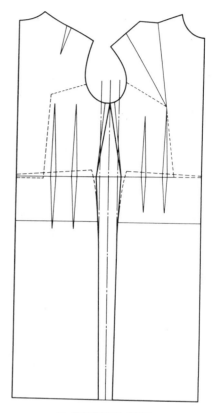

C. DEMIFITTED SHIFT

major problem in the unfitted shift is that of balancing the side seamline of the waist. The waist front usually is 1 inch wider than the waist back at the underarm level, and balance is achieved by first aligning back and front underarm points at the new underarm level and then taking enough away from the front and adding it to the back at the underarm to achieve balance. As a result of this equalization, the side seamline is moved forward at the underarm. (If it is desirable in production, the underarm seam of the sleeve can be shifted over at the underarm to match the seamline of the garment.) As a final step, the customary half-inch ease is added at the underarm and the shoulder dart is pivoted down to side seam.

Diagram C shows how the demifitted shift is made by splitting the differences between the fitted torso shift and the unfitted shift. (A similar technique was used in drafting the A-line flared skirt.) The slopers are lapped only half as much at the waistline and the waistline is widened only half as much at the side seamline as in the unfitted shift, and the take-up of the waistline darts is only half the take-up of the darts in the fitted slopers. In Diagram C the front-panel dart is shown centered below the bust apex and the back-panel dart is positioned to match it. The second dart is spaced midway between panel-dart seamline and side seamline. In the sketch a single dart is used in which the take-up of both darts is combined.

Fitted Princess-Line Slopers

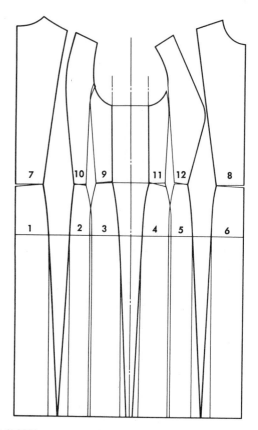

FITTED PRINCESS-LINE SLOPER

THE PRINCESS-LINE dress is the only vertically seamed cut-in-one structure that can be tightly fitted with much success. Its princess seamlines permit enough fitting to compensate for the front waist being wider than the back waist and for the figure being longer at the side than at the center. These two discrepancies, which are handled perfectly by the waistline seam of the waist-and-skirt dress, are the besetting problems of all cut-in-one structures. The diagram on this page shows how the gored skirt and waist slopers are combined to produce the fitted princess dress. Note that the skirt follows the development principles used for the gored skirts in Chapter 6. Much more flare can be introduced, too, than the minimum amount

shown in the diagram. The pattern pieces have been numbered to indicate the order in which they must be positioned.

The Skirt. Skirt sections are positioned first, aligned precisely on the 5-inch line to facilitate drafting. As always, a balance line is drawn in so that the back and front seamlines can be balanced properly. The side sections of both skirt and waist are split in this pattern development. (In a 10-gore structure they would remain as separate pieces.) The side back and side front of the skirt are each lapped ¼ inch and the darts thereby are shortened since a dart never needs to extend into a flare. The ¼ inch taken up by the back darts at the 5-inch line in the sloper can be lapped out of any gored skirt in which

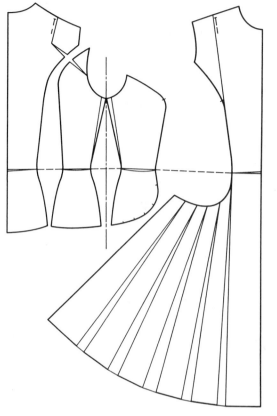

FITTED PRINCESS-LINE VARIATION

the flare extends above the 5-inch line. The front must be lapped the same as the back.

The Waist. The center panels of the waist are aligned on straight grain to match the center panels of the skirt. The small transverse wrinkle that the gap at the waistline represents can be eliminated only by easing the fit or cutting a waistline seam. The back side-seam section is positioned to join the skirt at the side-seam point. It cannot tip inward and therefore it usually lies parallel with the balance line. The princess section is positioned to join the skirt at the princess-line point and at the same time to match with the armhole of the side section where a slight lap develops. A compensating gap develops in the front causing the front

shoulderline to be lengthened slightly and the back shoulderline to be shortened slightly.

Variations. Other skirt styles can be combined with the gored waist in the development of attractive and practical princess variations. One is shown here and several others are illustrated later in the chapter. This variation combines a gored waist and a bell-flare skirt. In planning this garment the front panel of the waist is joined to the skirt as an initial step. Then the style line of the hip yoke is sketched on the pattern and the slashes for the flare drawn in. Then the yoke section is cut away and joined to the side and back sections of the waist at their common waistline. The skirt sections are slashed and spread to add the flare (back not shown).

187

DEMIFITTED PRINCESS-LINE SLOPER

Demifitted Princess and Bias-Cut Slopers

FLARE DEPENDS ON a fitted waistline, and the amount of flare tends to be proportional to tightness of fit. Thus a tightly fitted waistline can support a circular flare, whereas the unfitted shift can support no flare at all.

Demifitted Princess Sloper. Demifitted princess dresses are generally styled with the restrained flare of the A-line silhouette. If more movement is desired than this silhouette provides, either inverted pleats or a hemline flounce are introduced to supply it. Several demifitted styling variations are shown later in the chapter. The development of the demifitted princess structure consists merely of cutting apart a demifitted shift of desired styling and widening the skirt bottom by the technique regularly used for gored skirts. The diagram shows standard princess styling. The small diagram shows the A-line that was introduced by Dior, a style particularly well adapted to the demifitted silhouette.

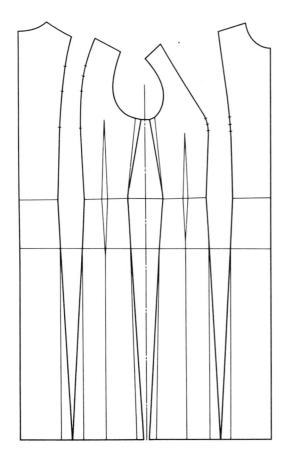

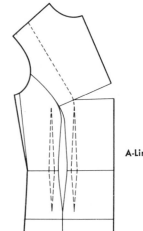

A-Line Princess

Demifitted Bias-Cut Shift Sloper. The inherent stretchability of bias permits it to mold a cut-in-one garment to the figure without darts at the waistline. Unless this exclusive molding feature can be used to advantage, however, the many troublesome characteristics of bias styling outweigh its good points. For this reason bias cut-in-one styling is infrequently used except in high-price garments. The drafting of the bias-cut 4-gore shift shown here is very simple. First, position the A-line skirt slopers (with half darts) on either side of the balance line with true bias planned at the normal straight-grain positions. Next, balance the back-waist sloper on the skirt waistline. Because of the bias cut the waist can overlap the skirt as shown. Shift the shoulder dart to center back and cut it away. Position the waist front to balance the waist back at the side seamlines. The waistline dart excess is theoretically pivoted to center front and cut away as is any excess in the back waist that protrudes beyond center back. As a final step (shown in the small diagram) the customary ½-inch ease is added at the underarm and then the shoulder dart is pivoted down to a low French-dart position on the side seam.

DEMIFITTED BIAS-CUT SHIFT SLOPER

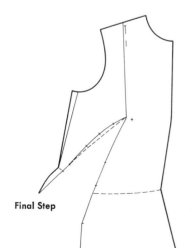

Final Step

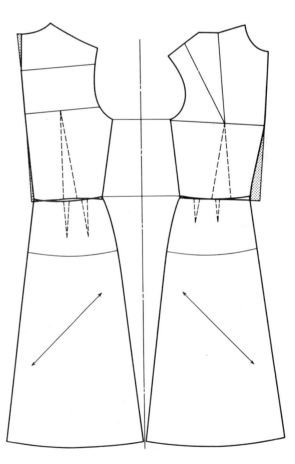

189

The Unfitted and Demifitted Shifts

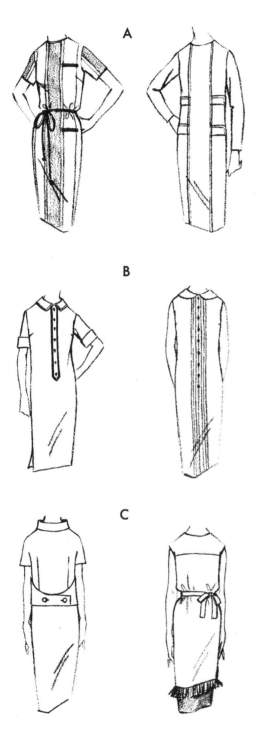

A

B

C

The Unfitted Shift. The simplest of all dress styles, the unfitted shift needs only a bust dart in front and a shoulder dart in back to shape it, and only a side seam to make a garment from its two pattern pieces. It relies heavily on its fabric for sales appeal. When the rectangular look of this shift is in fashion, examples of it are found at all market levels. The typical garments shown at the left, for example, range from $3.75 to $375.00. The standard styling of the unfitted shift is simple and is often both collarless and sleeveless. The feeling of this loosely fitted rectangular "composition" is strong, casual, uncluttered, and incompatible with detail.

BELTS. The shift on the left in A (for which the pattern was made on page 184) is shown with a tie belt because it was found necessary to overcome customer resistance to the shift's unfitted style. A shift cut to be worn straight, however, hangs short at the sides when worn with a belt, and the more tightly the belt is tied the more this tendency is evident. On the other hand, the belted shift in C is styled to be worn with a belt and will hang unevenly if worn unbelted.

STYLING. The dresses in A use vertical lines in simple styling that slims the figure; the dresses in B use different types of button-down styling that also slims and lengthens the figure. In the dresses in C, no attempt is made to lengthen the figure, instead the characteristic rectangular silhouette of the high-style trapeze is accentuated.

The Demifitted Shift. The modified silhouette of the demifitted shift is much easier to wear than the extreme trapeze silhouette of the un-fitted shift. The waistline of the demifitted shift is slightly indented by half-size darts (refer again to page 185) that produce a more flattering and far more popular silhouette than the unfitted shift.

KNITS. The demifitted shift is popular in knit-ted fabrics of wool, silk, acetate, linen, and cot-ton. The naturally soft, supple quality of knitted fabric permits an easy "skimmer" fit while it minimizes awareness that the waistline is not indented in the customary way. The dresses shown in D are of knitted fabric, the standard version of the shift on the left, again shown with a tie belt, and an interesting variation on the right in which the dart excess is caught and held by self-spaghetti ties. (On the back of the garment, of course, the darts are stitched closed.)

A-LINE. The extremely tailored button-down dress of herringbone tweed in E and the ex-tremely dressy costume of silk brocade beside it illustrate the wide variation possible in demi-fitted shift styling. Note that an A-line silhou-ette results when the garment is opened at cen-ter front and allowed to spread, as it does in the illustration on the right. The standard shift does not normally have capability for the A-line sil-houette, and either the bias-cut shift or the demifitted princess is used since both automati-cally have A-line styling. Both dresses in F show versions of the bias-cut A-line shift in which styling is usually kept simple. The capability of bias to mold subtly to the figure has such great style value that the addition of trimming as a rule is a thankless, lily-gilding procedure.

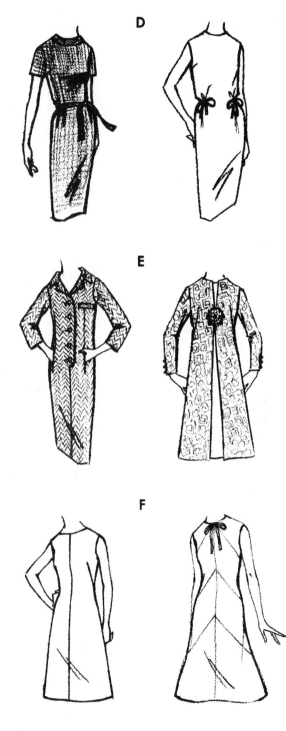

The Fitted and Demifitted Princess Dresses

A

B

C

The Fitted Princess Dress. This style has a young connotation because one must have a slim young waistline to wear it successfully—and it fools the eye into believing the waistline is still slimmer. To produce this illusion the princess lines must tend to converge at the waistline as is possible only in relatively small sizes. For this reason the fitted princess dress is not usually sold in women's or half-sizes, although variations of it, like the two dresses in C, are well suited to larger sizes in both styling and structure.

FLARE. The standard 6-gore princess dress shown in A, for which a pattern was made earlier in the chapter, has a more restrained silhouette than the 8-gore dress in B. The degree of fit and flare that is possible in any gored structure depends largely on the number of gores. A 6-gore dress cannot fit as snugly or flare as widely as can an 8-gore dress because there is a mechanical limit to the amount of fitting and flare at any one gore line. When a more exaggerated flare is desired, other techniques must be used. Flare is increased, for example, in the dress on the right in A by combining a circular skirt with a gored waist (the pattern for this dress was shown on page 186). Flare is increased by trumpet gores in the dress on the right in B.

PRINCESS PANEL. The dresses in C retain only the princess panel, substituting a separate waist-and-skirt structure for sides and back, with the seamline hidden under the partial belt. The eye-fooling combination of unbroken panel and segmented beltline effectively decreases an obviously heavy waistline and for this reason both of these cleverly designed dresses are much more wearable than their prototype, the fitted princess dress.

The Demifitted Princess Dress. This dress offers such excellent styling advantages that it is perennially popular, fitted a little more strictly perhaps in hourglass eras and relaxed a little more in shift eras, but never out of fashion. It has the long unbroken lines that make the princess dress so flattering and its easy fit is kind to figures that are no better than average. The A-line that Dior unveiled in 1954 to initiate the trend toward rectangular silhouettes was based on this demifitted princess dress, with the princess line moved far enough to the side that it was possible to use a partial dart at the bustline, as is illustrated in the jumper dress in D (for which a pattern is shown on page 188).

COAT DRESSES. The coat dress is a particularly appropriate type of styling for this demifitted silhouette. It is shown in E in both single- and double-breasted versions, while the dress in D (pattern on page 188) has a coat-dress feeling because of the double-breasted look of the buttons.

STYLING. A collar is not necessarily used on the princess dress. The small mandarin collar shown in E is the most popular collar type and deservedly so because it does not hide the princess lines. In addition, it has the same feeling that the lines of the dress exemplify. The demifitted princess structure is not mechanically suited to exaggerated flare, and if movement at the hemline is desired it can be introduced by cut-in inverted pleats or a flounce, both of which are illustrated in F. Pleats are more suited to casual styling, whereas the flounce gives a very dressy look. When the princess line curves over into the armhole rather than extending up to the shoulder, the effect of height is diminished while breadth at the shoulder is increased.

193

A

B

Two-Piece Dresses

Tailored Button-Down Two-Piece. The fitted torsoline sheath which was the first cut-in-one sloper to be developed in this chapter probably has its greatest dress use in the type of two-piece styling shown in A. These two-piece outfits differ from tailored suits in that suit jackets can be removed because they are worn over blouses, while here the jacket is not removable because there is no blouse beneath it. And a suit jacket is customarily lined since the inside shows when it is removed, while a lining is not necessarily used in a garment that is not removable.

The fitted jacket structure may be developed from either the torsoline sloper or the fitted princess sloper, depending on whether darts or gorelines are preferred in the styling. An extremely straight sheath skirt or an extremely full flared skirt can be used, or one of the pleated skirts, which are more comfortable than the sheath and more flattering to the figure than the full flare.

Casual Button-Down Two-Piece. Button-down styling can also be adapted to the casual look that is characteristic of the shift eras, as the garments shown in B illustrate. Here the demifitted shift pattern generally is used. The removable jacket at the far left closes casually with one button to show a striped jersey shell beneath. The seersucker two-piece in the middle has a very casually tied narrow belt of self-fabric. The top of the flannel two-piece next to it is styled almost like a man's pyjama jacket and is properly accented with a paisley scarf casually tucked into the unbuttoned neckline. Both silhouette and styling in these casual dresses are in contrast to the tailored two-piece dresses shown in A.

Casual Pullover Separates. Pullover separates
have great popularity for several reasons. They
can be styled in so many different ways that they
can serve many different uses, and whenever
tops and skirts can be sold separately, women
with figure problems are able to mix and match
sizes. All three pullover styles illustrated in C
are examples of these mix-and-match separates
that have the middy blouse as their parent
fashion, just as the tailored suit is the parent
fashion of button-down, two-piece garments.
The classic middy blouse with sailor collar is
shown at the far right with two standard variations. All three are based on the unfitted shift
sloper, cut across at the hip level, as is appropriate for the styling. For these casual separates
the sheath skirt, pleated skirt, or one of the
A-line skirts may be used.

Dressy Two-Piece Outfits. All three of the comparatively dressy two-piece dresses shown in D
avoid both the casual pullover look and the tailored button-down look and attain instead a
dressy look by a combination of structure, fabric,
and styling detail. The two-tone pastel linen
dress at the far right, the least dressy of the
three, closes with buttons down the back. The
dress in the middle, which is in the Chanel tra-
dition, needs only a short neckline zipper at the
back. Its fabric is a lacy tweed in a pale tone and
its trimming is of self-color satin edged with
hand crochet. This combination of casual structure with perishable fabric and trimming is a
technique frequently used to produce garments
that can serve a broad range of uses. The cocktail dress of heavy silk crepe, which is extremely
dressy, closes with an inconspicuous side zipper.
Its high-style pegged skirt and classically draped
overblouse are so perfectly coordinated that the
two-piece look generally associated with casual
styling is not apparent.

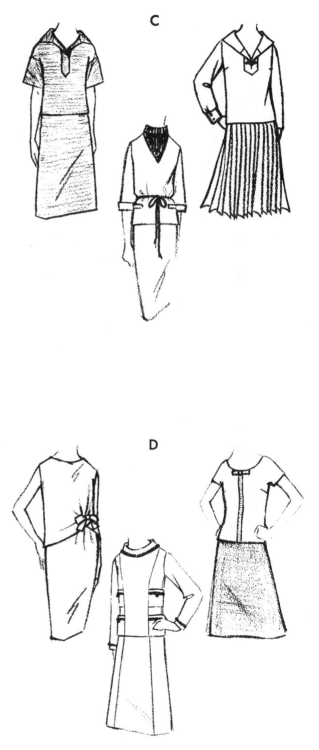

One-Piece Torsoline Dress and Variations

A

B

C

Fitted Torsoline Dress. The fitted one-piece torsoline dress, like its two-piece counterpart, is developed from the torso sloper which is cut across at the hipline to prevent the oversize front darts from extending down into the skirt in an objectionable way. The two dresses in A show one of the most popular types of torsoline styling in which the fitted bodice is combined with a pleated skirt. This low-waisted styling has the advantage of being able to use straight pleating rather than the more expensive contoured pleating that is necessary to fit pleats properly at the normal waistline. The bodice sections of the dresses in B are similar to those in A, but flared skirts are used instead of pleated skirts to give width to the silhouette at the hemline. For these tightly fitted bodice sections either the torso sloper or the fitted princess sloper can be used, depending on how other style features can be best coordinated. For example, the princess sloper is used for the bodice of a gored skirt while the torso sloper is used in combination with a flared skirt.

Demifitted Torsoline Dress. When the silhouette is relaxed at the waistline as shown in the two dresses in C, the width of the hemline is reduced. Exaggerated flare requires a fitted waistline for both mechanical and artistic reasons, but the demifitted silhouette can use no more than a restrained A-line flare. The two dresses illustrated have very similar silhouettes although each has different styling. The demifitted shift sloper is used to make the dress on the far left and horizontal style lines are drawn in at points where they can take care of the dart excess. The other more conservatively styled dress uses the demifitted princess sloper.

Variations. WIDE HEMLINE. When a wide hemline is desired in demifitted torsoline styling, it can be introduced in one of the two ways shown by the dresses in D. On the far right, an extremely full dirndl skirt, cut on true bias for a more subtle effect, is combined with the demifitted shift upper section. The more conservative dress beside it uses trumpet gores to produce an exaggerated hemline.

NARROW HEMLINE. Narrow hemlines are also possible with demifitted torsoline styling. The sheath skirt is rarely used, but the pegged skirt is very well suited to being styled with a lowered waistline in both one-piece and two-piece versions. The demifitted shift or princess dress can be cut off at the desired style line to furnish the upper section of the dress while the basic skirt replaces the lower section of the princess dress so that it may be slashed and spread to achieve the desired draped effect, as was shown on page 155 of Chapter 7. Many interesting and artistically sound styles can be developed by combining the lowered waistline with a pegged skirt because it is possible to exaggerate the silhouette at the hipline and retain the sound 5-to-8 proportion of waist to skirt.

BLOUSON SILHOUETTE. One of the most difficult silhouettes to handle well both artistically and mechanically is the blouson, two examples of which are shown in F, one with the sheath silhouette and the other with its pleated counterpart. To develop the blouson bodice, the unfitted shift can be cut apart at the desired beltline and the necessary amount of blousing added. The skirt of a blouson requires support, usually given by attaching it to an underwaist.

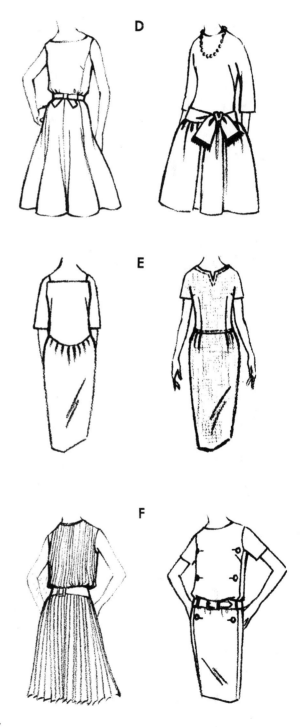

The Empire Line

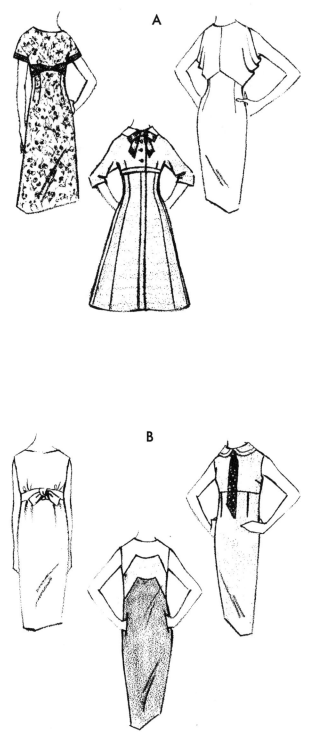

Fitted Waistline. The Empire line furnishes the most satisfactory structure for styling a fitted sheath that cannot be cut as a waist-and-skirt dress. In the dresses shown in A, the skirt types range from the fitted sheath through the restrained A-line to the flared princess-line silhouette, all of them with a tightly fitted waistline. Empire styling based on the sheath has been explained. Empire styling based on the fitted princess sloper is much more easily accomplished since the pattern is made simply by cutting the princess sloper apart at the desired style line for the skirt section and using the sloper waist pattern instead of the princess waist sections for the upper section. A-line styling, however, imposes considerable restriction on the location of the Empire line. A-line flare is developed by pivoting the sheath pattern for the skirt section of the dress, just as was done in the development of the A-line skirt shown on page 149 of Chapter 7, and the pivot can be no more than enough to close the top of the darts. Thus the more nearly the Empire line coincides with the normal waistline, the more flare possible, while no flare at all can be used at the upper limit of the Empire-line position.

Demifitted Waistline. Empire-line styling is particularly well suited to the eased waistline of the demifitted shift. Three different ways in which this structure can be styled are illustrated in B. The styling can be dressy when the dart excess is softly shirred, as shown at the far left, or it can be tailored when darts are used as strong style lines, as shown at the right. The middle illustration shows a cleverly styled dress in which three tones of linen are combined. Its shaped yoke sections take out the dart excess and furnish flattering style lines.

Demifitted Variations. Demifitted Empire-line variations can be based on the demifitted bias-cut sloper, the demifitted princess sloper, or the demifitted shift sloper, as the sketches in C illustrate. The dress at the far right is made from the A-line princess pattern, the dress in the middle uses the demifitted shift pattern, and the third dress uses the bias-cut pattern shown on page 189. As with the fitted Empire-line pattern explained on page 183, it is practical here also to substitute the regular sloper waist for the waist section of the sloper used in the development, since the waist or "yoke" section in Empire styling should fit like a regular sloper waist and be kept free of darts except for the partial dart below the bust, if the Empire line is not placed high enough to avoid it.

Unfitted Variations. All of the dresses shown in D are based on the unfitted shift sloper, which has a shoulder dart but no darts to take out excess at the waistline. The Empire line is necessarily high in this styling, often just above the bust apex, in which case the shoulder dart can be eliminated since the Empire line cuts across the tip of it. In effect, the horizontal Empire line replaces the vertical dart line for a high-style look, as the examples show. In each case a strong styling detail is used to center the attention near the face since there are no vertical lines in the body of the dress, as there are in C, for example, which the eye can use as a track up to the face. None of these three dresses attempts to lengthen the figure, except in the subtle way of contrasting a very short yoke section with a comparatively long body section, a trick used in evening wear with tremendous success because the contrast is greatly intensified when the skirt section reaches the floor.

C

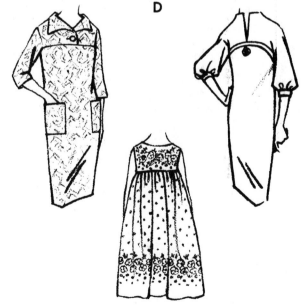

D

199

Chapter Nine

The Family of Sleeves

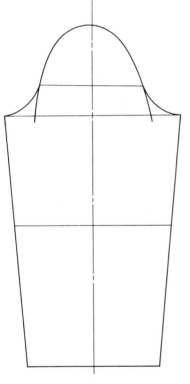

The "Sleeveboard" Sloper

THIS CHAPTER is entitled "The Family of Sleeves" to emphasize that all sleeves are offspring of a single common source—the sleeve sloper shown in the sketch. Sleeve styling, which is customarily developed through drafting (the dress form normally has no arms), presents a unique problem. The sleeve and the armhole of its waist must match one another as accurately as a jar or bottle matches the lid or cap that closes it, and the complexity lies in the fact that the sleeve has an entirely different curvature from its armhole. An intensive study of sleeves is undertaken in this chapter, in which practical drafting methods for all members of the sleeve family are presented in considerable detail since the prime necessity for a sleeve to fit perfectly causes styling to depend totally on structure.

Development of Sleeve Types

THE SLEEVE, much more than the waist, defines and interprets the silhouette. Sleeve shape, therefore, must be sensitive to many types of exaggeration. Although the sketches presented on this page show restrained examples of the different sleeve types, each of the types has a wide range of variation that is developed and illustrated in the body of the chapter. The basic sloper sleeve that is the parent of the entire sleeve family is not shown here because it is used only as a sloper. From it the long, fitted sleeves are developed and they too act as slopers.

opment from those used for the more or less cylindrical skirt and waist. The sleeve presents additional mechanical problems, too, because its requirement for body movement is far beyond that necessary for waist or skirt. An intensive study of the sleeve is undertaken in this chapter, and it is recommended that the student develop the complete range of sleeves first in paper and then in muslin to gain adequate insight into both their possibilities and their limitations.

One-Piece Fitted-Sleeve Sloper

Two-Piece Fitted-Sleeve Sloper

only as a sloper. From it the long, fitted sleeves are developed and they too act as slopers.

Sleeve styling depends to such a great extent on fit that drafting procedures are given more attention than is any other facet of sleeve development. The sleeve cap—where sleeve styling originates—is hemispherical in form and for this reason it requires different techniques of devel-

Sleeves are divided into three groups:

Type I: the rather dressy sleeves that are set in to the normal armhole.

Type II: the rather casual sleeves that require the normal armhole to be lowered and simplified.

Type III: the sleeves that are cut partly or entirely in-one with the waist.

THE FAMILY OF SLEEVES

Type I
Sleeves for
Normal Armhole

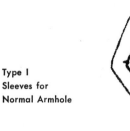

Leg-of-Mutton Sleeve   Puff Sleeve   Bishop Sleeve

Type II
Sleeves for
Lowered Armhole

Casual Sleeve

Type III
Sleeves Cut Partly
or Entirely In-One
with Waist

Raglan Sleeve   Kimono-Gusset Sleeve   Kimono-Dolman Sleeve

Development of Sleeve-Cap Oval from Armscye

Sleeve Shape. The upper section of the sleeve, which sets into the armhole of the waist, is called the "cap" of the sleeve (shown in A). The sleeve cap derives its shape from the armhole. The armhole, in turn, derives its shape from the *armscye,* as the area of the dress form that represents the arm is called.

Armhole Development. The upper half of the armscye is measured from the tip of the shoulder to the midpoint of the plate screw, but since the lower half of the armscye has no defining ridge like the upper half, the total length of the armscye must be found by doubling the length of the upper half. The *armhole of the waist* does not fit around the armscye of the dress form precisely, however, but must be lowered ⅝ inch at the underarm for lengthwise ease and increased in width by 1 inch for crosswise ease, as shown in the diagram.

Sleeve-Cap Development. The ease added to the lower half of the armhole requires the sleeve-cap opening, as represented by the *sleeve-cap oval,* to be enlarged a comparable amount at the underarm. The upper half of the sleeve-cap oval must also be enlarged in order to fit around the shoulder which protrudes beyond the body, as it is represented by the dress form. When both upper and lower halves of the sleeve-cap oval are lengthened by ⅝ inch, its width is automatically increased by ⅛ inch (1/16 inch × 2), as shown in diagram B.

DIMENSIONS OF SLEEVE-CAP OVAL. The sleeve-cap oval has a length-to-width proportion of 3 to 2. Thus when the length is 6 inches, as is used for Sizes 9–10, the width is 4 inches. The "grade factor," or amount of variation per size, in the misses and junior size ranges is 3/16 inch for cap height and ⅜ inch for bicep width. As a rule the top half of the armscye (from shoulder point to midpoint of plate screw) is measured to obtain the one measurement needed for sleeve-cap development. However, it is equally feasible to begin the computation with the correct bicep width (actual bicep circumference with ⅜ inch ease added) and to work back to establish correct armhole length. Since sleeve cap and armhole are interdependent, the measurement of either one can be used to compute the other.

The Arm-Direction Line. Note that the armscye has a forward pitch of ¼ inch to represent the direction that the arm takes as it hangs at the side. The arm-direction line, as shown in the B diagrams, is an important consideration in all sleeve development.

A. RELATIONSHIP OF SLEEVE TO ARMHOLE

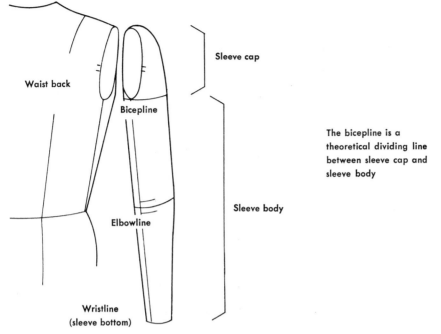

Waist back

Sleeve cap

Bicepline

The bicepline is a theoretical dividing line between sleeve cap and sleeve body

Sleeve body

Elbowline

Wristline
(sleeve bottom)

B. DEVELOPMENT OF SLEEVE-CAP OVAL

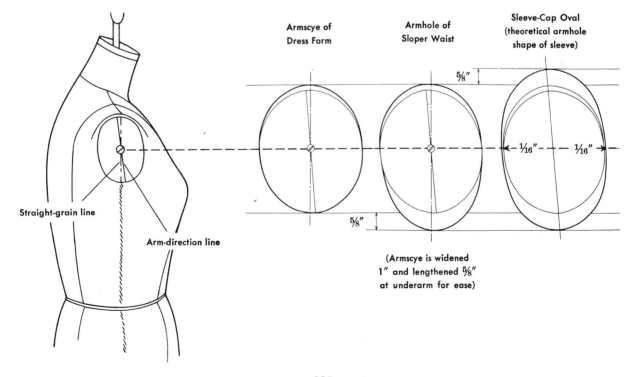

Straight-grain line

Arm-direction line

Armscye of
Dress Form

Armhole of
Sloper Waist

Sleeve-Cap Oval
(theoretical armhole
shape of sleeve)

5⁄8″

1⁄16″ — 1⁄16″

5⁄8″

(Armscye is widened
1″ and lengthened 5⁄8″
at underarm for ease)

205

Theoretical Development of the Pattern for the Sleeve Cap

THE SLEEVE-CAP OVAL developed on the preceding page represents the sleeve-cap opening as it appears with the underarm seam of the sleeve closed, as shown in A. The way the sleeve-cap oval furnishes the length and height measurements of the sleeve-cap pattern is shown in B. The theoretical relationship of the oval to the pattern is shown in C. Note that two ovals approximate the overarm section of the sleeve cap. Segments of two additional ovals form the small underarm sections and when the underarm seam is closed these segments represent the third oval. (The bicep width of the sleeve cap is equal to the combined width of three ovals.)

In Diagram D a single half-oval of double size (8 by 12 inches) replaces the two small (4 by 6 inches) ovals that were used in C to represent the overarm section of the sleeve cap. The resulting ovoid shape (as made with the French curve) accurately represents the overarm section of the sleeve, as shown in E. The completed sleeve cap is shown in F, with the overarm section tilted at the slight angle of the arm-direction line, and with the underarm sections added.

Derivation of Sleeve-Cap Dimensions

When $\frac{1}{2}$ armscye length is $2\frac{3}{8}$ inches
(as here shown)
Then armhole length is $5\frac{3}{8}$ inches
$(2\frac{3}{8}'' + 2\frac{3}{8}'' + \frac{5}{8}'') = 5\frac{3}{8}''$
And sleeve-cap oval length is 6 inches
$(5\frac{3}{8}'' + \frac{5}{8}'') = 6''$
And sleeve-cap oval width is 4 inches
$\frac{2}{3}$ of $6'' = 4''$
And bicep width is 12 inches
$(6'' \times 2)$ or $(4'' \times 3) = 12''$

The six diagrams on the facing page show the theoretical development of a sleeve cap. On the two following pages a practical step-by-step method for drafting sleeve caps according to this theory is presented.

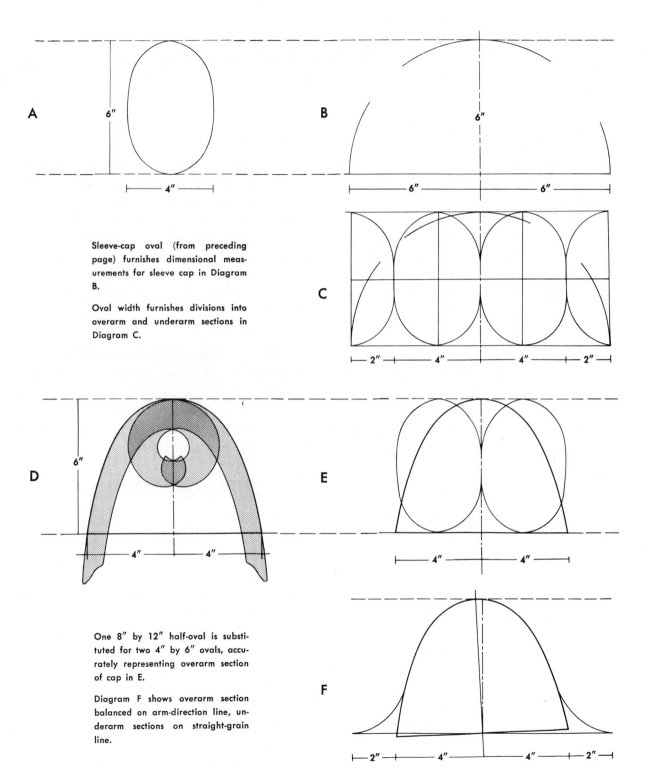

A

6"

4"

B

6"

6"   6"

Sleeve-cap oval (from preceding page) furnishes dimensional measurements for sleeve cap in Diagram B.

Oval width furnishes divisions into overarm and underarm sections in Diagram C.

C

2"   4"   4"   2"

D

6"

4"   4"

E

4"   4"

One 8" by 12" half-oval is substituted for two 4" by 6" ovals, accurately representing overarm section of cap in E.

Diagram F shows overarm section balanced on arm-direction line, underarm sections on straight-grain line.

F

2"   4"   4"   2"

207

Drafting the Sleeve Cap Step by Step

STEP 1. THE WIDTH-HEIGHT FRAMEWORK OF THE SLEEVE CAP (RULER AND COMPASS).

(a) Draw two grain lines on the pattern paper at right angles to one another on which to measure the bicepline (width) and the center of the sleeve (height) of the sleeve cap.

(b) Use the intersection of the two grain lines as a center for the compass to mark off the measured width and height of the cap. (The width of bicepline is double the cap height.)

(c) Measure over ¼ inch to the left at the top of the cap and at each end of the bicepline and draw in dotted-framework lines to act as axis lines for the tilted overarm section of the cap.

(d) Measure and use the compass to mark off the width of the overarm section of the cap on its dotted bicepline. (The overarm section takes up the middle two-thirds of the bicepline.)

STEP 2. THE OVERARM SECTION OF THE SLEEVE CAP (FRENCH CURVE).

Use the French curve as in Chapter 6 to draw the capline, first the front half, then the back half of the cap. Balance the French curve at the top of the cap for ½ inch (¼ inch each way from the dotted center line of the tilted overarm section) for Points 1–2 and at the intersection of the dotted bicepline and the overarm line for Point 3. The overarm section of a sleeve cap is bisymmetric when folded on its own dotted center line. When the cap is folded on the center-grain line of the sleeve, the back half is ¼ inch longer than the front half.

STEP 3. THE BREAKPOINTS AND UNDERARM SECTIONS OF THE SLEEVE CAP.

(a) Erase the dotted axis lines to avoid confusion. The grain lines of the sleeve serve as reference lines for this step.

(b) Use the compass centered on the intersections of capline and bicepline to establish the breakpoints (where the sleeve turns from overarm to underarm when on the arm) by marking off on the capline a distance equal to the distance from the compass point to the underarm end of the bicepline. Note that the back measurement is ⅛ inch longer than the front measurement, causing the breakpoint to be ⅛ inch higher on the back of the sleeve than on the front of the sleeve.

(c) Connect the two breakpoints to establish the breakline. The breakline does not change in relation to the body and to the waist sloper. It remains stable while the sections above and below it are enlarged or reduced in different types of sleeve styling.

(d) Draw in the underarm sections of the sleeve cap. Use the French curve, with Points 1–2 tangent to the overarm section of the sleeve for ½ inch above the breakpoint, and Point 3 touching the underarm end of the bicepline. The underarm sections of a sleeve are merely connecting sections that are drawn in this same way as a final step in drafting all set-in sleeves.

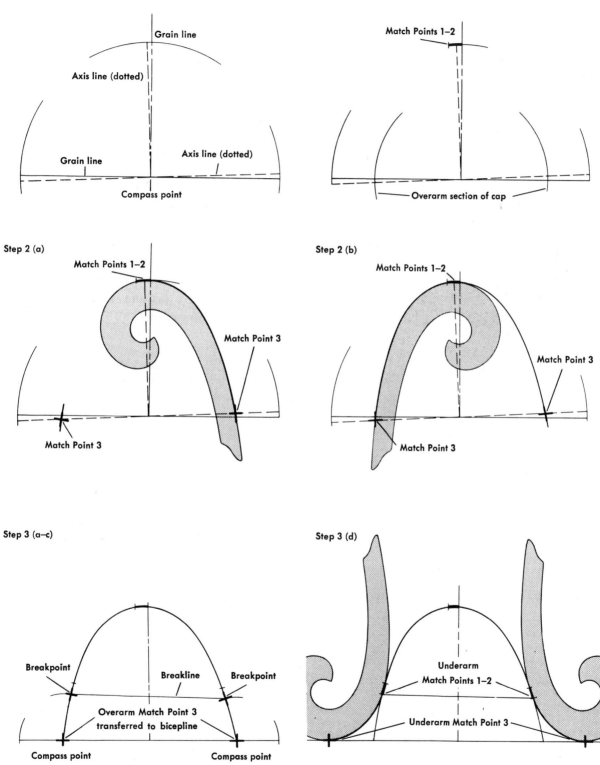

Step 1 (a–c)

Grain line

Axis line (dotted)

Grain line   Axis line (dotted)

Compass point

Step 1 (d)

Match Points 1–2

Overarm section of cap

Step 2 (a)

Match Points 1–2

Match Point 3

Match Point 3

Step 2 (b)

Match Points 1–2

Match Point 3

Match Point 3

Step 3 (a–c)

Breakpoint   Breakline   Breakpoint

Overarm Match Point 3
transferred to bicepline

Compass point   Compass point

Step 3 (d)

Underarm
Match Points 1–2

Underarm Match Point 3

209

Development of Body Section of Sloper Sleeves

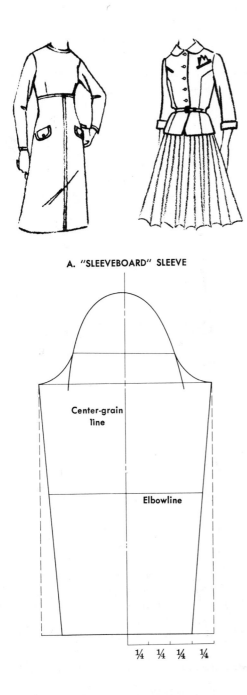

The Basic Sloper Sleeve (A). This sleeve is made from the sleeve cap that has just been developed by adding a tapered bisymmetric body section to encase the arm. The length of the body section can be varied to suit individual measurements. The standard position for the elbow is 1 inch above the midpoint of the body section measured on the center-grain line. The width of the sleeve bottom is three-fourths of the width of the bicepline.

A. "SLEEVEBOARD" SLEEVE

Center-grain line

Elbowline

¼ ¼ ¼ ¼

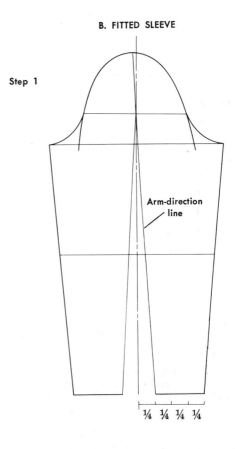

B. FITTED SLEEVE

Step 1

Arm-direction line

¼ ¼ ¼ ¼

The Tightly Fitted Sloper Sleeve (B and C).
The first step in the development of the tightly fitted sleeve is shown in B. The arm-direction line is drawn in on the sleeve sloper, from the capline to the wristline where it cuts off one quarter of the wrist width from the front of the sleeve. When an equal amount is cut from the back of the sleeve, the wristline is reduced properly for the fitted sleeve. In C a method for introducing the necessary ease at the elbow is shown. The back half of the sleeve is slashed ½ inch above and ½ inch below the elbowline, with a compensating slash at the bicepline, and when the back section of the sleeve is brought over to meet the front section at the wristline, the dart excess that is pivoted from the wrist to the elbow gives it enough room to bend.

The Demifitted Sleeve (D). The same technique is used to produce the demifitted sleeve. The wrist measurement of this sleeve is midway between the loose sloper sleeve and the tightly fitted sloper sleeve. This amount of shaping generally is used for three-quarter sleeves which look awkward and unbalanced if tightly fitted.

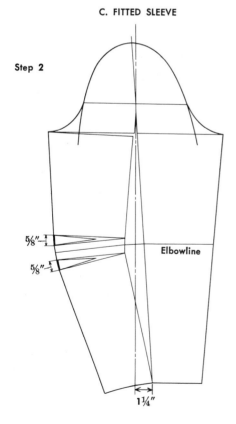

C. FITTED SLEEVE

Step 2

⅝"

⅝"

Elbowline

1¼"

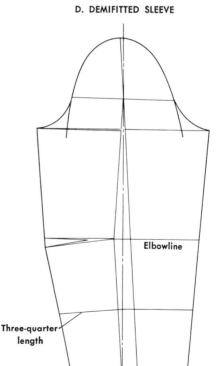

D. DEMIFITTED SLEEVE

Elbowline

Three-quarter length

The Leg-of-Mutton Sleeve

Minimum Expansion

Maximum Expansion

Short Sleeve

THE LEG-OF-MUTTON sleeve, with widened, exaggerated shoulderline and tight fit below the elbow, is most popular during the eras when the hourglass silhouette is in fashion. This sleeve is developed from the fitted sloper sleeve by slashing and spreading the two halves of the sleeve as shown in the diagrams. Cap height is increased proportionally to the new bicep width by adding one-half the amount by which the bicepline is increased. The French curve is shown in the correct position to draw in the new cap, tangent to the original cap for Points 1–2, and touching the new height mark at the center for Point 3.

The minimum expansion considered practical for these sleeves is ¼ inch on each half of the sleeve, as measured at the bicepline. Maximum expansion is reached when the back underarm seamline becomes a straight line. With greater expansion the underarm section of the sleeve does not fit properly into the normal armhole.

The short leg-of-mutton sleeve is developed by the same method, but uses the basic sloper instead of the fitted sloper, and slashes it on the center-grain line instead of on the arm-direction line. All short sleeves use the basic sloper because the body of a short sleeve is bisymmetric and thus centered on the center-grain line. A long sleeve is centered on the arm-direction line because its back half requires extra length and width.

LONG LEG-OF-MUTTON SLEEVE

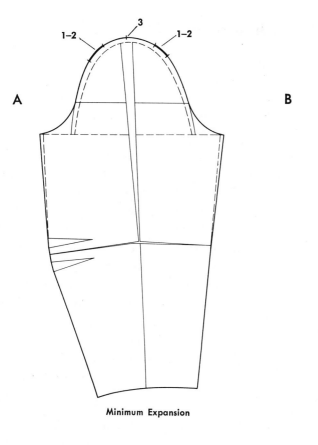

A

Minimum Expansion

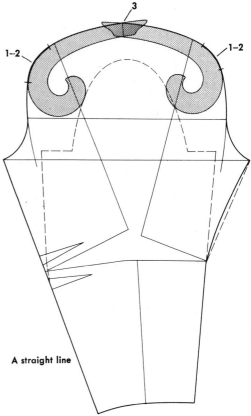

B

A straight line

Maximum Expansion

SHORT LEG-OF-MUTTON SLEEVE

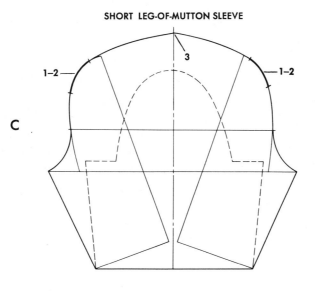

C

Development of the Puff Sleeve

The Standard Short Puff Sleeve (A). This sleeve is developed from the short leg-of-mutton sleeve shown in C on the preceding page. It is slashed on the center-grain line and pivoted out from the midpoint of the cap, as shown. The maximum amount of spread is reached when the underarm seamline of the sleeve becomes perpendicular to the new bicepline. The amount that must be added back to the cap to correct its shape is again one-half the difference between the old and new overarm section of the bicepline. For the open puff sleeve, the cap is spread only a moderate amount in drafting the leg-of-mutton sleeve, whereas in the "puff" development the sleeve bottom is pivoted far enough out to give the desired flared or circular effect.

The Long Puff Sleeve (B and C). In Step 1 a leg-of-mutton sleeve of the desired cap width is developed from the basic sleeve sloper, as shown in B. In Step 2 this sleeve is slashed on the arm-direction line (rather than the center-grain line) and spread the desired amount at the wrist. The method is the same as for the short puff sleeve.

For all of the puffed sleeves, fullness can be further increased by slashing and spreading the sleeve an additional amount at positions where the fullness is desired and then redrawing the cap and the bottom of the sleeve.

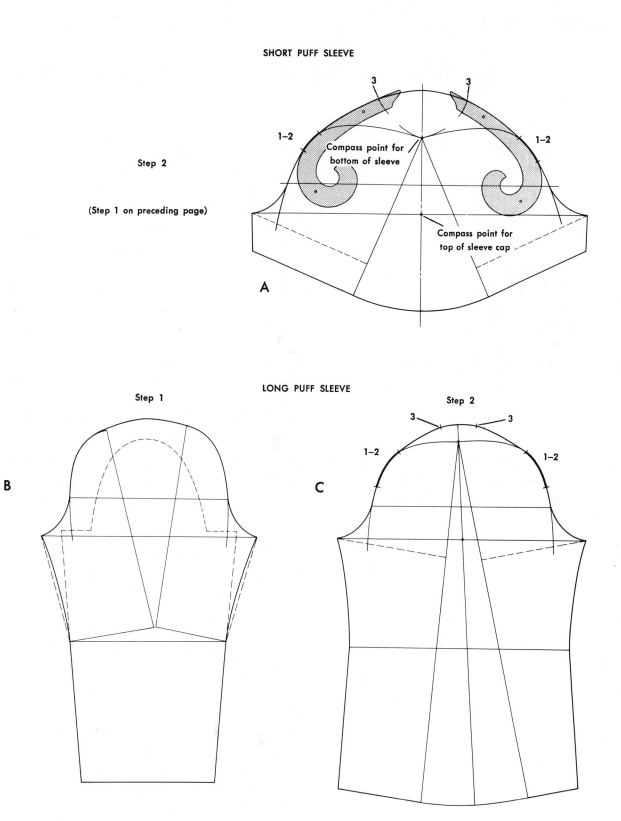

SHORT PUFF SLEEVE

Step 2

(Step 1 on preceding page)

3   3

1–2   1–2

Compass point for
bottom of sleeve

Compass point for
top of sleeve cap

A

LONG PUFF SLEEVE

Step 1   Step 2

B   C

3   3

1–2   1–2

215

Identification of Ease Provides the Two-Piece Sloper

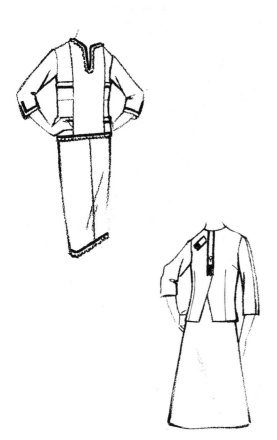

IDENTIFICATION of the ease that exists in the cap of the sloper sleeve becomes necessary for the development of all sleeves in which the cap is reduced because cap reduction is accomplished by the removal of this ease. The amount of ease in the back half of the sleeve can be identified by superimposing the back-waist sloper on the sleeve sloper, with breakpoints matching as shown in A. The amount of ease is the amount by which the capline of the sleeve is longer than the armhole line. Front ease, as measured to the center-grain line, is made equal to back ease, as measured to the arm-direction line, so that the sleeve may retain its initial balance. The regular sleeve slopers become the two-piece sleeve slopers when the ease segment of the sleeve is identified.

Drafting Steps. The drafting process is shown in B. First the ⅜-inch ease that exists at the bicepline (⅛ inch for each armhole oval) is marked off—half of it on each side of the arm-direction line. Next, lines are drawn to connect the elbow point with these two points. The two lines are continued up to the breakline where they are ½ inch apart. The French curve is then used to connect Point 1 at the capline (Diagram A) with Points 2–3, the segment of the line just drawn in between bicepline and breakline.

Two Uses. The two-piece sleeve sloper is used for drafting all raglan and kimono sleeves. It is also used for some set-in sleeves, in which a minimum of ¼ inch of the identified ease must be added back on each half of the sleeve cap, as shown in C. A set-in sleeve appears to be too small for its armhole without this slight amount of ease in the cap.

A. IDENTIFICATION OF EASE IN BACK HALF OF SLEEVE.

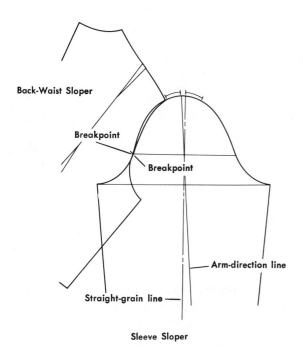

Back-Waist Sloper

Breakpoint

Breakpoint

Arm-direction line

Straight-grain line

Sleeve Sloper

B. DEVELOPMENT OF TWO-PIECE SLOPER SLEEVE

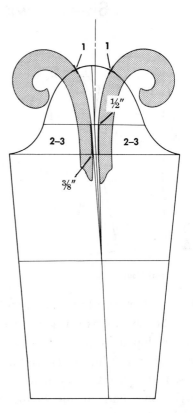

1   1

½"

2–3   2–3

⅜"

C. USE OF TWO-PIECE SLOPER WITH ONE-PIECE SLEEVES

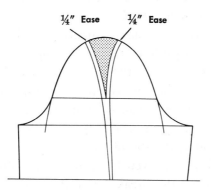

¼" Ease   ¼" Ease

217

Sleeves with Reduced Cap and Expanded Bottom

Short Blouse   Bell   Bishop

A SLEEVE automatically becomes wider at the bottom as the ease in its cap is reduced. Flared skirts are developed from the sloper skirt in this same way. When the hip darts are partly or entirely closed, the excess is automatically pivoted down to become flare at the hemline. In the sleeve the break level is chosen as the pivot point because the excess ease in the sleeve cap ends there, as was shown in C on the preceding page. The sloper sleeve is used for all of these flared sleeves. It is cut in half and the halves are pivoted from the break level. The sleeve bottom is automatically expanded in proportion to the amount that the cap ease is reduced. The maximum pivot is reached when the breaklines of the original sleeve reach the bicepline of the new sleeve, or at a position where the cap is only ½ inch larger than the armhole of the garment. After the two halves of the sleeve cap have been overlapped the desired amount, the top of the sleeve is smoothed by using the French curve, with the half-inch area above the breakline as Points 1–2, and intersection of the over-

arm line with the original bicep line as Point 3. The bottom of a short blouse sleeve can be made straight and hemmed if just enough pivot is used to bring the underarm to a right angle with the bicepline, as shown in A on the facing page.

Elbow-length sleeves as well as all long sleeves are cut apart on the arm-direction line instead of the center-grain line (which short sleeves use) so that the back of the sleeve can be wider than the front and thus give a better line, whether in a loose bell styling or as a bishop sleeve that is shirred into a cuff. If more than maximum expansion is desired, the expanded sleeve must be slashed and pivoted by the same technique that is used for circular skirts.

In the sketches, styling variations from short to long and from scant to exaggerated flare are shown. The amount of flare that can be managed at the sleeve bottom and the amount of ease that can be managed in the sleeve cap are two factors—often in opposition to each other—that determine the shape that sleeves of this important type must take.

BISHOP, BELL, AND SHORT BLOUSE SLEEVES WITH EXPANDED BOTTOM

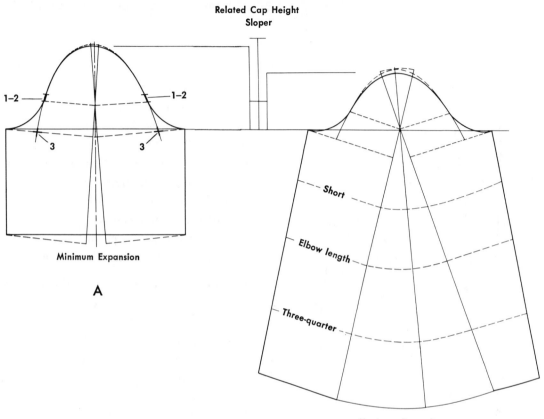

Related Cap Height
Sloper

1–2   1–2

3   3

Minimum Expansion

A

Short

Elbow length

Three-quarter

Maximum Expansion

B

Redrafted Sleeves for Lowered Armholes

THE SLOPER SLEEVE that fits the armhole of the sloper waist is the most tightly fitted sleeve that can be worn. The casual sleeve shown here is not suited to the silhouette of the fitted sheath waist, nor can it fit into the sloper armhole. Drafting changes must be made in the armhole as well as in the sleeve because the casual silhouette has ease throughout. The shirtwaist that was discussed on page 172 of Chapter 7 is an excellent example of casual styling.

Casual vs Fitted Sleeve. The body of the casual sleeve is wider and the cap is shorter than the sloper sleeve, as if the sloper had been cut from elastic and stretched. When the sleeve is thus widened and the curve of the capline somewhat flattened, an armhole is required that is not only correspondingly deeper but also less curved. First the new sleeve must be drafted, then the armhole of the sloper waist must be changed to match it. Note in both A and B that, although the underarm is widened and the cap is reduced, the break level of the sleeve cap remains at its sloper position in relation to the biceline. The maximum amount that the sleeve cap can be lowered, if the sleeve is to hang properly, is the amount by which the overarm section of each half of the sleeve is increased in width at the biceline (actually by half the sum of the two halves), but capline length can never be made less than armhole length, and the inclusion of ½ inch additional ease in the sleeve cap is generally considered desirable.

220

A

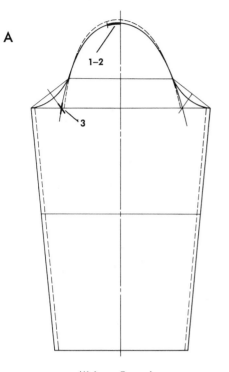

1–2

3

Minimum Expansion

B

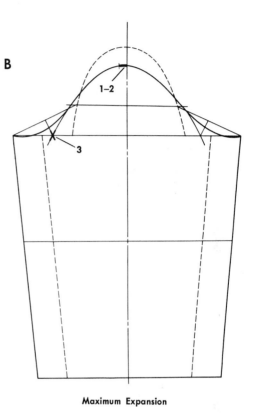

1–2

3

Maximum Expansion

Drafting the Sleeve. The new drafting points for the sleeve cap are found by first drawing a line to connect the breakpoint on each half of the sloper sleeve with the new widened underarm point. Then from the midpoint of this line a perpendicular is dropped that cuts through the bicepline, as shown in both diagrams. The point where the bicepline is cut is used as Point 3 for drawing in the sleeve cap, using the French curve in the same way it is used for drafting the sloper sleeve cap. As a final step the under-arm sections are drawn in with the French curve, again following the method used for the sloper sleeve. Note that although the break level of the new sleeve remains unchanged, its width increases at break level as the cap is lowered. A minimum redrafted sleeve (A) with matching armhole is often used instead of the fitted sloper sleeve when an easier fit is desired, both in developing expanded sleeves and in drafting the sleeves that are cut wholly or partly in-one with the waist.

221

The Reconstructed Armhole

WHEN THE ARMHOLE is redrafted for use with the new sleeve, the width of the waist is increased and the underarm is lowered in proportion to the amount that the sleeve is widened. In the diagrams on the facing page the sleeve has been widened by 1 inch (on the half), causing the width of back and front to be increased by ¼ inch at the shoulderline and at the underarm seamline, and the underarm to be lowered by ¾ inch. The same amount in width is added also to the armhole at break level that was added to the sleeve cap at break level. Since the front width of the sleeve cap is always increased more than the back, a greater amount is always added to the front waist than to the back waist at break level, as is necessary to straighten the extreme curvature of the front armhole line. There is a gradual change from the normal sloper armhole as it is lowered until finally front and back become practically identical.

The Armhole Line. The capline of the new sleeve must be used to draw in the lower section of the new armhole below the break level to establish an armhole that will match the sleeve precisely. The French curve cannot be used for this purpose because the required three match points are not available. The French curve can be used properly for the upper section of the armhole, however, by fitting it to the long line of the lower section.

The Shoulder Dart. The front shoulder dart is usually moved to the underarm position in a waist-and-skirt dress. In a very casual overblouse, with a small amount of dart excess, the dart may be lapped out at center front as was shown in Chapter 6, page 137. In casual sportswear of this type, the front of an unfitted overblouse is often cut without darts, like a man's shirt.

STEP-BY-STEP DRAFTING PROCEDURE

STEP 1.   Back Armhole and Side Seam

Armhole below Breakpoint: Copy the back-waist sloper. Drop a straight-grain line down from the underarm point for use in establishing the new underarm position. Superimpose the new sleeve on the waist, matching the original breakpoint of the sleeve with the armhole breakpoint. Pivot the sleeve down to a position where its underarm point touches the straight-grain line. Draw in the new underarm seamline from this point to the waistline, parallel with the original seamline. Trace in the lower half of the armhole line from the sleeve.

Armhole above Breakpoint: Fit the French curve to the lower half of the armhole line just drawn in and continue the line up to shoulder level.

STEP 2.   Front Armhole and Side Seam

Armhole below Breakpoint: Copy the front-waist sloper. Increase front shoulder width to match the width of the new back shoulder. Drop a straight-grain line down from the underarm point and mark the new underarm point at the same distance down as for the back. (Front and back seamlines are same length.) Draw in the new side seamline parallel to the original side seam. Superimpose the sleeve on the waist with underarm points matching and pivot the sleeve up until its original breakpoint meets the break level of the armhole. Trace in the lower half of the armhole line from the sleeve.

Armhole above Breakpoint: Fit the French curve to the lower half of the armhole line just drawn in and continue the line up to the level of the back shoulder established in Step 1.

STEP 3.   Shoulder Dart

Shoulder Dart Reduced: Copy the upper shoulder section of the waist front as shown and pivot it (the overlay) from the bust apex over toward center front until its shoulder point touches the new armhole line drawn in Step 2. The shoulder dart is reduced by the amount of the new theoretical dart in the armhole that is opened in order to lengthen the armhole above the break level.

Shoulder Dart Pivoted to Underarm: Mark the desired dart position on the underarm seamline. Slash in from this point to the bust apex and pivot the shoulder dart to the new position. As the dart is reduced, the amount that it may be shortened is proportionally increased. Here it is shortened by 2 inches.

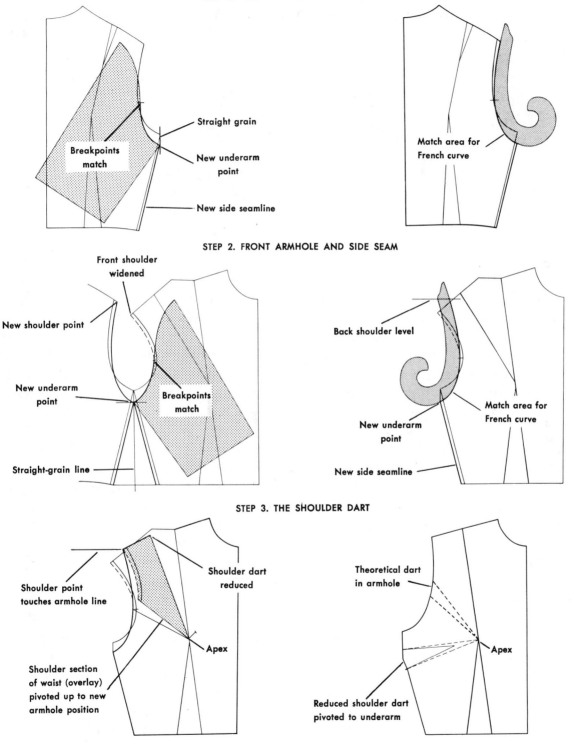

STEP 1. BACK ARMHOLE AND SIDE SEAM

Straight grain

New underarm point

Breakpoints match

New side seamline

Match area for French curve

STEP 2. FRONT ARMHOLE AND SIDE SEAM

Front shoulder widened

New shoulder point

New underarm point

Breakpoints match

Straight-grain line

Back shoulder level

New underarm point

Match area for French curve

New side seamline

STEP 3. THE SHOULDER DART

Shoulder point touches armhole line

Shoulder dart reduced

Apex

Shoulder section of waist (overlay) pivoted up to new armhole position

Theoretical dart in armhole

Apex

Reduced shoulder dart pivoted to underarm

Development of Raglan Waist-and-Sleeve Sloper

THE RAGLAN SLEEVE, which is cut partly in-one with the waist, offers still another type of sleeve styling. Raglan sleeves are more popular in eras when the trapeze silhouette is in fashion than in eras when the exaggerated shoulderline is worn because the cut of the sleeve produces a smoothly rounded shoulderline that accentuates the narrow-shouldered look, as shown in these sketches. This type of sleeve fits well and is not difficult to handle in production, but it is not used as often in dresses as it is in topcoats and raincoats. In dress styling the raglan line often interferes with other style details, and waists that leave the upper part of the chest free for trimming are more popular because they are easier to style.

The standard raglan is developed by superimposing the waist slopers on the two-piece sleeve sloper introduced on page 216. When the breakpoints are matched, as shown in A, the back waist matches the easeline of the sleeve since its position was originally determined from the shoulder point of the waist. The front shoulder point, however, falls about ½ inch below the easeline of the sleeve front and is raised to match the sleeve by pivoting that section of the waist by the method introduced on page 222. The front shoulder dart is then pivoted to the waistline as shown in B (or other seamline) to free the shoulder area so that the raglan line can be drawn in. It is drawn with the French curve and the standard position for it is shown, although any line that can be made with the French curve may be used. The back shoulder dart is not moved from its normal position but is pinned closed in the sleeve section after the raglan line has been put in, and is left as ease in the waist section. This raglan pattern of necessity has part of the waist section superimposed on part of the sleeve section, and, for use, the pattern pieces must be traced off onto separate pieces of paper.

Many styling variations are possible with the raglan structure. On the following page the two general types of variation are illustrated:

Type I: style lines cut lower on the chest to form yokes and princess lines.

Type II: style lines cut higher than the raglan line to form dropped shoulder effects.

224

A. WAIST AND SLEEVE SLOPERS OVERLAPPED

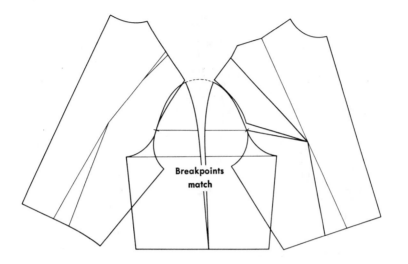

Breakpoints
match

B. COMPLETED RAGLAN SLOPER

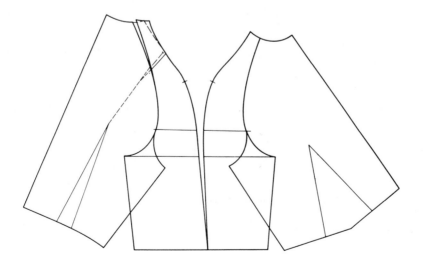

TYPE I   PRINCESS LINES AND YOKES

Raglan and Princess-Line Combination

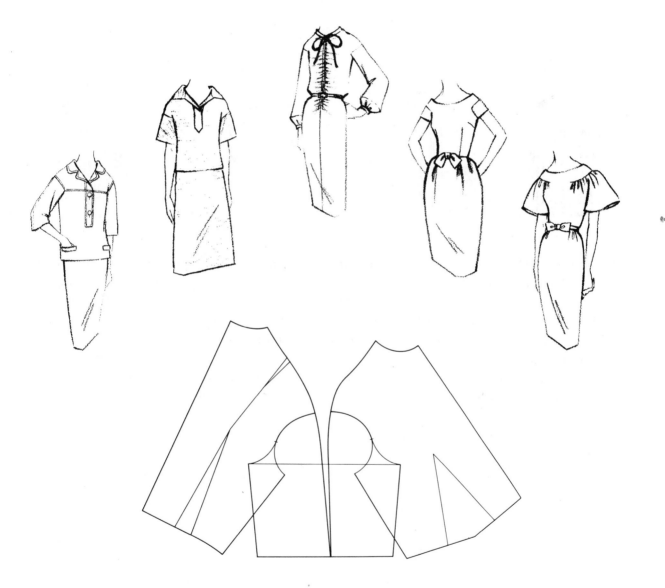

Raglan with Dropped Shoulder

Development of the Cut-in-One Kimono Sloper

THE BASIC KIMONO sloper like the raglan sloper is developed from the slopers for waist and two-piece sleeve. It can be used only for the cap sleeve, as shown in the sketches, since the underarm angle of sleeve to waist in the kimono sloper is too sharp to permit the arm to be raised. All kimono waists with sleeves require further development. Diagram A shows the rela-tionship of the kimono sloper to the raglan and the kimono-gusset structures in which angle of sleeve to waist is decreased sufficiently to cause the sleeve to hang like the set-in sloper sleeves. Diagram B shows the relationship of the kimono sloper to the so-called "high-kimono" waists in which the angle of sleeve to waist is increased enough to allow comfortable movement.

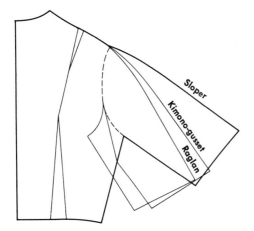

A. UNDERARM ANGLE DECREASED

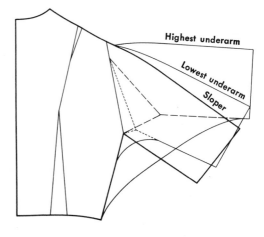

B. UNDERARM ANGLE INCREASED

Drafting of kimono waists must begin with the back because the dart excess in the back cannot be shifted from shoulder to waist, whereas the bust dart in the front can be moved as needed to bring the front armhole into alignment with the back armhole, as must be done to keep the two halves of the sleeve in balance.

The difference between the kimono sloper and the raglan sloper (page 224) is that the kimono waist and sleeve cannot overlap because they are cut in one. The back is developed by first bringing the shoulder points of waist and sleeve together, as shown in C, and since the sleeve is longer than the waist in this position, their underarm meeting point is approximately 1 inch below the normal armhole point of the waist. Next the front waist is positioned in relation to the sleeve to match the back-waist length from underarm to waistline. A small dart is pivoted into the armhole as shown to bring the front shoulder up to meet the sleeve cap. A straight line is drawn from underarm to shoulder to separate the waist and sleeve sections so that they can be cut apart for ease in handling.

The kimono pivot point, used to swing the sleeve up or down from its sloper position, is located at a distance above the breakline that is equal to the distance that the underarm point is below the breakline, as shown in the detail diagram. This pivot point is the theoretical center of the shoulder joint and thus is the pivotal point from which arm movement originates.

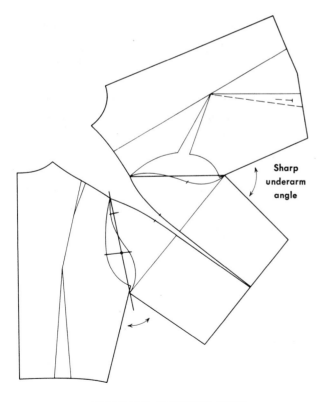

C. DEVELOPMENT OF KIMONO SLOPER

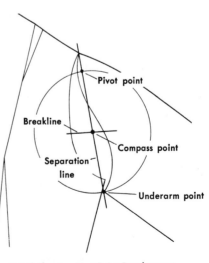

Detail Showing Pivot-Point Development

Development of Kimono-Gusset Waist and Sleeve

THE KIMONO-GUSSET and the raglan sleeves are similar in silhouette, but while in the raglan pattern the waist and sleeve overlap at the underarm to produce a proper fit, the cut-in-one kimono must be slashed and a gusset introduced to serve this same requirement. The kimono waist with gusset is developed by pivoting the sleeve section down from the pivot point designated on the preceding page. Pivoting the sleeve down spreads the shoulder slightly and causes the sleeve to overlap the waist at the underarm, as shown in the diagrams. The sleeve is pivoted down only far enough to permit it to hang like a set-in sleeve, since the greater the pivot, the longer the slash must be and the larger the gusset. The hinge point of the gusset is located precisely at the breakpoint, since that is the lowest position at which adequate hinge action for the arm can be obtained. Nor should the gusset be placed higher than necessary since it is an un-attractive "patch" and when placed higher it must be larger and thus more obvious.

First the back sleeve section is pivoted down, and then the front sleeve section is pivoted to match the back at the underarm and shoulder. The slash line for the gusset is drawn from underarm to breakpoint and the stitching lines for setting in the gusset are added on each side of the slash line, as shown, since they—not the slash—must determine the size of the gusset. The gusset generally is developed on the waist front since it may produce a wider gusset than the back and thus compensate somewhat for the fabric lost at the breakpoint where the seam allowance is reduced to nothing.

Note in B that the gusset for the short sleeve extends to the sleeve bottom, rather than being the standard diamond shape, and thus eliminates one of the "nothing" points that make the gusset such a problem in production.

A. DEVELOPMENT OF KIMONO-GUSSET PATTERN

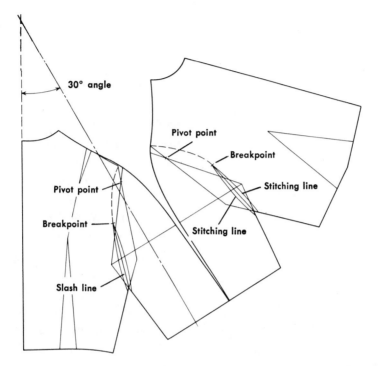

30° angle

Pivot point

Breakpoint

Stitching line

Pivot point

Breakpoint

Stitching line

Slash line

B. THE GUSSET

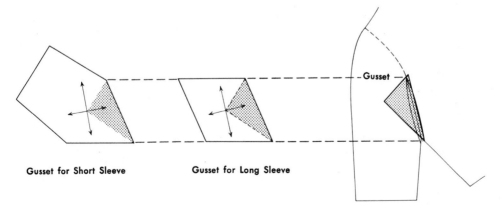

Gusset

Gusset for Short Sleeve

Gusset for Long Sleeve

Planning the Gusset

Development of the Kimono-Dolman Waist and Sleeve

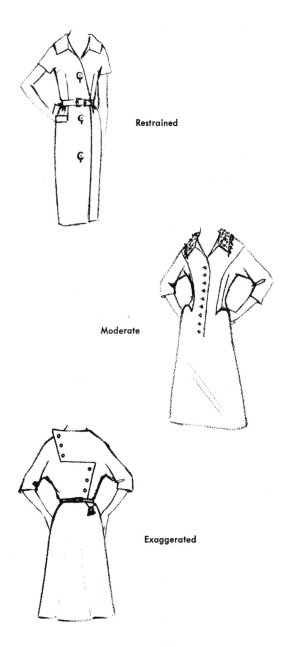

Restrained

Moderate

Exaggerated

THE HIGH-KIMONO WAISTS, developed by pivoting the sleeve section out from the waist section at the underarm, offer the simplest of all sleeve structures. Their style value lies in the soft, graceful folds formed by the excess fabric at the underarm, and thus they are restricted to fabrics that will fall softly such as crepes and jersey. The higher the sleeve section is raised, the more pronounced the folds become, and the more necessary that the garment be made of fabric that drapes well.

The minimum amount that the sleeve section is generally raised, for a waist with the highest underarm and fewest folds, is an amount equal to the distance from the pivot point to the shoulder point. The maximum pivot of the kimono-batwing is slightly less than half the length of the underarm seamline, an amount that causes the curve to begin at the waistline. The method for drafting all these sleeves is the same and is illustrated here by the moderately raised kimono-dolman.

The development of a graceful underarm curve requires the rather complicated drafting steps shown. The curve for the waist front and back are developed by the same method. These curves, however, are not identical because the angle of the front is greater than the angle of the back, but their linear length is the same and they match when stitched together.

THE UNDERARM CURVE

Step 1. Drop a line from the pivot point, bisecting the space between waist and sleeve. Extend the line down for a distance equal to the width of the space at Points W (waist) and S (sleeve) for Line 1–2.

Step 2. From Point 2 draw a perpendicular line over to the waist for Point 3.

Step 3. Measure down on the sleeve side a distance equal to 3–W on the waist side for Point 4. Draw a line from Point 4 to Point 2.

Step 4. On Line 4–2, measure a distance equal to 3–2. The small segment 5–2 furnishes the double match point for the curve.

Step 5. Use the French curve, tangent first to the waist and then to the sleeve for Match Point 1, and touching Line Segment 5–2, for Match Points 2–3.

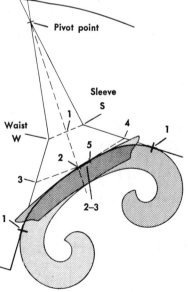

Detail of Underarm Curve

Stylized Variations

STYLIZED ARMHOLE

A

KIMONO VARIATIONS such as these have several good points. The pattern is cut into smaller pieces that are easier to manage in production; changes in grain can be made to improve fit; and wider variety in styling is made possible. Stylized kimonos are often mechanical masterpieces, with added ease introduced at strategic locations and darts replaced by attractive style lines.

Stylized Armhole (A). Diagram A shows a popular type of styling. The three-quarter sleeve is cut in one piece and the cap ease distributed to

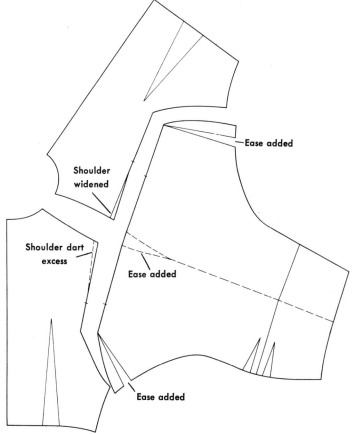

Shoulder widened

Ease added

Shoulder dart excess

Ease added

Ease added

improve the shoulderline. The shoulder has been widened to allow the sleeve to hang with fewer folds and the underarm has been increased to give added ease, thus correcting two inherent shortcomings of the kimono.

Kimono and Midriff (**B**). Diagram B shows a practical midriff variation of the kimono-dolman. The shoulder seam has been eliminated because, with the lowered neckline, the shoulderline is practically straight. The widened short sleeve gives ample room for arm movement, and the high midriff takes care of the dart excess.

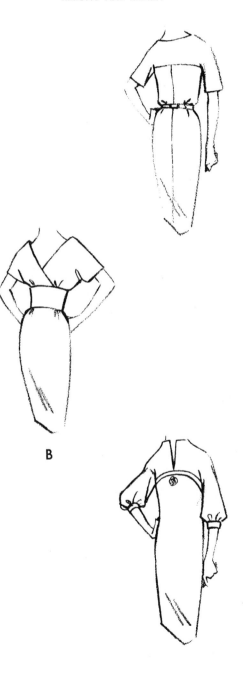

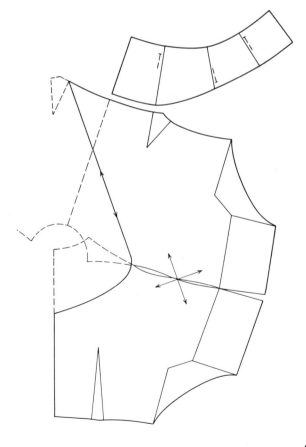

B

235

Chapter Ten

Collar Development and Styling

A couture showroom in Paris in the 1920's. The debutante slouch of the mannequins characterizes the "garçonne" or flapper era.

COLLARS that are as simple as a tie belt or a neck facing are shown on the following pages as an introduction to collar styling. The great majority of collars, however, are not styled in one of these two simple ways but have a soft roll or "stand" at the neckline so that they can more successfully accomplish their purpose of framing the face in a flattering way. Roll collars must be made by specific drafting techniques if better than trial-and-error results are to be enjoyed. Draping the roll collar puts an impossible demand on the designer who must work in the dark, for the effect of the collar cannot be properly appraised until after it is finished and basted into the neckline of its garment. In this chapter the commonly used types of roll collar are analyzed and for each is shown a rather simple drafting technique that will automatically give the desired depth, "stand," and distance from the neckline, which together constitute good collar styling.

Prototype Collars

COLLAR DEVELOPMENT began from two opposite directions—as a neckband at one extreme and as a neck facing at the other. The prototype collars shown in the two sketches on the near right are of such simple structure that they require no special pattern; those on the far right, which are each a step away from their prototypes, also can be made without special patterns because their use of bias grain achieves a softer effect that usually requires specially drafted collar patterns.

Band Collars. The simple band collars at the upper right are made from long bands of fabric that clean-finish the neckline and tie under the chin. The straight-grain band is necessarily narrow, but the bias band is wide enough to fold back on itself, as is possible only with bias. This wider band fits better and is more flattering because it is less rigid than the straight-grain band.

Flat Collars. The sketch on the near right below shows a collar that is hardly a collar but rather is the neck facing which has been put on the outside of the garment. Like a facing, this prototype collar can be cut directly from the waist pattern, with the same grain direction and the same shoulder seam. The collar beside it is different from it in two ways: it is cut in one piece without a shoulder seam, and its outer edge is not stitched down to the dress but left free. Note that it has the same grain direction as the waist at center back, but because there is no shoulder seam the grain is quite bias from the shoulder forward. To make its pattern, the waist front is laid on the back pattern with the shoulders overlapped at the outer edge. The combination of bias grain and edge reduction gives this collar a softer effect than is possible with the flat-facing type of collar.

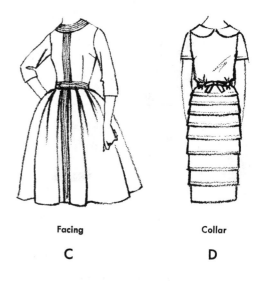

STANDING BAND COLLARS

Straight-Grain Fold
A

Bias Fold
B

FLAT COLLARS

Facing
C

Collar
D

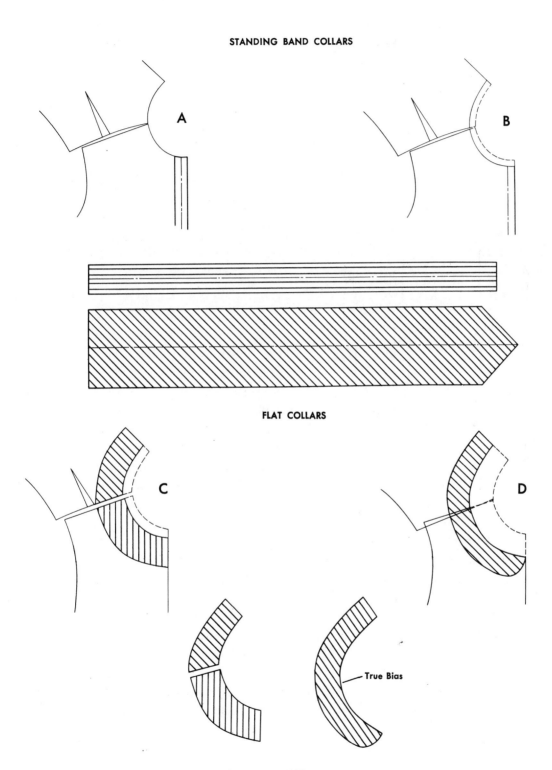

STANDING BAND COLLARS

A

B

FLAT COLLARS

C

D

True Bias

239

Introduction to Collars with "Stand" or Roll

THE TWO COLLARS sketched on this page, one with a round neck and the other with a V-neck, represent the great array of roll collars that occupy the center of the stage between neckband and facing. Roll collars are probably used 90 per cent of the time, although they are much more difficult to make than either of the other types, requiring the development of precise patterns that compare with sleeve patterns in difficulty. The soft roll at the neckline is responsible for both their complexity and their charm. The roll requires a hidden "stand" section that connects the visible portion of the col-

lar to the garment neckline. The development of collars with stand depends on two interrelated factors: the reduction of the outer edge of the collar to give it the proper contour so it can rise to meet the stand; and the addition of the stand section.

Development of Template. Collars must be individually planned. There is no standard collar pattern that can be used again and again like the sheath-waist pattern. For this reason it is practical to develop a "template" or master diagram that can be used as a basis for all types of collars, and the development steps are shown on the facing page. After the template is developed, information that increases its usefulness can be added, as shown on the next two pages, following which the use of the template in the development of collar patterns is demonstrated. The template furnishes an accurately balanced master pattern that can be used in all roll-collar development. For the template, the measurements from the waist slopers must be refined to a degree that makes it possible for the compass, ruler, and French curve to be used with the great accuracy necessary to produce perfectly balanced collars. Styling the outer edge of a collar is of secondary importance. Collar design lies in the optimum combination of collar depth, collar stand, and the position of the collar neckline in relation to the base of the neck or normal high-neck position.

THE COLLAR TEMPLATE STEP BY STEP

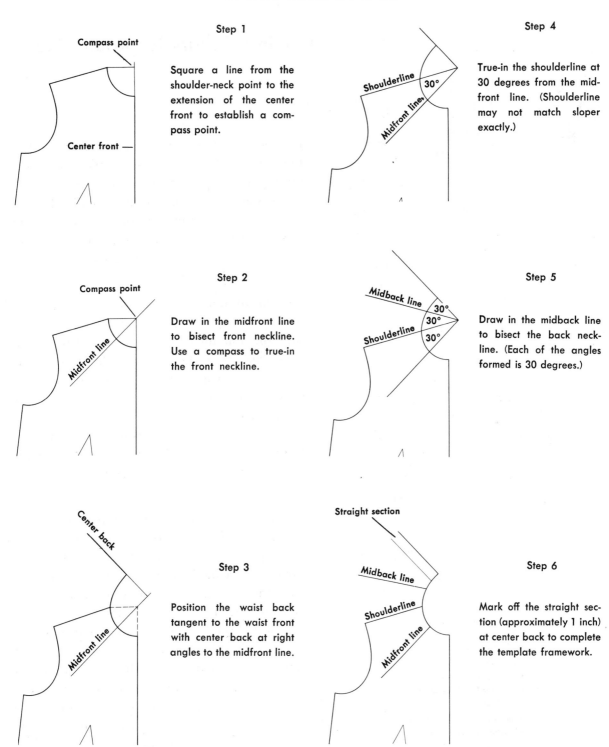

Step 1

Square a line from the shoulder-neck point to the extension of the center front to establish a compass point.

Step 2

Draw in the midfront line to bisect front neckline. Use a compass to true-in the front neckline.

Step 3

Position the waist back tangent to the waist front with center back at right angles to the midfront line.

Step 4

True-in the shoulderline at 30 degrees from the midfront line. (Shoulderline may not match sloper exactly.)

Step 5

Draw in the midback line to bisect the back neckline. (Each of the angles formed is 30 degrees.)

Step 6

Mark off the straight section (approximately 1 inch) at center back to complete the template framework.

Planning Collars for Round Necks

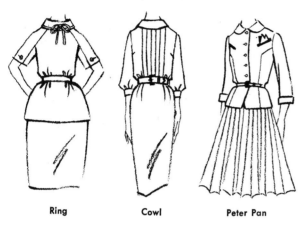

Ring   Cowl   Peter Pan

A. THE TEMPLATE

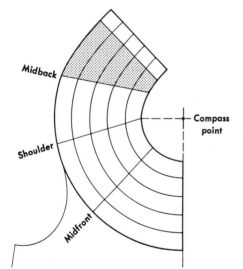

Use compass to draw lines from
center front to midback. Space the
lines at 1″ intervals for
convenient use.

Use ruler to draw lines in straight
center-back section. They are slightly
less than 1″ apart.

Use French curve to draw lines in
shaded section, connecting circular
front with straight back sections.

Location of Stand. In the sketches at the left, the plan of all three collars is the same, their difference in appearance resulting from a different stand location. The Peter Pan collar has stand at the back, the cowl collar has stand at the front, and the ring collar has stand all around. Pattern development for these collars is shown on the next four pages.

Amount of Stand. The amount of stand determines the angle of the collar to the body and thus the amount of garment area that lies beneath the collar. Note that in the introductory examples on page 239 the flat collar covers an area equal to its own area, whereas the band collar does not cover any of the garment. As the outer edge of a collar is reduced, it falls closer to the neckline, whereas its inner edge rises and depends on the added stand section of the collar to support it.

Use of the Template. The template developed on the preceding page is shown at the left with rings added at 1-inch intervals as an aid in planning collar reduction. From center front to midback the rings are circular, whereas in a small area at center back they are straight. (The neckline is straight for approximately 1 inch at center back.) The intermediate area is shown shaded in to indicate that the lines in that area must be drawn with the French curve. At center back it is necessary to make the concentric lines slightly less than 1 inch apart in order to keep center back perfectly straight.

B. EDGE REDUCTION IN RELATION TO STAND

Measuring the back of the collar   Measuring the front of the collar

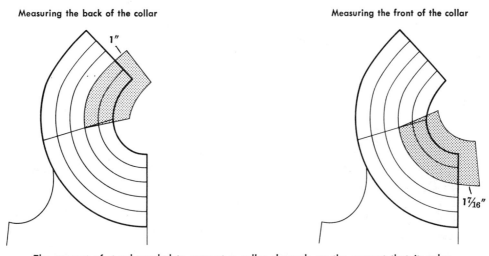

The amount of stand needed to support a collar depends on the amount that its edge is moved in toward the neckline. A collar of 3 inches depth is shown moved from its natural 3-inch position to a 2-inch position (first the back half, then the front half). The amount left over is 1 inch at back and approximately 1½ inches at front. When the edge of the collar is reduced by those amounts the collar will fit at the 2-inch position.

C. PLANNING THE FIVE LAP POSITIONS

Template divided into four sections   Template with five lap positions added

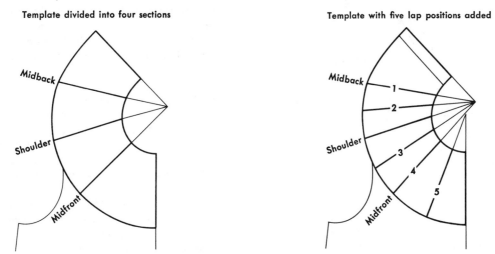

In theory the perfect way to reduce the edge of a collar would be to shrink it. In practice, however, any desired reduction can be made by slashing the collar and lapping its outer edge the correct amount, provided that the lap positions are so located that the 2 to 3 ratio of 1 inch in back for 1½ inches in front is maintained. The diagram at the left shows the template divided into four sections by the shoulderline (always the main dividing line) and midlines. The diagram at the right shows the sections split to furnish the five lap positions. Note that the segment at center back is not subject to reduction because its outer edge already has the same measurement as its inner edge.

243

The Roll-Collar Pattern Step by Step

REDUCING COLLAR AT OUTER EDGE

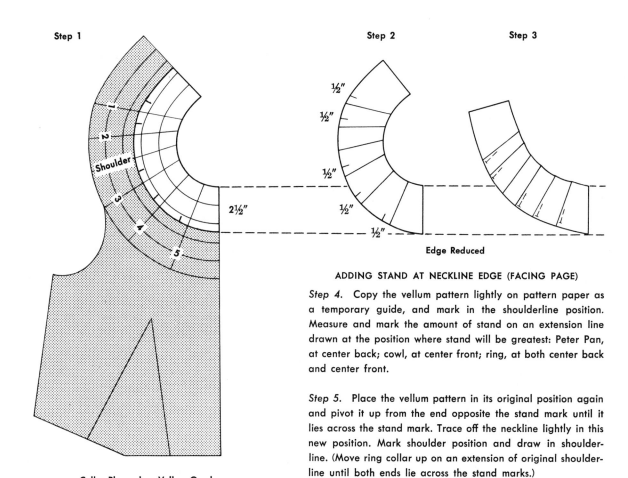

Step 1

Shoulder

2½"

Step 2

½"
½"
½"
½"
½"

Step 3

Edge Reduced

Collar Planned on Vellum Overlay

Step 1. Trace a collar of desired depth, using transparent vellum overlaying the template. Mark shoulderline and five lap positions. Measure and mark the planned amount of reduction at each lap position. Cut the collar out.

Collar Planned { Collar Depth 2½"
Collar Stand 1"
At the Neckline

Steps 2–3. Slash and lap the collar, as shown. All three collars are planned alike since all have the same depth and stand and are at the neckline.

ADDING STAND AT NECKLINE EDGE (FACING PAGE)

Step 4. Copy the vellum pattern lightly on pattern paper as a temporary guide, and mark in the shoulderline position. Measure and mark the amount of stand on an extension line drawn at the position where stand will be greatest: Peter Pan, at center back; cowl, at center front; ring, at both center back and center front.

Step 5. Place the vellum pattern in its original position again and pivot it up from the end opposite the stand mark until it lies across the stand mark. Trace off the neckline lightly in this new position. Mark shoulder position and draw in shoulder-line. (Move ring collar up on an extension of original shoulder-line until both ends lie across the stand marks.)

Step 6. Connect the new neckline point (points for ring collar) and the outer edge of the collar with a straight line which will act as the new center-edge line of the collar. Square across this line at stand level (here 1 inch above original neckline and draw in a line equal in length to the amount of the stand. Draw in parallel lines of the same length at the bottom edge of stand and at the bottom edge of collar.

Note. Step 7 is shown in detail on the following pages. The patterns at the bottom of this page are the finished collars after Step 7 has been completed. (Ring collar may close at front also since stand is uniform.)

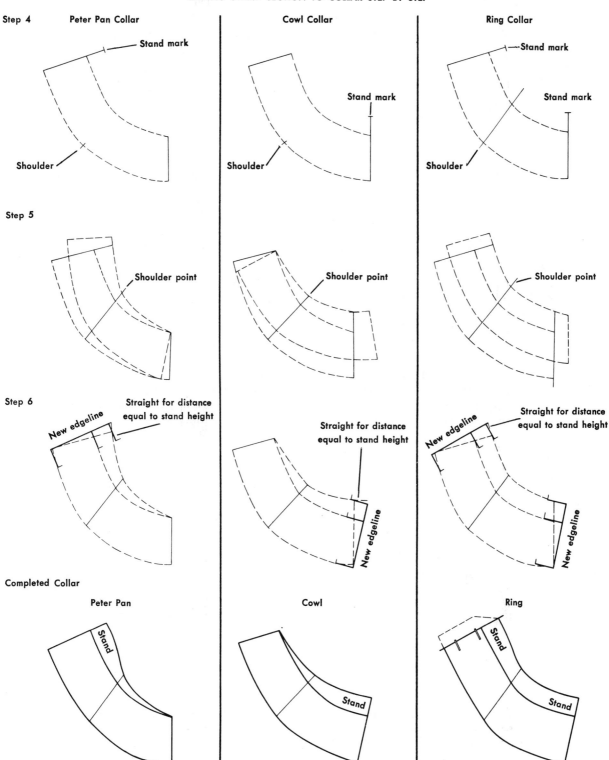

Step 4   Peter Pan Collar   Cowl Collar   Ring Collar

Stand mark — Shoulder — Stand mark — Shoulder — Stand mark — Stand mark — Shoulder

Step 5

Shoulder point — Shoulder point — Shoulder point

Step 6

New edgeline — Straight for distance equal to stand height — Straight for distance equal to stand height — New edgeline — New edgeline — Straight for distance equal to stand height

Completed Collar

Peter Pan   Cowl   Ring

Stand — Stand — Stand — Stand — Stand

Method for Using French Curve to True-in

Peter Pan Collar

Cowl Collar

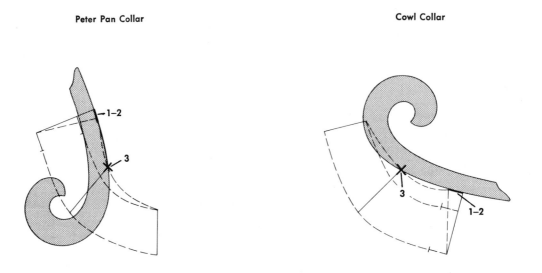

Step 7a. True-in the back half of the Peter Pan and ring collars, and the front half of the cowl collar. The collar outline that was traced off in Step 4 represents the visible section of the collar, and the amount added by the pivot in Step 5 and squared up in Step 6 becomes the stand section after the lines are trued-in with the French curve.

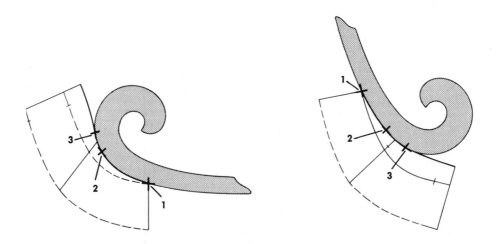

Step 7b. Position the French curve with Point 1 touching the front neck point of the Peter Pan and ring collars and the back neck point of the cowl collar, Point 2 tangent to the dotted neckline drawn in Step 5 and Point 3 tangent to the new neckline drawn in Step 7a above. Points 2 and 3 should be positioned at equal distances from the shoulder point.

Collar Line and Stand Line (Step 7)

Peter Pan Collar

Cowl Collar

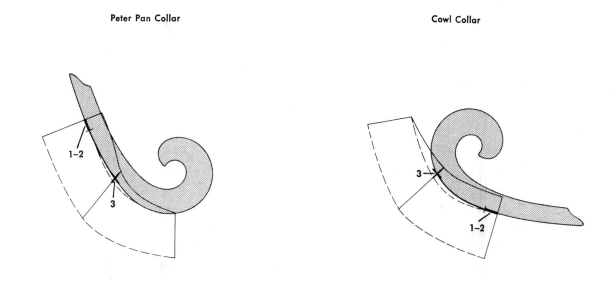

Step 7c. Measure and mark the stand height at the shoulderline, making it half the height of the stand at center back (here ½ inch) for the Peter Pan and cowl collars. For the ring collar, stand height is the same at all points. Draw in the stand line for the end of the collar that has stand.

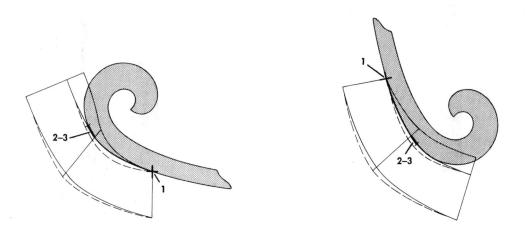

Step 7d. Draw in the stand line for the end of the collar without stand. Overlap the line drawn in the step above for ½ inch for Points 2–3.

Note. The purpose of the theoretical stand line is to furnish a base from which collar depth can be measured, which is made equal to the depth originally planned. (At the center back of the collar ⅞ inch is used as the equivalent of 1 inch at the shoulder.)

Introduction to Peter Pan Collars

THIS COLLAR TYPE was probably named for Peter Pan because it typifies youth and Peter Pan was the boy who refused to grow up. Peter Pan collars are used almost exclusively in infants' and children's wear. They also furnish a charming neck styling for adult wear.

Variation in Depth (A). Although the name Peter Pan is often applied to all collars for high, round, front-closing necks, there are more distinctive names that are applicable, as the sketches show. The name Buster Brown (a more roguish boy) identifies a collar that looks more typically boyish because it is higher and narrower than the Peter Pan, and the Puritan collar looks more demure than the Peter Pan because it varies in the opposite direction and is wider and flatter. All three collars in this group have the same 1-inch stand (which is as high as can be worn comfortably) in order to make the comparison more clear. A stand of ½ inch may be used, especially with the wider Puritan collar, but the important variable in the high-neck group is collar depth.

A. VARIATION IN DEPTH

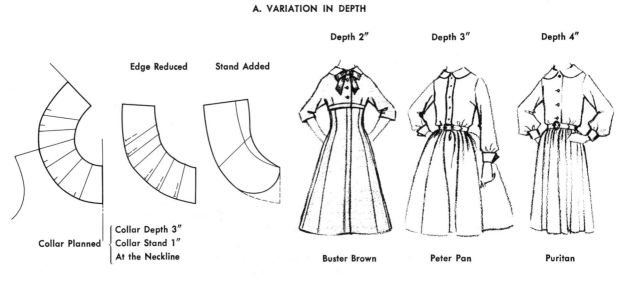

Edge Reduced   Stand Added   Depth 2″   Depth 3″   Depth 4″

Collar Planned   { Collar Depth 3″ / Collar Stand 1″ / At the Neckline }

Buster Brown   Peter Pan   Puritan

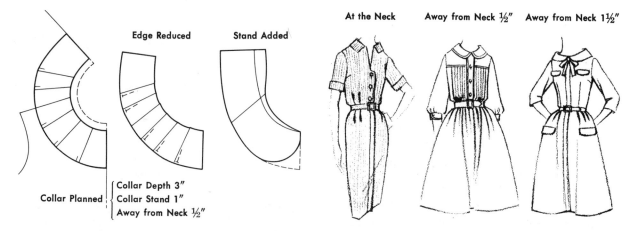

Edge Reduced   Stand Added

At the Neck   Away from Neck ½"   Away from Neck 1½"

Collar Planned { Collar Depth 3" / Collar Stand 1" / Away from Neck ½" }

Variation in Distance from Neck (B). When a lower, more comfortable neckline is used, the character of the collar changes in a different way. As a rule youth is expressed by a high collar line, while sophistication is expressed by a lowered collar line. The Peter Pan collar in the sketch at the near right has lost its identity because the neckline, in effect, has been left open. Although the collar on the middle dress of this group has the same contour as that shown on the middle dress in the group appearing on the facing page, its effect is more sophisticated be-

cause it is away from the neck. The collar on the dress at the far right, where the neckline has been lowered considerably, no longer bears much resemblance to its Peter Pan prototype.

Variation in Stand (C). As the neckline is lowered, the stand can be increased. (As a rule it is practical to increase stand no more than 1 inch for each inch that the neckline is away from the neck.) The sketches in this group illustrate how increased stand changes the character of a collar from conservative to extreme.

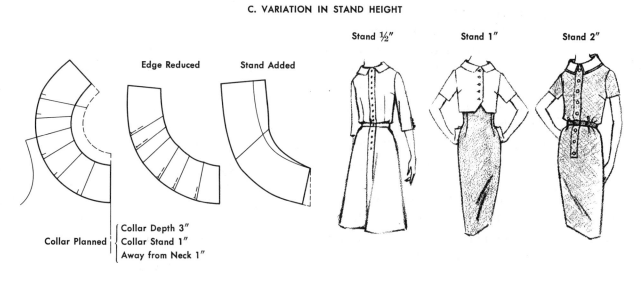

Edge Reduced   Stand Added

Stand ½"   Stand 1"   Stand 2"

Collar Planned { Collar Depth 3" / Collar Stand 1" / Away from Neck 1" }

Back-Closing Collars

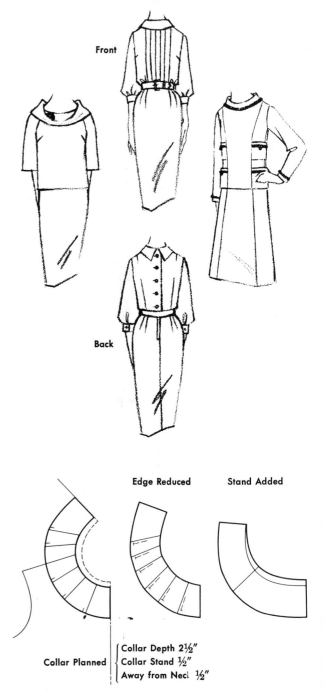

COWL COLLARS WITH FRONT STAND

Front

Back

Edge Reduced   Stand Added

Collar Planned

Collar Depth 2½"
Collar Stand ½"
Away from Neck ½"

WHEN A DRESS with a back closing is styled with a collar, the choice of collars is limited to the three groups of back-closing collars shown at the right. The development of the collar with front stand and with all-around stand was shown on pages 244–247, along with the more common Peter Pan collar with back stand. It is as easy to make one of these collars as another. Nevertheless, most dresses with collars close in front and most dresses without collars close in back. One reason may be that the collar is mechanically better suited to a front-closing garment because the neck is higher in back and lower in front, and a collar with a stand in back acts as a flattering frame for the face. A dress with a front closing often looks bare without a collar, whereas a dress that closes in back usually looks finished without a collar. All the dresses on this page are exceptions to this rule.

Back Closing. The back view for one collar from each group has been sketched to show the way the back closing is handled. The cowl collar and the Peter Pan collar simply meet at center back, but the ring collar must have a lapped closing to give it the distinctive ring silhouette. The crew collar on a pullover sweater (from which the ring collar takes its styling) avoids this awkward closing because knitted fabric can stretch enough to permit the head to be pulled through; but in woven fabric this advantage is lost. Fabric on true bias, however, can stretch enough to be used for a cowl collar. An illustration of the conversion of a regular collar pattern for use on a bias fold is shown on the last page of this chapter.

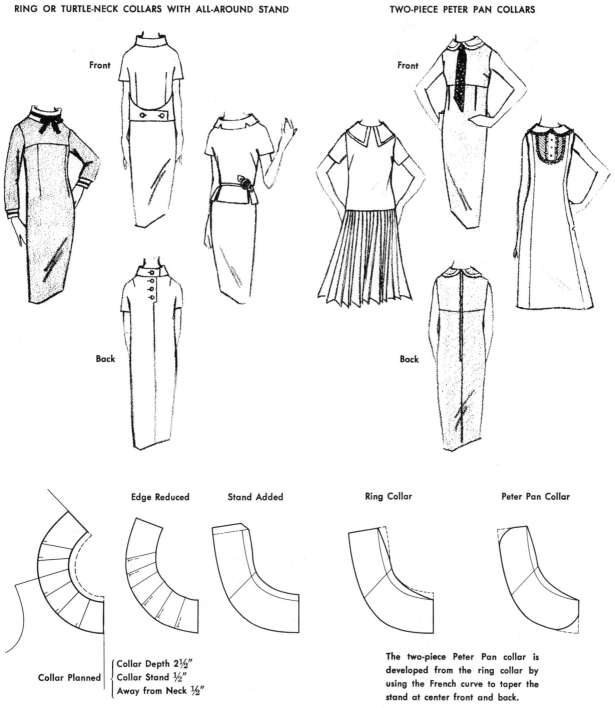

RING OR TURTLE-NECK COLLARS WITH ALL-AROUND STAND

Front

Back

TWO-PIECE PETER PAN COLLARS

Front

Back

Edge Reduced

Stand Added

Ring Collar

Peter Pan Collar

Collar Planned

Collar Depth 2½"
Collar Stand ½"
Away from Neck ½"

The two-piece Peter Pan collar is developed from the ring collar by using the French curve to taper the stand at center front and back.

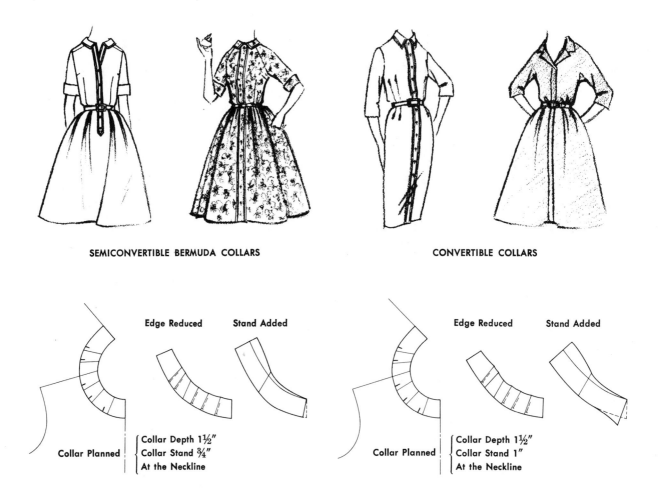

SEMICONVERTIBLE BERMUDA COLLARS   CONVERTIBLE COLLARS

Edge Reduced   Stand Added   Edge Reduced   Stand Added

Collar Planned   Collar Depth 1½"   Collar Planned   Collar Depth 1½"
   Collar Stand ¾"   Collar Stand 1"
   At the Neckline   At the Neckline

COLLARS for the round neck can be made both smaller and larger than the Peter Pan. Extremely small collars and extremely large collars are shown together here because both have similar proportions (although the looks they produce are quite opposite).

Small Convertible Collars. For a collar to be convertible, its outer edge must be straighter than the regular Peter Pan collar so that it can fit smoothly when open as well as when closed. A collar of 3-inch depth could be made straight enough to convert if its outer edge were reduced enough to require a 2-inch stand, but since a stand of more than 1 inch is impractical at the high neckline, the depth of the collar must be reduced enough to maintain the 3-to-2 relationship of depth to stand that convertibility requires. A collar of 1½-inch depth and a 1-inch stand thus becomes the standard formula for the convertible collar. In the semiconvertible Bermuda collar, the 1½-inch depth is generally retained, but the stand is ¾ inches or less. Its contour thus looks less straight and mannish, and it is straight enough that it can be partly converted, with the top button left open.

Peter Pan Type Collars

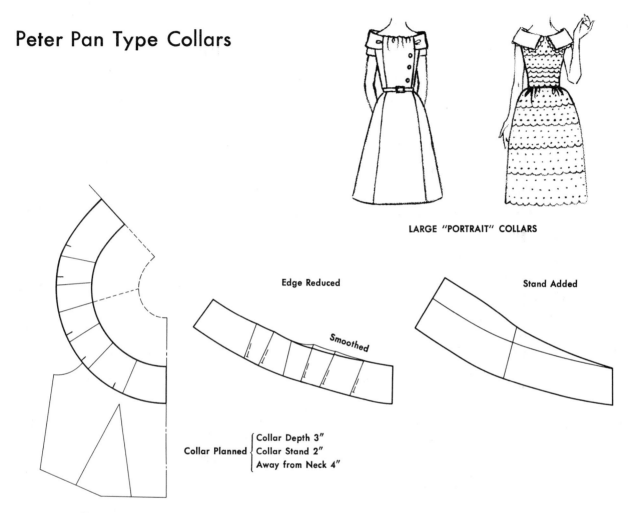

LARGE "PORTRAIT" COLLARS

Edge Reduced

Stand Added

Smoothed

Collar Planned { Collar Depth 3"
Collar Stand 2"
Away from Neck 4"

Large Portrait Collar. The large collar that sets well away from the neck and has a high stand resembles the draped effects that photographers in another era were prone to use, and thus it gets its name. The collar shown with the diagram was chosen because it offers an interesting comparison with the convertible collar, the one being a king-size version of the other. The neckline of this collar is 4 inches away, collar depth is 3 inches, stand is 2 inches. The amount of stand that a collar may have is limited both by its depth and its distance away from the neck. As explained in the discussion of Peter Pan collars on page 248, the stand should not exceed the distance away plus the 1-inch stand that a collar at the neckline can have. In theory this collar could have a stand of 5 inches (4 inches + 1 inch). However, collar depth is 3 inches, and stand can never be as great as depth, for when the two are equal, a straight band is the result. Therefore the maximum allowable stand for this collar is 2½ inches.

Note: As the outer edge of a collar is straightened, its neckline edge becomes increasingly distorted. It must be smoothed, as shown, so that it can furnish a usable neckline edge in the development steps that follow. This is particularly important with a large collar because the French curve is not long enough to be used in Step 7 for this purpose.

Separate Collars for V-Necklines

WAYS TO CONCEAL NECKLINE SEAM

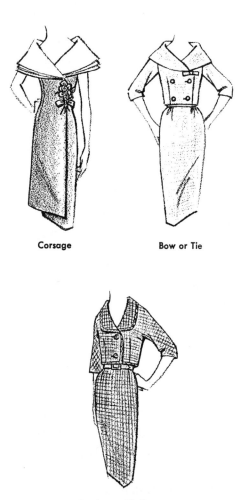

Corsage

Bow or Tie

Continuous Binding

A separate collar for a V-neckline permits an "away" look that is more dressy than can be obtained with the revers collars that are cut in one. When a separate collar laps like a revers collar, however, the point where it joins the waist at the edge of the garment is ugly and is generally concealed by one of the devices shown in the sketches above.

AS THE NECKLINE of a garment is lowered in front, its contour changes from round to more or less V-shape. The development of the rounded V-neckline and its collar is planned on the template in the regular way, as shown in Step 1 of the diagrams on the facing page. A new intermediate step must be introduced, however, in which the collar is spread at the neckline edge to give the desired neckline depth. The neckline actually begins to straighten at the back, as can be seen most clearly in the pattern for the large collar at the bottom of the facing page. Note that the back of the collar is spread slightly at the lap position adjacent to the shoulderline, by whatever small amount is necessary to keep the three front slashes of equal size.

Spreading the neckline edge of a collar is just as effective a means for reducing the outer edge as is lapping the outer edge since an inch added at the neckline straightens the collar the same amount that an inch subtracted from the outer edge straightens it. For this reason, when the neckline can be spread an amount equal to the planned reduction, no edge reduction is necessary in the front section of the collar. When it is spread less than the necessary amount, the remainder must be "lapped out" in the regular way, as shown by the small collar at the top of the facing page. The back neckline is never spread enough to eliminate the lap adjacent to the shoulderline, or to affect the lap adjacent to the center back at all.

DRAFTING NOTE FOR STEP 1

After the vellum collar is cut out, it is slashed and overlaid on the template to plan the lowered neckline by spreading the slashes. When the vellum pattern is spread ¼ inch at the back slash position near the shoulder, the lap at that position is reduced to ¼ inch.

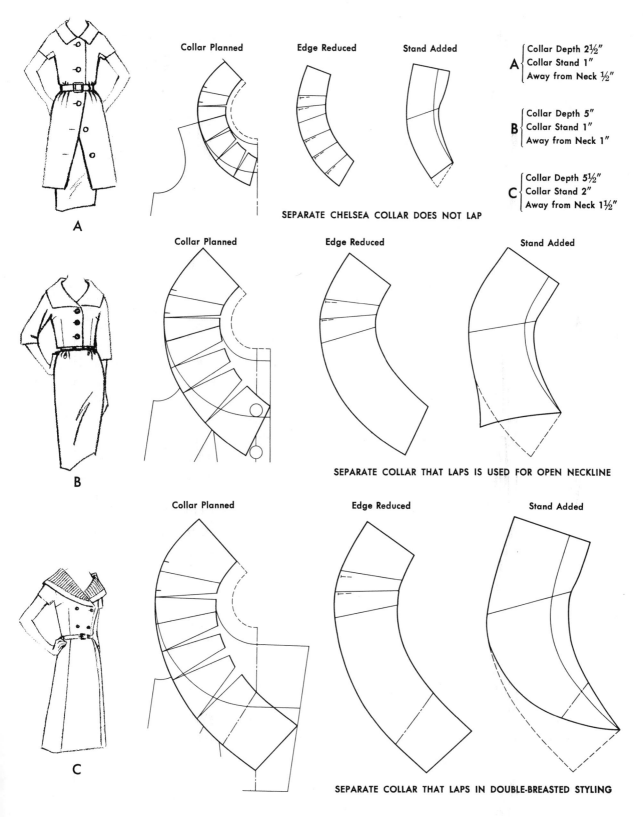

Collar Planned **Edge Reduced** **Stand Added**

A {
Collar Depth 2½"
Collar Stand 1"
Away from Neck ½"
}

B {
Collar Depth 5"
Collar Stand 1"
Away from Neck 1"
}

C {
Collar Depth 5½"
Collar Stand 2"
Away from Neck 1½"
}

SEPARATE CHELSEA COLLAR DOES NOT LAP

Collar Planned **Edge Reduced** **Stand Added**

SEPARATE COLLAR THAT LAPS IS USED FOR OPEN NECKLINE

Collar Planned **Edge Reduced** **Stand Added**

SEPARATE COLLAR THAT LAPS IN DOUBLE-BREASTED STYLING

V-NECK COLLARS

COMPARISON OF V-NECK COLLARS

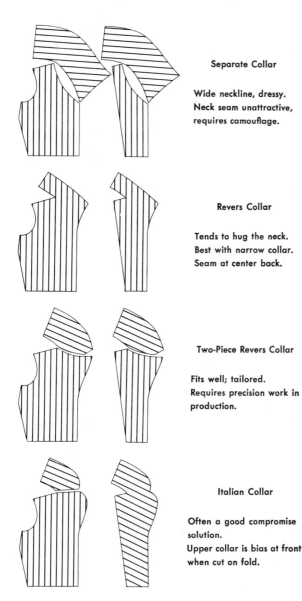

Separate Collar

Wide neckline, dressy.
Neck seam unattractive,
requires camouflage.

Revers Collar

Tends to hug the neck.
Best with narrow collar.
Seam at center back.

Two-Piece Revers Collar

Fits well; tailored.
Requires precision work in
production.

Italian Collar

Often a good compromise
solution.
Upper collar is bias at front
when cut on fold.

Comparison of Collar Types. Four types of collar that can be used for the V-neckline are shown above. The designer is always faced with deciding which type to use, since each has both advantages and shortcomings because of its construction. Patterns for the waist fronts, collars, and facings are shown because their mechanical differences generally form the basis for choice.

Introduction to Revers Collars

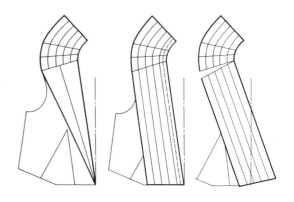

The Revers Template. There is a fundamental difference between the separate collar and the cut-in-one revers collar. Because the front section of a separate collar is curved, its outer edge is always larger than its neckline edge. But when a collar is cut-in-one with the waist front, its front neckline is a straight line—actually it is a fold in the fabric rather than a seamline. In theory, its outer and inner edges are the same length since both terminate at the point where a line from the midpoint of the shoulder, and at right angles to it, crosses the waistline, as shown above on the left.

The middle figure shows the template for V-necklines, with parallel lines drawn to represent the spaced neckline positions (concentric circles are used on the round-neck template). In theory, when the neckline is ½ inch away at the shoulder point, as shown, it is also ½ inch away at the waistline.

The figure on the right illustrates the template in use. As the collar neckline is raised at center front, the front section pulls away from the shoulderline, showing the theoretical amount that raising the neckline has added to the front edgeline. The front can have no reduction but instead receives the additional amount automatically added to it when the neckline is raised.

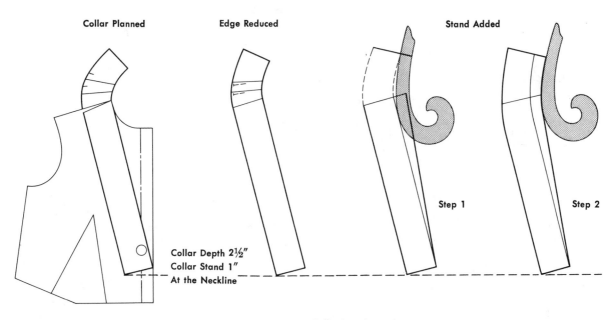

Collar Planned   Edge Reduced   Stand Added

Collar Depth 2½"
Collar Stand 1"
At the Neckline

Step 1   Step 2

Development of Shawl (Revers) Collar. Revers collars can be developed most easily as separate collars that are joined to the waist front at their common neckline as a final step, as shown in the diagrams on this page. The French curve can be used in a more simple way to true-in the collar lines of revers collars, since the amount of stand at the shoulder is equal to the stand at center back. The collar neckline, therefore, must be parallel with the stand line as far as the shoulder and can best be drawn in after the stand line has been established.

THE FISH DART. Note that although the collar is tangent to the waist at both the shoulder point and the center-front point, a gap exists throughout the intervening distance. This gap is known as the "fish dart" because it tapers to nothing at both ends. When it is stitched closed, the fish dart puts a slight curve into the too-straight neckline of the shawl collar and gives it a more graceful contour. In the two-piece revers collar shown on the following page, the fish dart has been pivoted to the seamline where the collar joins the revers (a trick that improves fit).

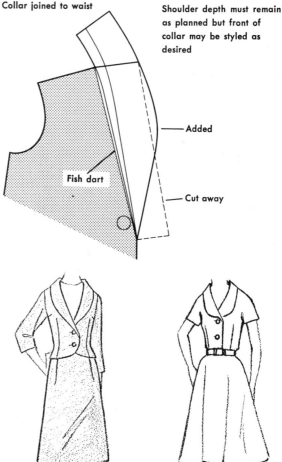

Collar joined to waist

Shoulder depth must remain as planned but front of collar may be styled as desired

Fish dart

Added

Cut away

257

V-NECK COLLARS

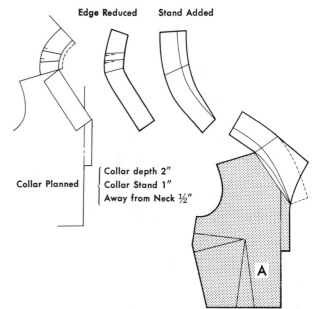

Edge Reduced   Stand Added

Collar Planned

{ Collar depth 2"
  Collar Stand 1"
  Away from Neck ½" }

A

Revers Collars with Center-Back Seam. Narrow collars where the center-back seam is not too noticeable, and stripes and plaids where the center-back seam can be mitered attrac- tively, use the shawl collar best. A technical weakness of this collar type is the shoulder point at which no seam allow- ance is possible.

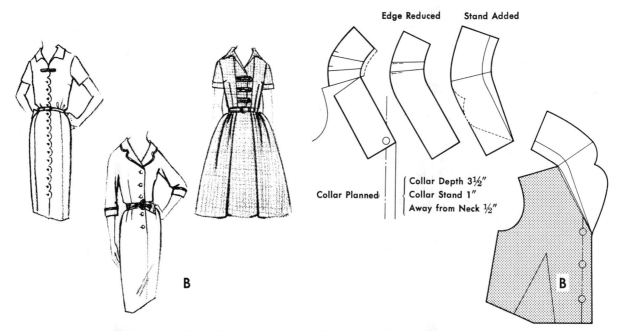

Edge Reduced   Stand Added

Collar Planned

{ Collar Depth 3½"
  Collar Stand 1"
  Away from Neck ½" }

B

Combination Italian Collars. The Italian collar looks like a two-piece notch collar, but it fits less precisely because only the under collar is cut separately. When the back of this collar is on straight grain, the front revers section is on the bias. For this reason the Italian collar is often more suitable for dressmaker styling than the two-piece notched collar.

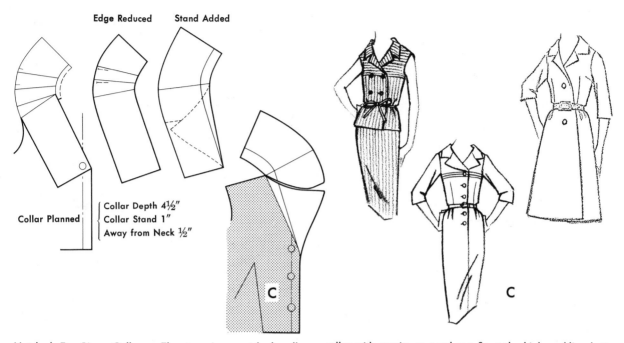

Edge Reduced   Stand Added

Collar Planned

Collar Depth 4½"
Collar Stand 1"
Away from Neck ½"

C

C

Notched Two-Piece Collars. The two-piece notched collar that is part of the standard styling of a tailored suit is used only with dresses that have a tailored feeling. The two-piece

collar with maximum stand can fit at the high neckline better than other revers collars because the notch introduces ease that allows the "fish dart" excess to be taken out.

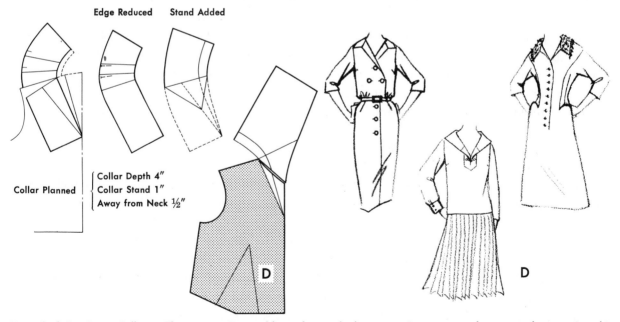

Edge Reduced   Stand Added

Collar Planned

Collar Depth 4"
Collar Stand 1"
Away from Neck ½"

D

D

Unnotched Two-Piece Collars. The construction problem of precise matching at the point of a notch is avoided by straight revers to which collars are attached without a notch. The

notch, however, gives ease at the outer edge, causing this styling to be better with the narrow revers of the middy than with the double-breasted dress above.

Introduction to Neckband Collars

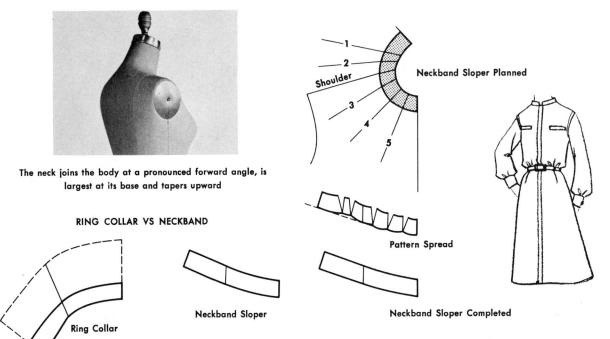

The neck joins the body at a pronounced forward angle, is largest at its base and tapers upward

RING COLLAR VS NECKBAND

Ring Collar

Neckband Sloper

Neckband Sloper Planned

Pattern Spread

Neckband Sloper Completed

Theory. To develop a neckband that will fit properly, a concentric ring must first be added to the template inside the neckline, as shown in the diagrams above. This ring can be handled like a collar excepting that its smaller edge is spread, whereas in a collar its larger edge is lapped. A neckband cannot be planned in the same way as a collar because the edge of the neckband that joins the garment is its larger edge. The neck is largest at its base and tapers upward as well as joining the body at a pronounced forward angle, as shown in the photo at the top of this column.

NECKBAND CONTOUR. One might think that an easier way to develop the neckband would be simply to use the stand section for the ring collar, but this is not true, as is illustrated by the two diagrams that are shown above. The larger edge of the neckband is its neck seamline; the smaller edge of a collar is its neck seamline.

Development. A simple method of neckband development is shown here. The back section of the inner neckband ring is slashed at the two regular slash positions and each is spread an equal amount until the neckband is straight as far as the shoulder (as is necessary to accommodate the neck). The front of the neckband is slashed at the three regular positions and each is spread the same amount as the back slashes (here ½ inch) in order to preserve the symmetrical contour of the pattern. A height of 1 inch is generally considered standard for a neckband because greater height is likely to be uncomfortable. By cutting down or adding to the sloper, the height can be varied as desired. Sketch B on the facing page shows a band of ¾ inch, for example. As soon as the neckband is moved away from the high neck position, greater freedom in height and amount of rise is possible as the other sketches on the facing page illustrate.

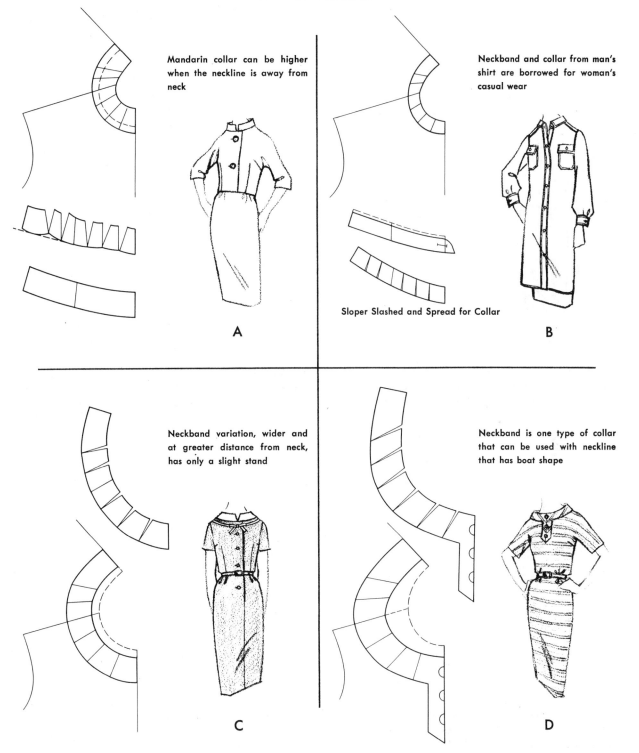

Mandarin collar can be higher when the neckline is away from neck

A

Neckband and collar from man's shirt are borrowed for woman's casual wear

Sloper Slashed and Spread for Collar

B

Neckband variation, wider and at greater distance from neck, has only a slight stand

C

Neckband is one type of collar that can be used with neckline that has boat shape

D

Roll Collars with Straight Outer Edge

Collar Planned
Center-Front Depth 5¼"
Center-Back Depth 7"
Shoulderline Depth 8¼"
Away at Shoulder 2½"
(Raglan Sloper)

Neckline of collar

Edgeline of collar

Collar with Draped Effect for Striped Fabric. When a striped fabric is used for a large portrait collar or when for some other reason a straight-grain edge is desirable, the collar can

be planned with the template overlaying the raglan sloper. Slashes are cut and opened enough to bring the center back and the center front of the pattern to straight grain.

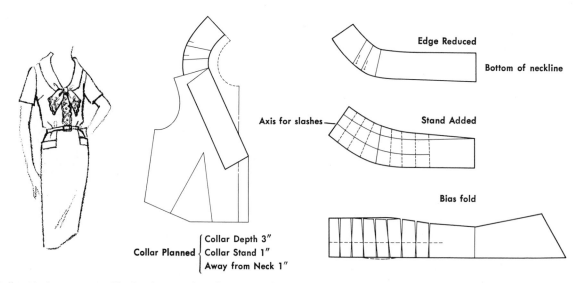

Edge Reduced

Bottom of neckline

Axis for slashes

Stand Added

Bias fold

Collar Planned ⎰ Collar Depth 3"
           ⎱ Collar Stand 1"
           ⎱ Away from Neck 1"

Collar Made on Bias Fold of Fabric. When the outer edge of a collar is a bias fold instead of a seam, as is often desirable with sheer fabrics, the collar must be straightened after the regular drafting is completed. Since bias will adjust itself

to some extent, the pattern can be spread on the inner edge and lapped on the outer edge. The stretchability of a fabric determines the distance that the pivot points should be from the edge of the collar.

Flat Collars with a Shoulder Seam

Collar Planned
Center-Front Depth 7″
Center-Back Depth 10½″
Shoulderline Depth 12½″
At the Neckline
(Raglan Sloper)

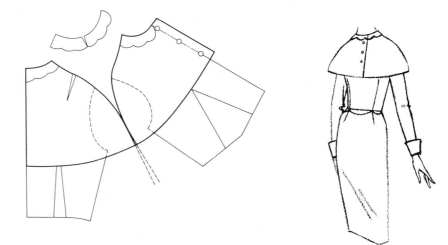

Fitted Cape or Bertha Collar. A large cape collar with a fitted silhouette can be planned quite practically on the raglan sloper since its sleeve section is pivoted down farther than on any other sloper. For a collar with more flare, one of the kimono slopers is more suitable for use. Large Bertha collars that require a shoulder seam are planned in the same way.

Collar Planned
Away at Center Front 2″
Away at Center Back, 6″
Away at Shoulder 2″
Collar Depth 4″
(Raglan Sloper)

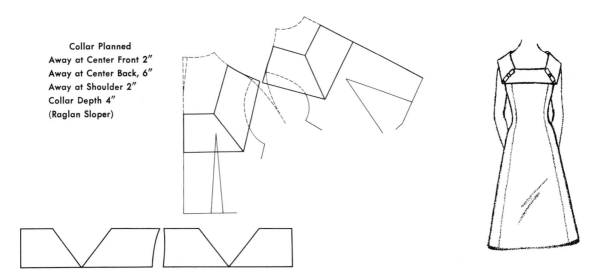

Collar with Mitered Corners for Square Neckline. A large square collar with mitered corners can be planned on either the raglan or the kimono sloper since both have the front shoulderline raised. When a square collar is made actually square, its neckline looks wider at the bottom than at the shoulder. When the side pieces follow the princess seam direction as shown in the pattern the illusion of a square neckline is created.

263

Chapter Eleven

The Effective Use of Trimmings

THE TERM "TRIMMING" is used with two rather different meanings in the apparel industry. In its first meaning it differentiates the accessory parts of a garment from its basic structural parts of waist, skirt, and sleeve. Trimmings thus include collars, cuffs, pockets, belts, ties, bows, and buttons. The term "trimming" also means to decorate, and in this equally important usage trimmings include the many techniques by which a garment can be individualized, by a strong spot of trimming to act as a center of interest, by some accent that will strengthen the garment's style lines, or by the application of some trimming technique that will add interest in a particular area of the garment.

This chapter is concerned with ways to add to sales appeal by improving the compositional quality of garment design through trimming. In the first half of the chapter the accessory parts that trim a garment are analyzed; in the latter half of the chapter commonly used trimming techniques are described.

The "Hard Chic" of the 1930's
Typified by Schiaparelli

"A sensation of the Openings was Schiaparelli's waistcoat '410,' very Beau Brummel indeed, with its high-waisted cut and its frills. Of black and white satin ribbon, ruffled and quilted, it goes over a black satin-jersey dress. The knitted ['madcap'] is from the same designer." Vogue, September 15, 1932.

Introduction to Trimmings

A. ACCESSORY PARTS

Belt, Bow,
and Buttons

Pockets

Collar
and
Cuffs

B. TRIMMING TECHNIQUES

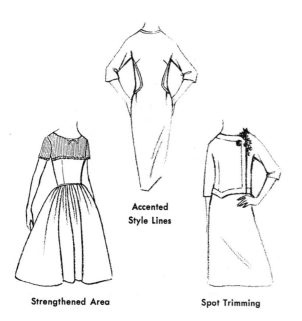

Accented
Style Lines

Strengthened Area

Spot Trimming

Accessory Parts of a Garment as Trimming (A).
All designers use the accessory parts of a garment in styling—only one dress among those shown on these two pages avoids them all—because they perform necessary services as well as furnishing effective trimming. Collars and cuffs supply an edge finish for neckline and sleeve bottom; pockets may be functional as well as decorative, and belts, ties, bows, and buttons are all "working devices" that hold their garment closed. Collars, cuffs, pockets, bows, and ties are usually cut and assembled "inside" the house as parts of the garment. Belts and buttons are purchased "outside" from firms that specialize in each of these important accessories and whose salesmen call on the designer with their lines of samples.

Trimming Techniques (B). The group of trimmings identified in this chapter as *trimming techniques* are purchased for the most part from trimming-passementerie firms that send salesmen to show their lines to the designer. These sample lines generally include hundreds of different ideas which their skilled operators can produce on the special types of sewing machines they use. A designer may choose from the samples shown or may prefer to plan original ideas which the trimming firms willingly carry out. The three dresses in B illustrate the three ways in which these trimming techniques are used:

Spot trimmings furnish centers of interest.
Trimmings that accent style lines intensify the garment's compositional pattern.
Trimmings that strengthen areas enrich undistinguished fabric.

266

Strong Simple Trimming   Intricate Styling

Trimmings Reflect Fashion Trends. Fashion trends have considerable influence on the type and amount of trimming used on a garment. During eras when simple, straight lines are most fashionable, trimmings are bold and simple, scaled-up to look "in-drawing" with the garments on which they are used. But when the hourglass silhouette and intricacy of design replace simplicity as the criterion of fashion, a great many scaled-down trimmings are often used. The two garments in C illustrate how properly scaled trimmings reflect fashion trends.

Trimmings Reflect Garment Price. Four dresses trimmed with Schiffli embroidery are used in D to show the way in which trimmings can reflect the price of their garments. The very high-price dress, a Paris original, is made entirely from fine-quality embroidered organdy with an excellently finished scalloped edge. The "better" dress next to it also uses fine-quality embroidered and scalloped batiste, but in a much smaller amount. The budget dress uses less embroidery that is much lower in quality and expensiveness because the scallops do not form the edge. The basement dress, which cannot afford scallops, cleverly camouflages this fact with inexpensive rickrack.

The Effective Use of Trimmings. A sensitive application of the fine-arts principles discussed in Chapter 5 results in an effective use of trimmings. Many of the illustrations from that chapter are used again in this chapter since they offer such excellent suggestions for using good composition, flattering lines, and good taste in the selection and application of trimmings and trimming techniques.

D. GARMENT PRICE

Couture (Import)   Better Dress

Budget Dress   Basement Dress

A. TAILORED BASIC DRESSES

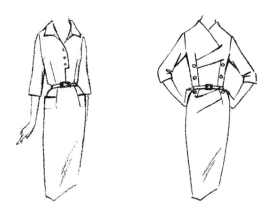

B. CASUAL BASIC DRESSES

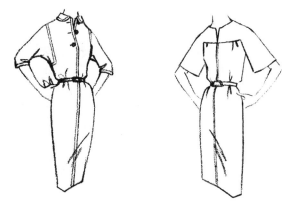

C. SOPHISTICATED OVERSKIRTS

Styling with and without Collars

ONE SAFE WAY to style a dress is to start with the basic sheath and glamorize it with a strong flattering collar, a technique that was discussed in Chapter 5. But dress styling cannot always follow this simple formula. Many dress types besides the sheath generally must be included in a line, and the question of the need for a collar arises for every dress. A collar is not a substitute for a neck facing, as beginners in design often assume. It is always an added expense that must be justified by its contribution to the sales appeal of the garment. The sketches on these two pages show pairs of dresses that are similar in type and silhouette; those on the left have collars and their twins on the right are collarless. Collars for dresses with front openings are shown on this page, and the less common types of collars for dresses that open in the back are illustrated on the facing page.

Collars with Front Openings. Collars generally are used for button-down necklines, and the three dresses with collars illustrate standard, artistically sound methods for styling them. The collarless dresses beside them are exceptions to the rule and must be justified. The tailored dress at the top of the page avoids both a collar and a collarless look by a neckline that is brought up to resemble the wrapped effect of a scarf and is coordinated with the rather intricate styling of the midsection. A collar is not needed on the typical "basic" dress in B since the long, strong T-line design is scaled up to furnish adequate design strength with distinctive simplicity. The collarless dress in C, designed by Balenciaga, has great elegance due to its flawless proportion which would be weakened by a collar. As a rule, however, button-down necklines are not in this "masterpiece" category and need to have collars.

Collars with Back Openings. Collars for back openings must be justified because they are not usually needed to terminate the eye track as they are on front-buttoning dresses. The two dresses in D are remarkably similar in feeling as well as in silhouette, the one of plain organdy with a crushed satin cummerbund and the other of embroidered organdy with a plain organdy collar. The proportions of the plain dress, with its uniform rhythm in the tiers of the skirt and diminishing rhythm in skirt to cummerbund to tiny sleeve, form an excellent and eye-satisfying composition to which any addition would be superfluous. In the embroidered dress the diminishing-rhythm pattern depends on the collar rather than the sleeve for its final step, and a plain collar subdues and unifies the busy pattern of the embroidery while making an effective frame for the face. The dress in E is a standard example of Empire structure, which seldom has a collar. Its twin, however, requires a strong collar to draw the attention up from the waistline and to balance the difficult length of the overblouse. Both dresses in F offer satisfactory ways to direct attention upward. The composition of the collarless dress is strong and simple, whereas the dress with collar is comparatively complex. Balance is again involved and the narrow band collar stands in the same relationship to the waist as the wide midriff stands to the skirt. The collar here, as in the two examples above, performs an important function in the design.

D. YOUNG PARTY DRESSES

E. HIGH STYLE AND TAILORED

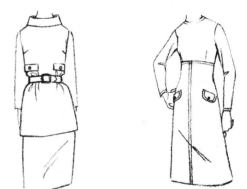

F. HIGH STYLE AND DRESSY

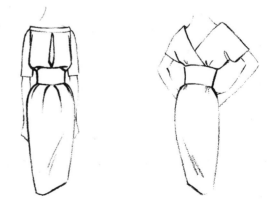

Styling with Cuffs

Collars and Cuffs as Color Accents. The collars shown on the preceding page were all of self-fabric, as is common when collars are used alone (and they are more often than not). A contrasting collar—without cuffs—must be of enormous size in order to balance the composition, as shown at far right in A, or its color must be repeated as a secondary balancing detail. Cuffs alone are used infrequently, and the same principle applies to contrasting cuffs as to contrasting collars. The color of the cuffs must be repeated in some other style detail if the composition is to look unified. Cuffs should never be the strongest accent on a garment because they are peripheral to the composition. Some stronger detail must pull the eye to a more central point and from there lead it to the face, as is well illustrated by the print dress in A, which is trimmed effectively with plain fabric that picks up one of the colors of the print. Note that in both of the collar-and-cuff dresses illustrated, the cuffs are narrower and thus weaker repetitions of the collar.

Tailored Collars and Cuffs. Strictly tailored collars and cuffs faithfully copy men's styling. The shirtdress copies the man's shirt, which down to its last detail of cuff and placket is so well engineered that no unfinished seam remains to show when a man rolls up his shirt sleeves. Here women's styling does not exactly follow. The roll-up sleeves in B are plain sleeves with a hem—a scheme that keeps production costs down and retains the proper casual look at the same time. Between these two classic types of shirt cuff, a variation is shown. Little variety is possible in styling cuffs for shirt sleeves because their greater width and casual feeling almost demand classic cuff styling. The roll-up cuff is so well suited to the casual look that it has been widely adopted for sportswear separates, as the outfit at the far right illustrates.

Cuffs for Softened Sleeves. The four dresses in C illustrate a more feminine type of collar and cuff styling that has developed from classic shirt styling, probably by way of the Russian blouse, an example of which is shown at the far right. In all four examples shown in this group, the sleeves are gathered in at the bottom and so require a cuff of some type to control the fullness. The simple, rather narrow band cuff customarily used is both mechanically sound and artistically appropriate. Typical "classic" neckline styling is shown by the print dress with a Peter Pan collar and flowing bow tie, truly the most feminine expression of a man's collar and tie that can be imagined. Other types of collar styling are also appropriate for these soft sleeves. Both the bishop and the puff sleeve are set into the normal armhole in a regular fitted waist, which, of course, is suited to being styled in a wide variety of ways. For this reason the styling of the collar is not limited in the way that shirt collar styling is limited (the shirtwaist has its own casual, eased sloper) but can use any type of collar suited to the styling of the dress. The important consideration is that collars and cuffs made in self-fabric can never be star performers like the contrasting collars and cuffs in A, but rather are members of a team that must work in cooperation with the other design details.

**A. Contrasting Collar and Cuffs
Furnish Strong Trimming**

**B. Convertible Shirt Collar
Is Used with Classic
or Roll-up Cuffs**

**C. A Choice of Collars
with Feminine Versions of
Tailored Cuff**

271

Pocket Styling—Usually with a Balanced Pair

POCKETS ARE an indispensable feature in menswear but they are used rather infrequently in dress styling. Their inherently tailored look limits their use for one thing, and for another they always add to the cost of production. In addition, pockets are strong design features that are difficult to coordinate with other style details unless they can be planned with particular attention to the rhythmic repetition of their style lines. Pockets are of two types: "patch" pockets that are attached to the outside of the garment "like a patch," and inset pockets that are inside the garment, with a slash of some type for their opening. Pocket flaps may be used (to hold them shut), the top of the pocket may be trimmed with a shaped band that looks like a working flap, or flaps may be used alone as pure decorative details (example on page 275). A single pocket is used occasionally, but as a rule the more fool-proof arrangement of pockets in pairs is preferred since their placement is thus less critical for good composition.

Tailored Styling. Tailored styling can imitate menswear in the use of pockets, with excellent effect, as the three examples in A illustrate. The standard formula of a small neat collar, 4-hole "suit" buttons, a classic belt, and slash pockets is successfully repeated season after season, whether high fashion dictates the hourglass, as shown in the two-piece suit dress, or the shift, as shown in the tweed coat dress. And for every season the tailored classic daytime dress is deservedly popular.

Dressy Styling. Each of the dressy garments shown in B uses pockets for a different reason. The short evening dress of bengaline at the far right interprets a casual look by its two slash pockets inset into the A-line seam of the skirt. The intricately draped taffeta afternoon dress (by Dior) uses a single slash pocket with supreme mastery as an important factor in its compositional balance. The cocktail shift of off-white silk brocade contrasts the formality of the fabric with the most casual type of patch pocket and thereby gives a multipurpose usefulness to the dress that is not inherent in silk brocade.

Casual Styling. Casual styling uses pockets well and often because the principles on which casual styling rests are functionality and comfort. Garments for casual wear should have pockets; and pockets frequently are used as the main feature of the design because of their generally purposeful look. Pockets that actually can be used should be of suitable size. Thus practicality, which is always a strong feature in casual styling, dictates skirts that are full enough to permit large pockets to be used without showing ugly bulges. And the pockets should have workable flaps that hold the pockets closed when the wearer bends over, and tabs that keep the belt in place and at the same time prevent the corner of the pocket from tearing out, as patch pockets tend to do. In addition pockets should furnish artistically planned style lines that strengthen the composition, as illustrated by all three dresses in C.

A. TAILORED STYLING

Neat inset pockets contribute to tailored image

B. DRESSY STYLING

Pockets give strong weight needed for artistic balance

C. CASUAL STYLING

Functional pockets are dominant style feature

Double Pairs of Pockets Contribute to Varied Looks

DOUBLE PAIRS of pockets usually are arranged with one pair above the bustline and the other pair at the hipline, producing an interesting composition in which both waist and skirt are divided into horizontal segments that can be proportioned in individually planned variations. The proportional relationship of breast pockets to hip pockets is often 5 to 8. (One of the dresses illustrated here also was used in Chapter 5 to represent the 5-to-8 Golden-Mean proportion.) Because pocket contour is a repetition in miniature of the contour of the waist or skirt on which it is used, a pocket that is the proper size for the waist will be too small for the skirt. Note in the illustrations that skirt pockets and flaps are scaled up to coordinate properly with the larger skirt area. The garments shown here are grouped in the same three categories used for the preceding page, although the styling of a garment with four pockets is quite different from one with two pockets.

Tailored Styling. Four-pocket styling, as illustrated by the two typical examples in A, can give to the composition a scattered effect unless other stronger design details are added to achieve artistic balance. Multiple pockets cannot furnish the single strong center of interest necessary for good design. The two-piece costume at the far right relies on its bulky contrasting sweater to bring the eye to the neckline and in this way to subdue the pockets. The button-down dress works the pockets into its comprehensive design scheme of collar and cuffs, buttons and belt which together form unified force that directs attention to the wearer's face.

Dressy Styling. The two-piece outfit was designed by Chanel, who has never seemed to worry about production costs. Her approach to design is expert and individual, and has harmony and balance. Here she has used four pockets cleverly set into the princess-line seam so that they become integral parts of the rhythmic repetition pattern of this beautifully balanced tweed outfit. The fashion for multiple pockets on loose jackets trimmed with braid is so closely associated with this great designer that the term "Chanel jacket" is as universally understood as "French cuff" or "bishop sleeve." The young taffeta dress beside the Chanel outfit has actual inset pockets in the skirt while flaps without pockets are used in the waist. Both pairs of flaps are placed strategically to strengthen the illusion of a slim waistline fostered by the other styling details. The center-front fold conceals the button-down closing and furnishes a strong track that draws the eye to the flattering neckline.

Casual Styling. The casual-separates outfit in C is similar to its tailored counterpart in A in pocket arrangement and welt-seam accent. But the casual outfit is sleeveless and substitutes flaps for pockets, narrowing its occasion use to the leisure-playclothes range, while the example shown above can be dressed up or down by the type of sweater, blouse, or scarf that is worn with it. The simple piqué dress shown in C relies entirely on its pockets for design interest. Their envelope shape piped with a contrasting color strongly directs the eye upward while emphasizing the casual simplicity of the styling.

A. TAILORED STYLING

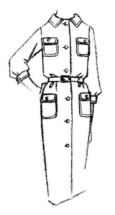

Patch pockets with button accent dramatize a coat and suit feeling

B. DRESSY STYLING

Less tailored pockets act as accent in subtle combinations of design detail

C. CASUAL STYLING

Pocket flaps are dominant style feature in strong simple design

Belt Styling with Buckles

THE BELT has been amusingly defined as an artful invention of the dress manufacturer to trick customers into buying garments that do not fit. And it is true that the waistline of the average dress is too large for the average customer and that a belt minimizes this defect. On the other hand, a sale is seldom lost simply because this usually easy alteration needs to be made, whereas a customer will seldom buy a dress in which the zipper will not close when she attempts to try on the dress. A properly coordinated belt can do a great deal for a garment, both on the hanger, where it helps to make its dress "look the money," and on the wearer, where it slims the waistline and often acts as an important element in the design, as illustrated by all the examples shown on the facing page.

The Expensive Belt. The cost of a belt depends on how much material is required, on how expensive the material is—some varieties of leather are very costly—and on the amount and quality of workmanship entailed. The belt at the right in A is made from fine-quality suede with a buckle in silver filigree of excellent quality and design that can also be used on other garments. The crushed kidskin belt on the dress of houndstooth tweed is also of excellent quality as is apparent in its turned edges, generous width, and contoured buckle. Belts of these types have sufficient strength to be the center of interest for their garments and for good design require only some track for the eye up to the neckline, which properly scaled buttons can often supply.

Classic Belt Styling. The contoured belt shown at the right in B is of good polished calf leather with a turned and stitched edge. It too is the only trimming used on its dress, matching it in color and segmenting the waistline in a flattering way with a wide oval buckle. A smart basic daytime dress of good quality can enhance its "better-dress" appeal with this type of understated styling. The strength of a belt depends on its width and its sharpness of contrast with the dress. Although a slim waistline is made to appear slimmer by a wide contrasting belt, the opposite holds true for the thick waistline of the larger sizes to which a wide or contrasting belt tends to draw attention. The print dress shown in B is representative of women's and half-size styling. Its rather narrow belt of self-fabric illustrates the standard type of belt used and it is flattering because it blends into the composition and does not cut the waistline.

Belts to Catch the Eye. Inexpensive belts must be used on inexpensive garments, but the necessity remains for them to furnish their share of sales appeal. The belt at the far right in C is an example of the exciting type of belt that is used effectively in the junior dress market where the average young customer is more responsive to variety than to quality merchandise. Inexpensive novelty belts also must be used on casual summer cottons such as the one on the near right in C. The belt shown is well designed and much less expensive than a belt made entirely of leather. When novelty belts are nicely coordinated with their dresses, they add considerably to sales appeal.

A. EXPENSIVE BELTS

Softly draped kidskin with fine self-buckle

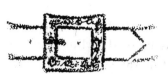

Silver filigree buckle on fine suede belt

B. CLASSIC BELT STYLING

Self-covered belt backed with leather

Contoured belt of polished calf with turned and stitched edges

C. BELTS TO CATCH THE EYE

Leather combined with braided cord

Leather belt with two-tone fancy buckle

Belts with Bows and String-Tie Belts

AS A RULE a belt with a buckle is more suitable for casual and tailored styling and a belt with a bow instead of the conventional buckle is more appropriate for softer and dressier types of styling. But there are so many well-styled, dressy garments that have belts with buckles that no general rule can be laid down. Belt styling like the styling of other design details depends on the excellence of the designer's taste. One reason that buckles are so much more widely used than bows is that they permit easy adjustment to individual waistline size. String ties, of course, are the most completely adjustable of all. Commercially produced belts with bows instead of buckles must fasten either with a concealed adjustable closing underneath the bow or with a buckle at the back, neither of which arrangement is as practical as a belt that simply buckles or a string tie that simply ties. In the illustrations on the facing page typical examples of bow belts and string-tie belts are shown.

Belts with Bow Buckles. The printed acetate jersey dress on the far right in A has a leather-lined bow belt of grosgrain that matches the binding used to clean-finish the neck and armholes. It is often easier to have a belt made from the trimming fabric used on a garment than to find a leather belt that is available in the entire range of colors in which the garment is offered. Moreover, use of the same fabric ensures against differences in dye lot which can cause obvious mismatching, particularly when a belt must coordinate with binding. The self-fabric belt on the other dress in A uses a bow rather than a buckle to dress up its basic-sheath, everyday plainness in the least expensive way.

Passementerie Cords and Leather Thongs. Novelty belts of the type shown on the far right in B include metal chain belts as well as the cord and tassel belt illustrated. Both are faddish and never widely popular, but one or two are often included in a line for variety. The leather thong belt in B is as understated as the cord and tassel is bold. Leather thongs have exceptional popularity in casual eras and they are well suited to casual styling at all times, combining well with tweeds, homespuns, and rough linens. They are particularly appropriate with pullover separates as shown in the illustration. The belt illustrated is made from a narrow strip of thin leather, sewn like spaghetti and trimmed at the ends with metal coins.

Self-Fabric Ties. The cost of a belt is always a factor in styling. When an extravagant belt is the *pièce de résistance* that sells the dress, other trimming often is held to a minimum to keep the price of the garment within bounds. At the other end of the scale, however, economy often forces the use of a self-belt. Of course, any belt that must be made outside by a belt manufacturer is more expensive than a belt that can be made in the workroom. The dress at the far right in C has a spaghetti belt made from long bias strips of fabric that are stitched and turned. Here two thin spaghetti strands are used together, matching the corded piping that trims the neckline. For the two-piece dress in C, a wider strip of self-fabric on lengthwise grain has been stitched and turned to make the tie belt that furnishes just the right casual touch for this beautifully designed cocktail dress by Givenchy. In this case, design sensitivity rather than economy was the controlling factor in belt choice.

Self-fabric backed with leather

Grosgrain backed with leather

B. LEATHER THONGS AND PASSEMENTERIE CORDS

Leather spaghetti with coin drop

Passementerie cord and tassel

C. SELF-FABRIC TIES

Clean-finished strip of self-fabric
casually tied

Double spaghetti tied in a casual
bow

Bows as Center of Interest

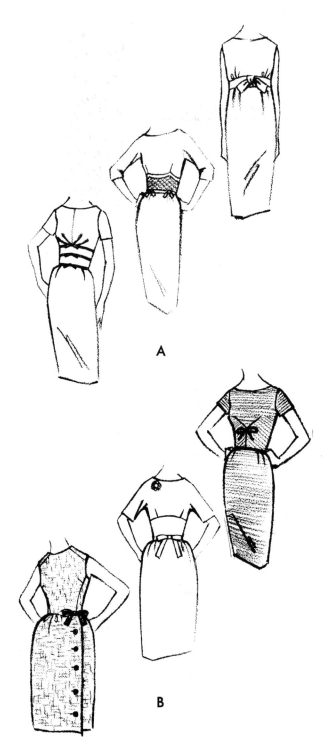

A

B

A BOW CAN be an effective replacement for a belt as the sketches on the left illustrate, but since a good belt generally is viewed by the average customer as a reliable gauge of value, other features must compensate when a belt is not used. Value factors that are apparent on the hanger include interesting fabric, good buttons, jeweled pins, and hand work such as binding, strapping, and tailored buttonholes. Simplicity of styling is also a sales factor because its quality look is associated with high-price garments in which excellence of cut and workmanship replace details as the criteria of value.

Bands That Imitate Belts. Applied bands replace belts in the three dresses in A, all of which have interest centered at the midriff. The Empire dress uses a wide inset band of self-fabric instead of a belt. In the other two dresses the narrow bands of strapping are properly scaled down for the generally restrained feeling of the other styling details. The center of interest in all three dresses is the bow detail; each is designed to effectively direct attention upward.

Bows Alone. Bows used on the three dresses in B create the illusion of a belt. The spaghetti bow on the bengaline sheath covers the awkward junction of darts and center seam and also draws attention to the segmented midriff. Although small, it is a strong center of interest because of its focal position. The dress in the middle has a gentle self-bow that segments the waistline and supports the jeweled pin on which interest centers. The dress at the far left uses a strong bow as center of interest to subdue the buttons that trim the skirt. It relies on its lacy mohair fabric for sales appeal and on the wearer's own costume jewelry for help in strengthening the rather weak track for the eye.

Bows in Draped and Laced Effects. When a bow takes over as the sole performer in trimming a dress, the effect resembles a gift-wrapped box. The box itself is neat and simple, permitting the ribbon and its bow to be the dominating, eye-filling feature. Two different techniques fall into this rather specialized category.

BOWS WITH DRAPED EFFECTS. All three dresses in A are imports with such strong, extravagant styling that they would be considered showcase dresses. A buyer who does not expect to make "runners" out of styles such as these often buys a limited number for display to show subtly that the department knows fashion. Note that all three dresses have a simple sheath silhouette, like a neat package, while the bow detail either drapes or appears to drape the fabric into a pattern of sculptured folds. In each dress the bow is the strong focal point, supported by converging lines, and in all dresses the styling provides a strong track from the bow to the face.

BOWS WITH LACED EFFECTS. Using ribbon or self-fabric, bows with laced effects are just as dominating as bows combined with draped folds, but they have less high-style feeling and thus are more wearable. The eyelets through which the ribbon is threaded must be clean-finished, usually by the tailored-buttonhole technique, and this hand-done detailing gives the same appeal that buttonholes for buttons give to a dress. Note that the ribbon used for the lacing in the dress at the near right is the same width as for the bow, whereas in the other dresses the bow is considerably wider than its lacing. All three dresses are of the cut-in-one type that can use scaled-up trimming, and bows with lacing should be scaled up in this way because of their use as the sole design feature.

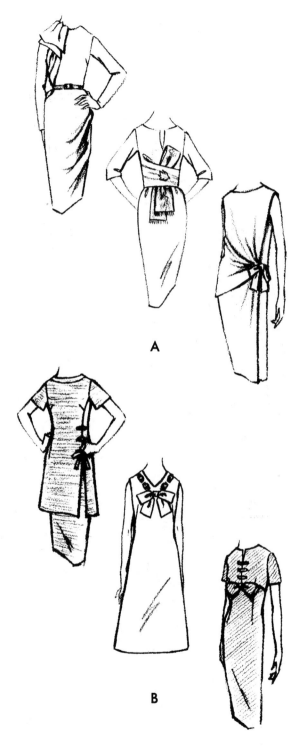

A

B

Bows at the Neckline

A

B

NECKLINE BOWS are not interchangeable parts that can be switched from dress to dress. The particular flavor of a bow that is used sensitively can accent its dress very effectively. The type of collar on a dress depends on the shape of the neckline, but the essence of both collar and bow summarize the mood of the dress.

Collars and Bows of Self-Fabric. Self-fabric collars and bows tend to look conservative and generally are used on dresses that have gentle style lines which they can dominate. Note that in each of the dresses in A the bow is scaled to the composition as a whole, giving adequate strength to pull the eye effectively, but not overpowering the other details of the styling.

Contrasting Collars and Bows. Contrast is used on dresses in which it is necessary to exert force of sufficient intensity to prevail over strong style lines or interesting fabric. Note how each of the three dresses shown in B compares with the dress above it in A. Much stronger accent is needed on the Empire shift than on the basic sheath dress above it. Cut-in-one styling requires stronger accent than the smaller scale of waist-and-skirt dresses. Note how the cool, sophisticated image of the blouson dress of dotted voile is well summarized by the crisp organdy collar and carelessly tied bow, just as a gentle conservative image is expressed above it by the soft self-collar and bow with embroidery touches. The two Peter Pan collars also express quite different images, both young, but the linen collar with satin ribbon is a young sophisticate, whereas the self-collar and bow above belong to a descendant of Kate Greenaway.

Bows Used at the Neckline without Collars.
Bows can camouflage the hard line of a plain
neck, draw the eye upward, and summarize the
styling just as bow and collar combinations do.
In the sketches at the right, three dresses of entirely different styling are illustrated although
each has a long style line to act as a strong
track for the eye. In each dress the bow also
adds an indispensable finishing touch. In the
bias shift it takes away from the monotony of
the triple diagonal seamlines. In the two-piece
outfit it gives necessary balance to the compositional weight of the skirt. In the waist-and-
skirt dress it is strong enough in size and color
contrast to tone down and thus unify the force-
ful inverted pleats with their accented seamlines and the exaggerated sleeves.

Paired Bows at the Neckline. All three illustrations in B show typical women's dressy garments with small twin bows just below the open
neckline. This type of styling is used often for
large sizes where the top of the dress needs to
counterbalance and distract attention from the
ungainly torso. A pretty neckline on a simple
dress is one sure formula for sales appeal in this
particular market area. The two plain-color
dresses combine long lines, rather tailored
styling, and dainty trimming that large women
generally prefer, skillfully using V-shapes to
lengthen the figure and draw the eye strongly
upward. The print dress, of course, relies more
on the smoke-screen effect of its pretty allover
pattern than on line, and the plain-color coordinated bows of velvet ribbon furnish a most effective trimming.

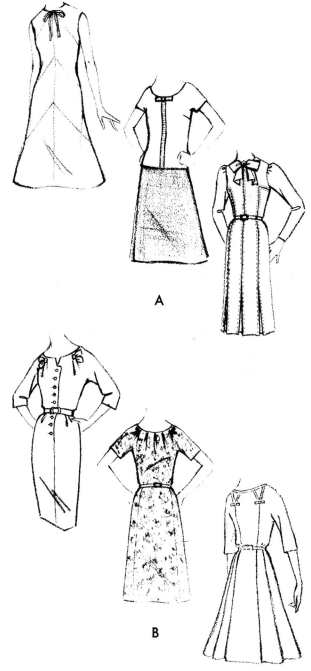

A

B

283

Button Styling

ALTHOUGH THE ZIPPER seems to be the almost universally used closing device, there are a number of styling situations in which the button is preferred. Dresses with front closing (as shown in the three dresses on the near right of the facing page) almost always button down since buttons accentuate the long-line closing while they perform their useful service. For the tailored classic dress (as shown in the three dresses at the far right) buttons are an almost indispensable part of the "image." In any removable jacket, buttons are the standard closing device. Back-closing blouses are buttoned as a rule, unless they have only a neck opening, because buttons are less clumsy than the separating zipper—the only alternative for a blouse that opens all the way. Blouson effects have a more graceful silhouette when the closing is buttoned, and in this styling a zipper is always avoided.

Button Selection. Buttons should be selected during the planning stage of garment development since the size and design strength of buttons combine to determine the number needed, and the number used always must be a definitive factor in their placement. The sketches on the facing page show different button arrangements that are often used for dresses. When buttons are used below the belt, part or all the way down, the strength of the belt becomes a factor in placement, with the buttons on either side placed to give an illusion of equal spacing, rather than being evenly spaced by measurement. Very small buttons, as shown on the two dresses at the bottom of the page, are seldom functional because buttoning them is tedious when they are spaced closely enough to scale with the garment. Occasionally the twin arrangement is used to scale up small buttons.

The Buttonhole Extension. The larger the buttons, the wider the buttonhole extension must be to maintain good proportion. Generally the extension can be made approximately the width of the button, as shown in the diagram. The buttonhole is placed off center as shown at the left, but the button is attached at the center line of the garment. Off-center placement is necessary because a button sets at the end of a buttonhole, not at its midpoint. Horizontal buttonholes are used whenever possible because in a vertical buttonhole the button pulls ineffectively against its side. Only very small buttons that are closely spaced or on which there is little tension can use vertical buttonholes.

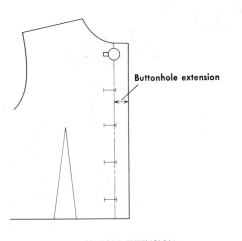

Buttonhole extension

THE BUTTONHOLE EXTENSION

LARGE BUTTONS (65 line to 40 line)

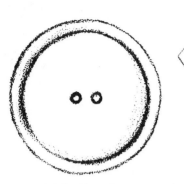

2-Hole Volume Plastic
65 line

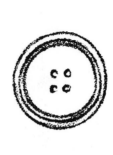

Classic 4-Hole Plastic
45 line

MEDIUM-SIZE BUTTONS (36 line to 30 line)

Carved Plastic Shank
36 line

Metal Filigree Shank
30 line

SMALL BUTTONS (24 line to 16 line)

Dyed Ocean Pearl
24 line

Self-Covered Half-Ball
16 line

285

Button Selection

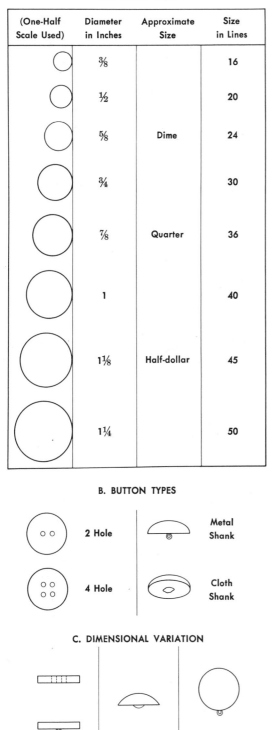

A. BUTTON SIZES

(One-Half Scale Used)	Diameter in Inches	Approximate Size	Size in Lines
	3/8		16
	1/2		20
	5/8	Dime	24
	3/4		30
	7/8	Quarter	36
	1		40
	1 1/8	Half-dollar	45
	1 1/4		50

B. BUTTON TYPES

2 Hole

4 Hole

Metal Shank

Cloth Shank

C. DIMENSIONAL VARIATION

Flat   Half-Ball   Full Ball

Size. Buttons are sized by their diameter in "lines," with 40 lines equal to one inch. The most commonly used sizes of buttons for dresses are shown in A. Some of their appropriate uses are illustrated on the facing page.

Type. Buttons are divided into types (B) according to the method of attachment to their garment. The most common types have either two or four holes for sewing them on. Shank buttons look more dressy than buttons with holes because their attachment is concealed.

Contour. Most buttons are smooth, round, and comparatively flat—qualities that make them easy to button, light in weight, and able to use the smallest possible buttonholes. Buttons of irregular shape easily get out of alignment on a garment, and rough surfaces are difficult to get through the buttonhole, so such novelty buttons are best used solely as trimming, only pretending to button. Self-covered buttons do not have holes but are attached by means of a cloth shank. They are usually "half-ball" rather than flat since the dome shape of the half-ball not only is easier to cover with cloth but also has greater design strength than a flat button without holes.

Materials. A wide variety of standard materials is used for buttons and many unusual novelties come on the market each season. Pearl leads the button industry in volume because of its use on men's shirts and children's clothing as well as on dresses and blouses. The most popular buttons for women's dresses are the plastics, which range from very high to very low price and provide a designer with a stimulating range of selection.

Self-Covered
70 line

Molded Plastic
with Metal Shank
55 line

Carved Imported Plastic
36 line

4-Hole Molded Plastic
34 line

Florentine-Finish Metal
28 line

2-Hole Volume Plastic
40 line

Individualized and

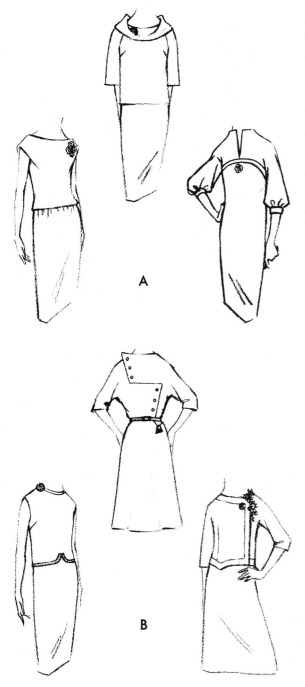

A

B

Jeweled Ornaments. A jeweled pin or a large, fancy button often furnishes an appealing luxury look on the hanger as well as a satisfactory center of interest when the dress is tried on. The simple lines of the cut-in-one dress rely on color, fabric, and this type of expensive-looking trimming to a much greater extent than the waist-and-skirt dress with its more complex structure and compatibility with belts, buttons, and fancy necklines. When a button or pin of gold or beads is sensitively coordinated with the color of the garment and scaled to it in size, it can furnish a very believable illusion of the wearer's own real jewelry.

Passementerie Ornaments. On dresses for 9-to-5 daytime wear, fancy jeweled ornaments are not generally appropriate. The same need for a strong focal point may exist, as the dresses in B illustrate, but their tailored rather than soft styling calls for less dressy ornaments. The handsome, white ottoman two-piece costume by Cardin is trimmed with a beautifully carved white button and a bunch of black patent-leather grapes. The Dior dress beside it uses a monogrammed suede bangle that matches its belt and buttons. (This dress was used as an example of asymmetrical balance in Chapter 5, page 91.) The two-piece separates outfit at the far left has contrasting braid binding with a stylized raffia ornament at the neckline. Passementerie trimmings of the types illustrated by this group of dresses are often used when a touch of color is needed. The designer works out an original idea with a representative of one of the many trimming firms which then provides the item in "sizes and colors."

Expensive-Looking Trimmings

Trimming for and with Colorful Prints. Trimming for prints and trimming with prints is more difficult than trimming for and with solid colors. For one thing, a print fabric looks different in different color combinations and when a dress is offered in three or four different colorings, as often happens, color combinations for each often must be individually planned. On light backgrounds the print color that has the greatest contrast can often be picked up in the trimming, but on dark grounds the most contrasting print color may be too light and weak to make effective trimming. The illustrations in C show successful examples of multicolor trimming. A colorful scarf is used on a plain, casual, two-piece outfit. A pocket is trimmed with a colorful beaded floral motif in an expensive Vera Maxwell classic dress; and a cashmere sweater is effectively appliquéd with motifs from the silk print of its dress.

Trimming with Tailored Buttonholes. The tailored, "bound" buttonhole always has hanger appeal because the handwork that goes into it keeps it out of the volume market as a rule. The junior dress on the near right, however, is a volume dress. It uses one huge nonoperative buttonhole that reduces production cost while retaining the hand-done, better-dress implication. The bolero beside it uses buttonholes of contrasting color to proclaim its "quality" aspirations while economizing on a dress devoid of trimming, as is often the formula in budget jacket dresses. The high-price, two-piece costume at the far right combines four small buttonholes with good self-fabric appliqué in a subtle and appealing design.

289

Style Lines Strengthened with

Welt and Slot Seams. Composition in a garment is strengthened when style lines are accented, in the same way that composition in a painting is strengthened by using broader and darker lines in some areas than in others. Welt and slot seams are simple techniques by which the style lines of a garment can be strengthened and, by contrast, side-seam and other construction lines that do not contribute to the design can be deemphasized. Welt stitching is the name given to a machine top-stitch made at a spaced distance from the edge or seamline of a garment. A slot seam is a double welt seam, usually with a strip of fabric underneath. When the style line is left free, the strip beneath it, often of contrasting color, shows in a subtle and interesting way. In place of machine stitching, hand-picking and saddle stitching are occasionally used for accent. The junior dress at the far left is an example of this technique, with wool yarn in a contrasting color that coordinates with the novelty belt. Contrasting stitching is always stronger than self-color and generally is used sparingly.

Multiple-Needle Stitching. Most trimming firms have multiple-needle machines by which a number of rows of stitching (or tucking) can be made simultaneously. The garments at the left show different effects that can be obtained by this technique. The band and collar on the button-down dress are accented with a triple row of stitching. The trimming on the dress in the middle has a dimensional appearance that results from a layer of sheet cotton being used underneath the fabric to give it a puffed effect. The fabric itself in the outfit on the far left—a spongy bouclé—produces its own dimensional look when stitched in quilted squares.

Stitching and Contrasting Accent

Binding and Banding. Binding for the edges and banding for the seamlines are stronger as well as more expensive trimming techniques than stitching. Banding and binding usually take some form of contrast, in color, material, or grain direction. The bolero jacket is bound with hand-cut bias binding that matches the shell bodice of the outfit. Binding the edges of a short jacket (illustrated also on the preceding page) is effective and mechanically practical since it eliminates the need for facings. Hand-cut bias always looks expensive because it is obviously hand-done while its "poor relation," commercial bias binding, is used principally on aprons and housedresses because it obviously is machine-made. Narrow bias strips that are made like spaghetti, but pressed flat, are known as "strapping." The dress in the middle, of wool trimmed with satin strapping, would usually be sent outside; the band on the checked dress, however, can be top-stitched and therefore could easily be made inside in the workroom.

Cord and Braid. Self-cording, as illustrated by the dress at the near right, is made by covering thin upholstery cord with bias fabric. The difference between it and spaghetti is that it is not clean-finished since it is either inset, as at a waistline, or used for finishing a free edge. Here the neckline edge is corded to match the spaghetti belt. Passementerie cord and braid are closely related and frequently combined. Here cord alone is used for the elongated frogs on the bolero outfit of menswear worsted, and braid alone is used on the separates outfit at the far right. Narrow soutache braid of this type has many applications, among them the sailor collar of the middy blouse and reembroidered lace.

Gentle Accents or

RUFFLES

SMOCKING AND PUFFING

FRINGE

Ruffles. When gentle rather than strong accent for style lines is desired, ruffles that are made by gathering or pleating self-fabric are an attractive solution, offering dimensional depth as well as movement. The ruffle of crisply pleated lace on the shift of sculptured crepe illustrated at the left contrasts with the strong lines of the garment in a gay and charming way, and the gathered ruffle that acts as a yoke for the casual dimity dress beside it adds a gentle feminine touch to the rather stark styling of the dress.

Puffing and Smocking. Puffing is used as an insertion to outline a wide hem. These little bands of self-fabric, whether compressed by pleats or gathers, can act as attractive border design for garments made of printed fabric. The type of smocked yoke shown at the left on this so-called "baby-dress" styling is often made with machine smocking rather than the expensive hand smocking, which often produces an unwieldy amount of fullness. Any desired amount of fullness can be used in conjunction with machine smocking, which is cut and handled like a piece of embroidery.

Fringe. Self-fringe has the same feeling of movement as a pleated ruffle but lacks its practicality. Self-fringe, which must be made by pulling out the cross threads of the fabric, is shown on the plaid dress. Many fabrics do not have enough body to produce adequate fringe, or are woven of such fine yarns that fringing is impractical, and, of course, self-fringe can be made only on straight grain. Passementerie fringe, which is in the same family as cord and braid, is shown on the bolero dress. This practical commercial type of fringe is available in many unusual and decorative patterns.

Strong Accents

Scallops. Serrated edges are so hard and strong that great restraint is necessary in their use or they weary the eye with their multiple curves and corners. The dress on the right, with button-down scallops, is a typical woman's dress, complete with a tiny bow and a long row of tiny buttons to aid the scallops in slimming and lengthening the figure. The two-piece outfit beside it, by Cardin, interprets scallops very differently, recognizing their power to stand alone, where they subtly slim the waistline.

Points and Sharp Corners. These are so strong that they must be used very sparingly. Two examples are illustrated that show their use in coordinated styling of pocket and neckline detail. Part of the appeal of all these curves and points lies in the fact that they are obviously hand-done. This appeal is not adequate, however, unless they also serve some useful purpose, a principle that applies in some measure to all trimmings. Thus the trimming on the tweed dress has more charm than the trimming on the button-down sheath because it has more purpose.

Trapunto Work. Trapunto can add a much greater dimensional depth to trimming than is possible with the multiple-needle stitching shown on the preceding pages. It is made by inserting padding between the outside garment piece and a lining, and then stitching around a stamped design (lining side up) to produce the desired shape. The lining is held taut but the outside fabric is not and this imbalance produces the "relief" effect. The styling of both of the dresses illustrated is kept very simple because the repoussé effect of the trapunto, coupled with the sharp angles of the designs, has an unusually strong impact.

SCALLOPS

POINTS AND SHARP CORNERS

TRAPUNTO WORK

Tucks and Tucking

A. TAILORED STYLING

B. FEMININE STYLING

TUCKS ARE planned individually for a garment; tucking is made by the yard. The result is the same, and tucks and tucking are both interesting to the eye because of their dimensional depth and rhythmic repetition. Multiple-needle tucking, a technique which all six dresses on this page illustrate, is made commercially on a special sewing machine with "multiple" needles that work simultaneously to produce perfectly spaced tucks in fabric by the yard, imitating to a degree the dainty hand-run tucks used to trim imported lingerie and blouses.

Tucks are made on yard goods whenever possible, from which the garment pieces are then cut, because this seemingly wasteful procedure is much less expensive than sending out the cut pieces of a garment to be individually tucked. Multiple-needle tucking can be made economically only on yard goods. Tucks of various widths and spacings can be planned by a designer and executed by a trimming firm whose sample lines have many novelty tucking ideas.

Tailored Styling. When machine tucking is used sparingly to trim matching plain fabric, it often acquires greater distinction than its cost implies, as the three cotton dresses at the left illustrate. Tucking acts as a ladder for the eye rather than being of itself a center of interest, and because it does not have intrinsic design value, it is much easier to use than the stronger techniques shown on the preceding pages.

Feminine Styling. The three dresses shown above furnish examples of machine tucking combined with Val (Valenciennes) lace. The dress at the right combines tucking with a ruffle of Val edging for a younger and more feminine look than its counterpart shown in A. The young dress in the middle also uses Val edging to soften the line where tucked and plain fabric join. The dress at the left in which tucking and Val insertion are combined gives an expensive hand-done illusion by coordinating the skirt with its waist in a clever and interesting way.

294

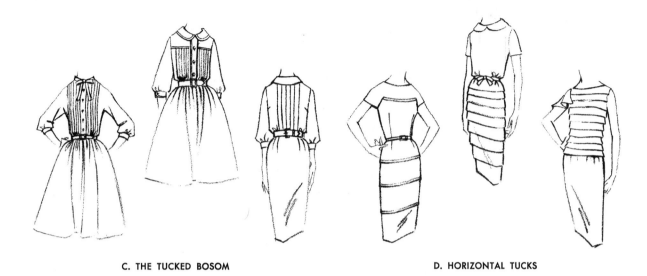

C. THE TUCKED BOSOM   D. HORIZONTAL TUCKS

The Tucked Bosom. This very popular type of styling must always provide mechanically for handling the dart excess and must also guard against a narrow look at the shoulderline. The three dresses illustrated above solve these problems in attractive ways. The first dress is made of soft cotton voile, and its sheerness when tucked produces a charming thick and thin effect while its softness permits all of the dart excess to be eased in at the waistline. The narrowed look of the waistline gives an illusion of width at the shoulder that is increased by the absence of an armhole seam and by the small band collar that takes nothing from shoulder width. The shirtdress in the middle uses a yoke in its clever styling which keeps the shoulders broad and takes out part of the dart excess as well. The silk faille dress at the right uses three box tucks that do not extend far enough to the side to interfere with the underarm dart and that permit the waist dart to be hidden under the outside fold, while the scale of the cowl collar

and other details combine effectively with the wide tucks in a subtle and unified composition.

Horizontal Tucks. Tucks that run horizontally cannot be made by the multiple-needle technique except when fabric can be used on crosswise grain, as is sometimes possible in a full dirndl skirt, for example. Otherwise these infrequently used horizontal tucks must be individually planned. The linen dress on the left in D shows a simple use of horizontal tucks that is practical in medium-price lines. The silk crepe dress beside it, with graduated spacing, is of course much more expensive to produce; and the chiffon dress at the right takes both time and skill in the making and is proportionally high in price. For this dress a shaped lining is used over which bias folds of chiffon are attached one above the other, with a seam under the left arm. The effect has particular charm because the apparently symmetrical tucks conform to the contour of the body.

Uses of Lace

Dyed Cluny Lace

Hand Crochet

Dotted Swiss

Eyelet Batiste

Venetian-Type Lace

Embroidered Batiste Yoke

ALL LACE originally was made by hand and so precious that it was used only for church vestments and decoration and on the apparel of nobility. The invention of machine-made lace has made it plentiful but it still remains a dressy trimming because it looks rich and perishable. Sheer laces are more appropriate for evening wear than for daytime wear but less delicate types of lace are in good taste for general wear.

Hand crochet and the rather substantial looking laces that have a similar feeling furnish an interesting trimming for daytime dresses. The two dresses at the upper left, both of wool and with simple tailored lines, are very effectively accented with this scaled-up type of lace.

Lace trims delicate sheer fabrics in a practical and appropriate way. Both of the very sheer dresses shown at the left use lace as an edge finish to avoid the necessity for a facing that would show through in an ugly manner. Both of these dresses also use narrow Val lace ruffles for styling accent. Its dimensional quality is strong enough to "compose" the busy all-over pattern of the fabric and bring it into drawing, and at the same time the delicate feeling of the narrow lace is extremely compatible with the delicacy of the fabric.

The mending stitch is used to make embroidered, lacy-looking batiste collars and yokes such as the one shown at the lower left. This very narrow, tight overcast joins pieces of fabric so firmly that, after the seam allowance (which is not needed) is cut away, they appear to be one. This mending technique is used for both of the dresses in C, joining the batiste yoke to its dress and joining the dyed-lace midriff and cuffs to the dress beside it.

and Openwork

The lacy look implied in openwork is more in keeping with daytime wear than is actual lace. Six different techniques by which these peek-a-boo effects can be produced are shown at the right, each of them particularly adapted to different styling situations.

Self-spaghetti and self-strapping can be worked into innumerable lacy openwork effects. Two restrained examples are shown at the upper right, both having the advantage of using self-fabric and of being rather inexpensive.

Hemstitching and fagoting look superficially alike, but are made by very different methods as the diagrams below illustrate. Machine hemstitching is shown combined with Val lace at the near right. This technique offers a good imitation of hand hemstitching and is used in preference to it because it is relatively inexpensive, although like self-fringe it cannot be used on a curved edge. Fagoting can take any shape and often replaces hemstitching for this reason, although it is such an expensive technique that it is usually restricted to better dresses.

Eyelet beading, different types of which are made by the yard, offers an inexpensive substitute for hemstitching. Some types of beading are planned for ribbon to be run through, while others are self-sufficient; those that have finished edges can be used at a neckline, and those that are not finished must be inset.

Spaghetti

Strapping

Hemstitching

Fagoting

Eyelet Beading

Eyelet Beading

OPENWORK TECHNIQUES

Hemstitching   Fagoting   Eyelet Beading

Embroidery and

Narrow-Band Embroidery

All-Over Embroidery

Specially Planned Embroidery

EMBROIDERY, like lace, was originally made only by hand. This association with handwork continues to give an expensive aura to the machine-made embroidery that has now replaced hand embroidery in general apparel usage. A look of dimension or depth determines quality to quite an extent, and depth ranges from the very obviously machine made that looks flat and thin to the rich dimensional effects that imitate hand embroidery very convincingly.

Schiffli embroidery, named for the Swiss manufacturer who invented the process, is made in widths ranging from the narrow eyelet beading of the preceding page to full fabric width and can cover the fabric completely, be confined to a border along one edge, or be spaced to suit a designer's individual requirements.

USES OF SCHIFFLI. One dress at the upper left shows an inexpensive banding that combines rickrack for an effective edge; the other dress shows an expensive banding that is edged with heavy dimensional scallops. In the group below one dress shows an all-over pattern on chiffon; the other one shows a spot pattern on linen, both made, as it happens, with the same styling. The two dresses at the bottom of the page show Schiffli patterns in which the width of the embroidery and its content are especially designed. In the dress at the far left, for example, the self-color embroidery repeats the horizontal lines of the tucked midriff and the triangular shape of the shoulder tabs in subtle repetitive motifs, and adds a row of curved shapes for variety in this excellently planned embroidery.

Other Special Trimmings

Monogram   Scallops

Burnout Yokes

Crochet Beading

SPOT EMBROIDERY. Monograms that are made from the initials of the wearer are obviously individually and expensively done. The few dress houses that specialize in this work design simple classic dresses suitable for monogramming. Fake monograms used on volume items are in a different category entirely. Scalloped edges that are not on straight grain are in the class with true monograms, however, since they must be individually embroidered, as illustrated by the dress on the far right.

BURNOUT YOKES. The high-price silk crepe dresses in this group have burnout yokes. For this technique, a piece of sheer fabric with a floral or conventional pattern stamped on it is basted behind the yoke area. The stamped pattern is mended to the dress fabric. Acid is then applied to burn out the parts of the dress fabric not in the mended design, leaving a sheer yoke with an attractive embossed self-fabric pattern.

CROCHET BEADING. Beading of this exquisite type is very expensive but even when used sparingly on a garment it adds an appealing luxury touch. The pastel crepe dress on the right uses white chiffon with seed beads of a tone deeper than the dress for its trimming. The other dress uses contrasting beads on self-fabric. To make crochet beading, the desired design is stamped on the left (wrong) side of the fabric which is then held taut in special beading hoops. The beads are strung on a long thread and a special crochet-type beading needle is pushed through the fabric again and again to catch one bead at a time until the design is completed.

Chapter Twelve

The Effective Use of Fabric

THE USE OF FABRIC in design has been purposely left for the final chapter in this book because fabric choice is conditioned by market-segment types, house-image concepts, fine-arts principles, and garment structure, as well as by the dictates of high fashion. In practice fabric selection is an initial step in design, but in theory it is the deepest and the most difficult facet of design for the beginner to comprehend. Within the limits of a single chapter only an outline of this broad subject can be presented, but no reading matter, however detailed or definitive, can take the place of actual practice. Fabrics must be handled, draped on three-dimensional forms, and tried out in actual garments before a designer can select and use them sensitively.

Balenciaga's supreme genius in handling fabric is clearly shown in this timeless dress of slubbed Italian silk. From Vogue, April 1, 1962.

Chapter Preview

FABRIC IS A TOOL with which to design. Fabric selection and style development are a tandem pair that must pull together. Experienced designers look at fabric lines early in any design season in order to get inspiration, and they choose fabrics "to design to" as well as fabrics to use for styles already planned. In less expensive markets where patterned fabrics are widely used, fabric choice is often more important than style development; but in every level of the market, the right fabric makes the designer's task easier and more rewarding.

crisp to the touch. In this chapter surface interest and texture will each be analyzed. These factors are considered separately for clarity in presentation although in practice both of them must be considered together. Their relationship is usually the prime factor in determining the suitability of a fabric for its intended use.

Development of Surface Pattern of Fabric. The fabrics first woven by man necessarily had a rough, homespun appearance because of the primitive nature of his tools and technical skills. Prehistoric man in colder climates had first used

**Plain Fabric without
Surface Pattern**

**Geometric Pattern
on Fabric**

**Naturalistic Pattern
on Fabric**

Fabric selection places immediate restrictions on design. The most obvious restriction is *suitability:* warm fabrics for winter; cool for summer; rich, perishable fabrics for dress; and coarse, durable fabrics for play and casual wear. Another limiting factor in fabric selection is the eye appeal or *surface interest* of the fabric; and the third limiting factor is the *texture* of the fabric, whether it is sheer or bulky, or soft or

animal pelts for clothing, eventually learning to cure and tan the hides which could then be fashioned into actual garments. The natural decorative taste of man caused him to decorate skins with paint and embroidery; and when he learned to weave he used contrasting colors to form stripes and borders to satisfy this same desire for color and decoration. Thus surface interest is as old as clothing itself.

PLAIN FABRICS. The eye enjoys wandering over any patterned surface, from fleecy clouds to precise grille work. Many types of surface interest have been developed expressly to relieve the monotony of plain fabric. Rich, expensive, plain fabric has a true beauty, but much of the fabric used in the garment industry cannot afford the quality yarns and workmanship necessary to produce it. Beautiful plain fabric requires only excellent cut, but inexpensive plain fabric usually does not have the inherent draping qualities necessary to produce attractive body-molding lines and therefore requires trimming to camouflage its shortcomings or pattern to cover them.

GEOMETRIC PATTERNS. Geometric patterns are an outgrowth of the primitive homespun into which ribs or self-color patterns were introduced or threads of different colors were woven. Geometrics are attractive to the eye but they require careful planning and matching at seamlines. They are generally best in tailored or casual styling unless made of rich fabric, and thus their use is somewhat restricted.

NATURALISTIC PATTERNS. These are descended from embroidery and painted design. Their great popularity is due to their ability to camouflage undistinguished fabric. Since they also tend to hide the style lines of a garment, they require simplicity of design and depend on expert selection and use of their surface pattern for their appeal.

DISTINGUISHED PLAIN FABRIC

TYPICAL GEOMETRIC PATTERNS

TYPICAL NATURALISTIC PATTERNS

303

Surface Interest in Fabric

Fabric-Pattern Analysis. The geometric and naturalistic pattern types introduced on the preceding page constitute the material for the first part of this chapter, in which surface interest is analyzed. The diagram on the facing page shows the relationship of geometric and naturalistic pattern types to each other; and it serves to introduce two additional pattern types that result from a mixture of geometric and naturalistic motifs:

Geometric Patterns. Textured patterns, stripes, and checks and plaids that are woven, printed, or knitted.

Conventional Patterns. Naturalistic motifs that have been stylized, often beyond recognition, and reflect geometric influence.

Naturalistic Patterns. Principally florals, although other motifs may be used, ranging from leopard spots to candy canes.

Dots and Spots. Natural curved forms that are simplified until their content has been destroyed, arranged in geometrical formation to resemble a checked pattern from which the connecting bars have been obliterated.

Fabric patterns have been divided thus into a small, workable number of generic groups that have common characteristics in order to furnish a practical basis for the analysis of their limitations and possibilities in apparel design. In each of the four pattern groups shown in the diagram, the middle figure represents a "pure" pattern type, and the figures at either side of it represent closely related pattern types that have developed from the pure type. Adjacent groups

are similarly related to each other, whereas groups that stand opposite one another have antithetical relationships. The geometric group, for example, consists of man-made, straight-line, nonrepresentational patterns. The naturalistic group, at the opposite extreme, consists of natural, free-form curves used to express meaningful content. The conventional group represents a compromise in which naturalistic content is made to conform to geometrically organized space. And the dot group represents a compromise in which a nonrepresentational concept is used to express the curved, naturalistic principle.

Special Requirements of Patterned Fabrics Used in Apparel Design. Adaptability to use on three-dimensional forms is a special requirement of all patterned fabric suitable for use in apparel design. Fabrics for apparel are not used flat, like rugs or wall paper, but must be molded around the body. A pattern on fabric must retain its effectiveness when seamed, darted, gathered, or draped. It must also look as well in motion as in repose, since the body is in motion a good deal of the time. The stronger the fabric pattern, with hard and definite outlines, the more difficult a styling problem it presents; conversely, the softer the outline of the pattern, the easier it is to use in garment styling. Textured patterns, where the outlines are only a soft blur, are almost as easy to handle in design as plain fabric, but strong geometric and naturalistic patterns present problems that tax the most experienced designers. On the following pages specific requirements of different fabric-pattern types are analyzed in relation to their most appropriate uses in apparel design.

FABRIC-PATTERN TYPES

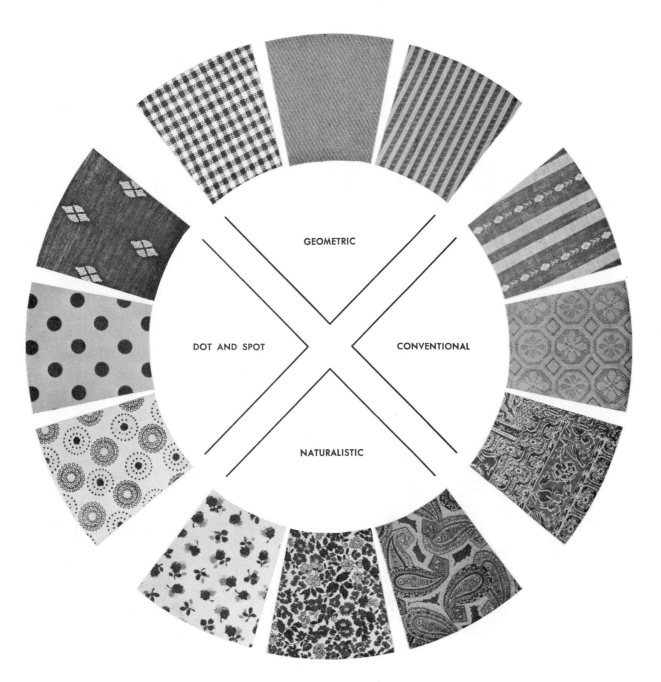

GEOMETRIC	CONVENTIONAL	NATURALISTIC	DOT AND SPOT
Gingham	Fancy Woven Stripe on Dimity	Paisley on Acetate Jersey	Novelty Dots on Cotton
Left-Hand Twill	Woven Silk Brocade	Naturalistic Floral on Cotton	Coin Dots on Flat Crepe
Striped Chambray	Block Print on Linen	Stylized Floral on Silk Crepe	Geometric Motif on Jersey

Winter-Wear Geometrics

WINTER GEOMETRICS were born when the first tailored suit for a woman was created by the Parisian designer Doucet in 1888. It copied the man's business suit and began the trend toward women's 9-to-5 business wear. The winter-geometric category has been broadened to include both very dressy and very casual fabrics, but the original concept remains to furnish fabrics that are still related to men's tailored suitings, although lighter in weight, softer in hand, finer in scale, and brighter in coloring.

Garment styles for geometrics generally are planned directly in the fabric, since the fabric pattern to a large degree dictates its own best styling which depends on both the mechanical limitations and possibilities of the pattern and the dressy-to-casual feeling that the texture of the fabric imparts to it. Checks and plaids are usually styled with some use of bias to direct the eye upward, and stripes often use bias to break the monotony of their straight lines. Trimmings are usually simple and tailored: a collar, a belt, buttons, perhaps pockets; thus allowing the fabric to capitalize on its own great appeal.

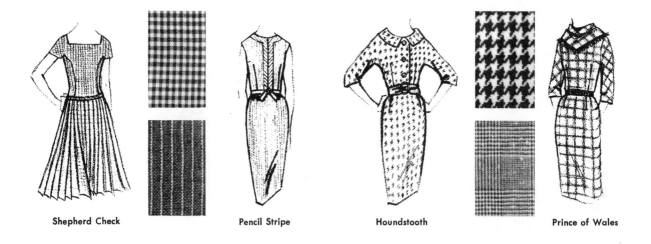

Shepherd Check   Pencil Stripe   Houndstooth   Prince of Wales

Small Stripes and Checks. These staple woolens are widely used for both men's and women's tailored suits as well as for dresses. Small checks are especially popular as dress fabrics, being both easy to style and easy to wear. They are practical, bright, and less conspicuous than the bolder and more colorful plaids.

Bolder Checks and Plaids. Houndstooth patterns shade gradually from dark to light, making less vivid contrasts than regular checkerboard squares. Prince of Wales checks and Glen plaids use thin lines grouped together in interesting but gentle patterns. These larger plaids are popular as dress fabrics because their impact is weakened, making them easier to wear.

Gabardine   Thin Hopsack   Corduroy   Bengaline

Monotone Woolen Geometrics. Woolens with diagonal weaves and other dimensional geometric effects are appropriate for fine daytime dresses because of the rich appearance of the fabric. They require styling that is suited to their individual fabric patterns although twilled weaves are so unobtrusive that they are often treated as plain fabrics.

Monotone Cords and Ribs. Silk and worsted ottoman and bengaline are used primarily for dressy wear because of the richness of their cross-ribbed patterns combined with the dressy connotation always inherent in silks. Corduroy, a velvety fabric with vertical ribs, can be used only for general and casual wear because it is made from cotton.

Slubbed Knit   Textured Tweed   Herringbone   Bold Plaid

Country Tweeds. The "country" look of tweedy fabrics may come from a heather yarn mixture, or a combination of a lighter warp yarn with a darker filling in a broken twill weave. In knit goods a combination of muted colors in thin cross stripes is often used effectively. Casual styling is most appropriate for country-tweed fabrics.

Heavy Tweeds and Strong Plaids. These bulky woolens are better adapted to separate skirts and coats than to dresses because they require such strong simple styling. In using plaid for a dress the size and complexity of its pattern dictate the styling to a great extent. Note how the plaid in the dress above cuts the figure at nicely proportioned levels.

Summer-Wear

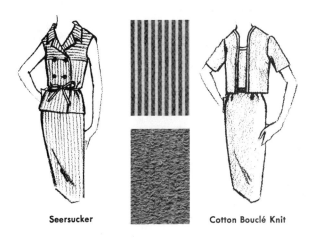

Seersucker   Cotton Bouclé Knit

Bulky Textured Fabrics. Bulky cottons are part of the casual trend. Seersucker has been disciplined by easy-care processes and blended with synthetics to become an almost perfect fabric for casual summer wear. Interesting weaves and easy care features combine to popularize summer knits which have the advantage of looking best in very simple styling.

SUMMER GEOMETRICS copy the woven geometrics of winter, but since summer fabrics are usually much lower in price than winter fabrics, many summer stripes and checks are printed rather than woven. Printed stripes on lengthwise (warp) grain are widely used and easy to work with, but printed checks present a problem because their cross-stripes seldom run true (straight with the grain). Checked and plaid gingham, in which the patterns are woven, are used in preference to printed imitations of them in all but very inexpensive lines.

The examples of printed geometrics shown

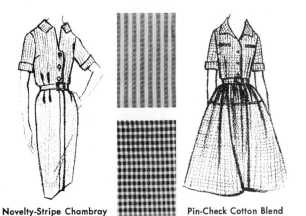

Novelty-Stripe Chambray   Pin-Check Cotton Blend

Checked Gingham   Plaid Gingham

Narrow Stripes and Tiny Checks. Small woven patterns are practical because their patterns do not require matching. The more sedate stripes are often used in women's classic styling with either a sheath or a discreetly gored skirt that women prefer, while the checks are better suited to the dirndl skirt and younger styling.

Woven Ginghams. As checks and plaids become larger, their matching problems require greater skill and taste. Most geometric patterns are not square. Warp stripes are usually closer together than filling stripes in order to look well balanced. For this reason a plaid can rarely be used on true bias as shown in the example above.

Geometrics

Windowpane-Check Organza

across the bottom half of the page are relatively easy to style. Printed stripes present no serious problem and soft outline and broken checks are widely used especially in sheer fabrics. But when accurate matching at the style lines cannot be avoided because it is a style feature of a dress, woven geometrics must be chosen in which the pattern runs perfectly true. Cottons avoid matching problems whenever possible. Woolens, on the other hand, are able to use styles that require matching much more easily, because the woven geometric patterns of wools automatically run true.

Printed Plaids. Geometric plaids in contrasting colors are not woven into sheer fabrics as a rule but are printed instead. The transparency of the fabric does not call for the tailored type of styling to which woven plaids are suited. Softer, broken patterns such as the one shown in the example are more compatible with sheers than are more formal patterns.

Awning-Striped Denim

Striped Synthetic Knit

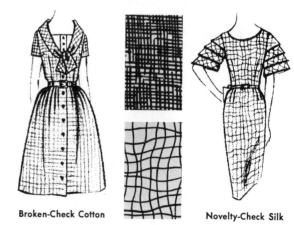

Broken-Check Cotton

Novelty-Check Silk

Bold Printed Stripes. Striped patterns that combine colors or stripes of different widths are popular for casual summer wear. The bolder the pattern the simpler the styling must be to scale with the gay fabric design. Some simple adaptation of the miter technique is often used, with the back of the waist kept on straight grain.

Printed Checks. Checked patterns on cotton and silk are printed rather than woven, either to keep down the price or to give a softer, less tailored pattern. Geometric patterns that are loosely drawn (as in the examples) lessen the matching problem. Even so, the successful styling of these printed geometrics requires great design skill.

Conventional Patterns

Cotton Dimity with Fancy Woven Stripes. Fancy stripes may be woven with a simple design of the type popular in men's shirting, or they may use lacy openwork similar to hemstitching, either alone or in combination with self-color stripes or embroidery in striped effects. All are appropriate for summer dresses that are less dressy than the styles for which organdy and dotted swiss are suited.

CONVENTIONAL patterns combine the impersonal rhythm of stripes with the soft natural charm of florals in patterns that are more versatile than geometrics and better suited to general daytime wear than the naturalistic floral patterns. Conventional patterns have an ancient and distinguished lineage.

Woven. Even in ancient times, taste and technical skill attained high excellence and the magnificence of brocade was evolved. Brocade patterns, which are so often based on the diamond shape, furnish inspiration for a wide range of conventional prints. Designers of knit goods

Woven Brocade in Conventional Diamond Pattern. Brocades were originally woven with gold and silver threads in small diamond patterns in which stylized floral motifs were centered. The double-filling technique developed from brocades is used for many types of modern woven fabric having surface patterns that are more complex than the strictly geometric stripes and plaids.

Matelassé Effect in Knitted Brocade Pattern. Jacquard processes in knitting have been developed to produce patterned double-knits with a dimensional depth equal to woven matelassé. These patterns achieve an effect of depth that printed patterns are incapable of producing, but the characteristically casual feeling of the knitted ground fabric limits their styling to jackets and casual two-piece costumes and tailored dresses.

have adapted brocade patterns to produce double-knit matelassé designs, and the embroidery industry, too, has borrowed the diamond brocade pattern for use in eyelet batiste, with small floral motifs used as centers for the diamonds.

Printed. In India and Persia during the Middle Ages, exquisite formal patterns were printed by hand on hand-loomed fabrics from wooden blocks hand carved with conventional patterns. The first printed cottons to reach Western civilization came from India to inspire paisley prints and bayadere borders as well as modern block prints.

Bayadere Stripes on Cotton Voile. Highly colored striped scarves were first used as costumes by Hindu dancing girls. Modern adaptations usually retain a slight oriental flavor in their wide conventionally patterned stripes that are most flattering when narrow and wide stripes alternate. In conservative patterns bayadere stripes make an excellent choice for women's summer sheer dresses.

Cotton Print in Conventional Pattern. Patterns of this type cover the fabric ground so well that they can use inexpensive cotton-print cloth. Because of the formality of their conventional patterns, they have a greater sophistication and a wider appeal in inexpensive cottons than do the true florals with their necessarily naturalistic coloring. These patterns too must "flow" to be in the best of taste.

Block Print on Linen. Conventional designs that are carved into wooden blocks which are dipped into dye and pressed onto fabric produce patterns of great charm because of the hand-done imperfectly registered pattern reproduction. The block-print technique is associated with quality fabrics. Less expensive roller prints that copy block-print patterns are widely used even though the imitation is obvious.

311

Naturalistic Patterns

THE CRITERION for a well-designed floral pattern is that it subtly flows so that it can lead the eye up to the face on its gentle curves, rather than holding the attention fixed on any single motif in the pattern. Strongly outlined floral patterns require simple, direct styling since they furnish their own best trimming, while very softly outlined floral patterns can be handled almost like plain fabric.

Choosing floral patterns involves practical as well as artistic considerations. Large floral patterns have long repeats, and matching a 16-inch repeat may waste much more fabric than matching a 4-inch repeat. Some florals are "one-way," and require all garment pieces to be cut in the same direction (like pile fabrics). Other florals not technically one-way nevertheless tend to look as if two different fabrics were combined when some of the garment pieces are cut straight grain and others on a bias. Multiple-direction patterns that have no layout restrictions are practical, but often dull. An attractive floral pattern usually has some styling limitation, and a designer must plan styles not affected by it.

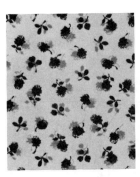

Up-and-Down Print

One-Way Print

A Spaced Pattern of Stylized Floral Motifs on Silk Crepe. Small, spaced formal patterns of this type have great popularity for rather tailored two-piece dresses and costume suits as well as for simple wearable dresses like the one in the sketch. Many of these spaced florals tend to hold the attention on their strong individual motifs rather than furnishing the flowing track for the eye, and careful selection is necessary.

Bold Sophisticated Black and White Print on Peau de Soie. A white or black pattern on a contrasting ground has great sophistication, especially if the pattern is bold, smart, and flows rhythmically. When garment styling is also bold and smart, the result can be stunning. Strong, exciting patterns are high fashion and their ground fabric is often distinctive in order to be properly suited to extreme garment styling.

Multiple-Direction Print

Multiple-Direction Print

Paisley Print on Synthetic Jersey. Paisley is one of the most satisfying and justly popular patterns that can be used for printed fabric because of the wonderful flow of its rhythmic design. Paisleys are more sophisticated than true florals, and their disciplined design is adaptable to color combinations in interesting ranges that are not available to the florals which must stay rather close to natural pastel coloring.

Light and Shadow Print on Cotton Voile. Naturalistic floral prints can be softened until they represent mere shadows cast by sunlight. These soft prints resemble other textured patterns and are just as easy to style and as easy to handle in production as a plain fabric. In addition, they do not show spots and wrinkles as plain fabrics do, and thus they are very practical with considerable appeal to conservative women.

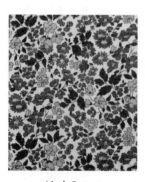 

4-Inch Repeat

16-Inch Repeat

Dainty All-Over Floral Pattern on Sheer Cotton. Liberty lawn in soft, charming patterns represents a type of cool, sweet, summer cotton print that is popular for both junior and women's dresses. Simple styles with full skirts are generally chosen since the fabric ground is so well covered by the print that intricate style lines are wasted because they cannot be seen.

Naturalistic Floral Pattern on Rayon Flat Crepe. The frankly pretty floral either in a monochromatic color scheme or in soft pastel multicolors is a staple in every women's dress house. These florals offer an appeal to large women that plain fabrics cannot match. The soft print blurs figure outlines and delights the eye with an attractive pattern instead, while its flowing curves direct attention pleasantly upward to the face.

Dot and Spot Patterns

THE DOT IS the strongest of all decorative forms because it is totally self-contained, and the absence of content gives to dots a purely emotional connotation of freedom and joy. Dots are associated with balloons and clown costumes. Dots are young and gay, and even when deliberately toned down they do not seem matronly. Successful use of dots generally depends on the reduction of their intensity in one or more of several possible ways:

Decreasing the Size. Dot strength is directionally proportional to size.

Decreasing the Purity. Any content that weakens the circular shape or the solid tone value decreases impact.

Weakening the Color Balance. Use of spacing that has less or more than optimum strength reduces impact.

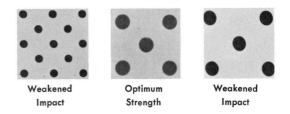

Weakened Impact	Optimum Strength	Weakened Impact

Decreasing the Color Contrast. Black dots on white have the greatest contrast. White dots on black are less intense because color is stronger than absence of color. As tone contrast between dot and ground is lessened, the impact of the dots is also reduced.

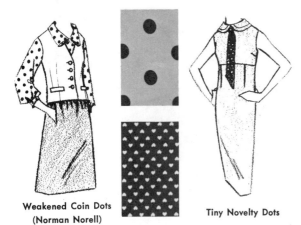

Weakened Coin Dots
(Norman Norell)

Tiny Novelty Dots

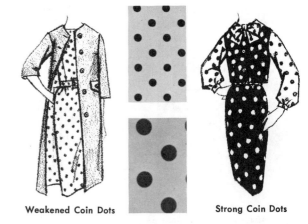

Weakened Coin Dots

Strong Coin Dots

Coin Dots as Trimming. Dots are the most popular of trimming patterns. Their self-containment makes them compatible with a plain fabric of the same ground color, and because of their great strength, a small area of dotted fabric can supply artistic balance for an entire dress. In the examples, note how dot size is coordinated with dot area.

Pure Coin Dots. Dots are practical as a companion coat lining for a dress since they do not restrict the use of a coat to its original dress as floral linings necessarily do. Colored dots on white make companion white dots on color seem less intense. This charming use of strong coin dots, here in a red and white combination, is perennially popular.

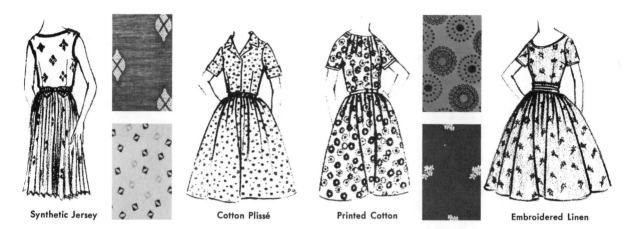

Synthetic Jersey   **Cotton Plissé**   **Printed Cotton**   **Embroidered Linen**

Geometric Spots. These novelty patterns are less popular than either the parent plaid or the true dot. They are best when the eye is led outward as both of the examples illustrate. A square in space is like a cage from which the eye works to escape, whereas a true dot permits free eye movement because of its pure natural form.

Novelty Floral Spots. Floral spots are only one step away from the spaced floral. In the novelty patterns above the motifs are set in geometrical planned space but retain a fragment of content. The motif may be repeated exactly or turned a quarter turn to furnish a set of four motifs, or it may use the same outline with varied content.

Dots on Voile   **Graduated Dots**   **Confetti Dots**   **Typical Foulard Dots**

Softened Coin Dots. When dots are printed on a sheer fabric like cotton voile, they are softened and, as their impact is decreased in this way, they become more dressy and more sophisticated. Dots printed in a series of related tones on opaque fabric, although softened in coloring, do not look dressy and are better adapted to general daytime wear.

Gentle Foulard Patterns. Small dots in closely related tone values are used on foulard or surah. These gentle dots are decreased in contrast and in purity, and are weakened in proportional color balance. They gain dignity in return and are more popular than any other member of the dot family, with wide acceptance for daytime wear in all market segments.

A. FABRIC HAND

Taffeta   Flat Crepe   Crepe

Crisp   Medium or General Purpose   Soft

Exaggerated Silhouette   Normal Silhouette   Exaggerated Silhouette

B. FABRIC WEIGHT

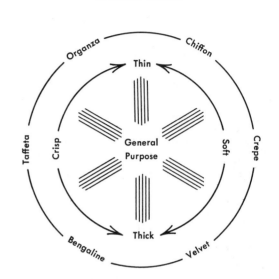

"HAND" AND "WEIGHT" are textural qualities of fabric that can often be more readily felt than seen. The interaction of these two qualities determines the silhouette capability of a fabric and thus restricts the types of styling for which it can be successfully used.

Hand (A). Hand can be illustrated by a comparison of three commonly used, medium-weight silk fabrics: taffeta, a true crepe like Canton crepe, and the so-called "flat crepe" that is widely used both as a plain fabric and as the ground fabric for many prints. Taffeta has a *crisp hand* that results from the use of hard-twist yarn in filling as well as in warp. True crepe has a *soft hand,* which comes from the use of crepe yarn, in which strands of hard-twist yarn are twisted together in the reverse direction, or to a shrinking process after the fabric is woven. Flat crepe has a *medium hand* because of the harder twist yarn used in warp than in filling (just as it is in muslin, as explained on page 122,

Chapter 5). Flat crepe, rather than either taffeta or true crepe, is generally used when the normal silhouette is desired, because it is less expensive and its normal hand is well adapted to the normal silhouette. Taffeta and true crepe, with their extreme hand, are generally used with more-or-less exaggerated silhouettes which their crispness or softness can capitalize on.

Weight (B). Weight can also be illustrated by a comparison among silk fabrics. Thin, sheer silks may be crisp like organza or soft like chiffon. Both are woven from high-denier (fine) yarns. Heavy or bulky silks may be crisp like bengaline and brocade or soft like velvet. Bulkiness may be produced either by use of heavier yarns or cords in warp or filling, or by one of the special weaving processes such as are used for jacquards, brocades, or pile fabrics. These extreme fabrics are suited for exaggerated silhouettes and generally are used only when styling specifically calls for them.

Silhouette Development

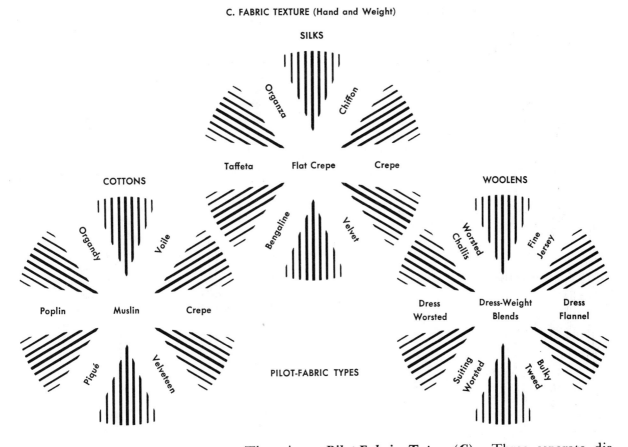

SILKS

Organza Chiffon

Taffeta   Flat Crepe   Crepe

COTTONS   WOOLENS

Organdy   Voile   Bengaline   Velvet   Worsted Challis   Fine Jersey

Poplin   Muslin   Crepe   Dress Worsted   Dress-Weight Blends   Dress Flannel

Piqué   Velveteen   PILOT-FABRIC TYPES   Suiting Worsted   Bulky Tweed

INTERACTION OF HAND AND WEIGHT. The crispness or hand of a fabric combines with and interacts on its weight. When extreme textural qualities that are a combination of hand and weight are arranged opposite one another as shown in Diagram B, it is easily seen that general-purpose qualities characterize fabrics that are neither extremely thin, thick, soft, nor crisp, and for this reason can be used best for the normal silhouette. Note that there are no hard demarcation lines separating these qualities. Instead, they blend into one another around the circle, and from the perimeter into the general-purpose center.

Pilot-Fabric Types (**C**). Three separate diagrams are used above to designate pilot-fabric types for silks, cottons, and woolens. In these diagrams the hand and weight qualities used in B are replaced by commonly recognized fabrics that are chosen to represent various textural qualities. On the following pages these fabrics act as pilots or leaders with which other fabrics that can be used for the same types of silhouette are grouped, and for which styles that are suitable are illustrated. As has been here explained, perimeter fabrics are generally chosen for exaggerated silhouettes, and general-purpose fabrics for the normal silhouette.

Silks and Synthetics That Imitate Them

GENERAL-PURPOSE SILKS

Silk Broadcloth
Flat Crepe (French Crepe)

Many Synthetics, Blends,
and Mixtures That Imitate
Various Silks

Slubbed Synthetic Blend

Rayon Faille

Satin-Back Acetate Crepe

Silk Flat Crepe

CRISP SILKS

Thin

Mousseline de Soie
Silk Organdy
Organza
Pongee
Chiffon Taffeta

Medium Weight

Faille
Jacquard Weaves
Satin
Acetate Sharkskin
Slubbed Weaves
   Douppioni
   Shantung
   Silk Linen
Taffeta

Thick

Brocade
Cords
   Bengaline
   Ottoman
Satin-Back Crepe
Matelassé
Peau de Soie
Slipper Satin

SOFT SILKS

Chiffon
China Silk
Crepes
   Crepe de Chine
   Georgette
   Meteor
Foulard
Silk Jersey
Bemberg Sheer
Triple Sheer

Crepes
   Canton
   Charmeuse
   Marocain
   Romaine
Synthetic Jersey

Four-Ply Crepe
Mossy Crepe
Velvets

SILKS ARE WORN the year around more or less as dressy garments. The more that a silk resembles linen or wool, the less dressy it is. When it looks extremely perishable like chiffon, velvet, or brocade, it is considered very dressy.

General-Purpose Silks and Synthetics. The four dresses shown on this page represent the multitude of rather conservative styles that are produced every season in general-purpose silks, whereas the dresses on the facing page require fabrics particularly suited to their less conservative styling.

Crisp Silks. Crisp silks (on the near right) are used to produce different silhouette effects. Crisp, sheer silks produce a diaphanous, bouffant effect; medium-weight silks impart a crispness to the silhouette; thick silks have a molding quality that subtly defines the silhouette.

CRISP SILKS

Thin

Organza

Chiffon Taffeta

Medium Weight

Douppioni Silk

Rayon Taffeta

Thick

Brocade

Silk Ottoman

SOFT SILKS

Thin

Triple Sheer

Foulard

Medium Weight

Synthetic Jersey

Crepe Romaine

Thick

Four-Ply Crepe

Velvet

Soft Silks. Soft silks (on the far right) are also used to produce particular effects. The soft drape of chiffon and the airy flow of foulard make fabric in these soft-sheer categories ideally suited for the look of cool, expensive styling. The crepes have a draping quality matched by no other woven fabric and equaled only by jersey. Crepe is used also to connote luxury, and for this reason a dress detailed with expensive lace or fagoting usually uses a pure silk crepe even though the styling does not demand it. Perishable velvet is so dressy that it is seldom used for daytime wear. The extremely tailored body lines of the high-style import at the bottom of the page make it more suitable for daytime wear than is often the case with velvet.

Cottons, Linens, and Synthetics

GENERAL-PURPOSE COTTONS		
Broadcloth	Madras	Print Cloth
Calico	Muslin	Sateen
Chambray	Oxford	Seersucker
Gingham	Percale	Synthetics and Blends

Percale

Gingham

Print Cloth   Broadcloth

CRISP COTTONS   SOFT COTTONS

Thin

Dimity	Batiste
Dotted Swiss	Lawn
Eyelet Batiste	Handkerchief Linen
Organdy	Voile
Point d'Esprit	
Plissé	
Thick and Thin Stripe	

Medium Weight

Dress-Weight Linens	Cotton Crepe
Linen Blends	Linen Crepe
Linenlike Synthetics	Cotton Knits
Poplin (Cotton Taffeta)	Linen Knits

Thick

Bedford Cord	Knits
Butcher Linen	Bouclé
Denim	Fancy
Gabardine	Pile Fabrics
Matelassé	Corduroy
Piqués	Terry Cloth
Rep	Velveteen
Sail Cloth	
Tapestry	
Twill	

COTTONS HAVE always been for summer, wools for winter. But when the development of synthetics that has characterized this century began to make inroads on the cotton market, cotton manufacturers developed new weaves and finishes that not only offer competition to the synthetic market but to woolens as well, making "winter cotton" a standard dress fabric, and producing a new and exciting range of bulky cotton fabrics suited to high-fashion summer styling.

General-Purpose Cottons, Blends, Synthetics. The four dresses on this page represent the great segment of this market, which includes the commonly used plain-color, printed, and woven geometric designs in medium-weight, general-purpose fabrics.

Crisp Cottons, Linens, Synthetics. These are naturally divided at the near right into the three groups. Crisp sheers are decidedly dressy and

CRISP COTTONS

Thin

Organdy — Eyelet Batiste

Medium Weight

Cotton Poplin — Dress Linen

Thick

Butcher Linen — Matelassé Piqué

SOFT COTTONS

Thin

Batiste — Cotton Voile

Medium Weight

Cotton Crepe — Cotton Knit

Thick

Waffle Knit — Velveteen

young. Crisp poplin and linen weaves and many winter cottons are suited to rather tailored styles that require fabric with crispness and body without excessive bulk. Heavy cottons that are offshoots of men's work-clothes fabrics are suited to the casual separates that spring from the same source. Bulky cottons derived from the fancy weaves of brocade and matelassé are ideal for more dressy high-style silhouettes.

Soft Cottons, Linens, Synthetics. These fabrics (above) are ideal for rather dressy summer wear in the thin and medium weights. The cotton and linen knits and the synthetics that imitate them are well adapted to casual styling in a soft rather than a crisp silhouette, whereas the thick velveteen and corduroy are true winter cottons and may be styled in either a casual or a semidressy way.

Woolens, Worsteds, and Synthetic Blends

GENERAL-PURPOSE DRESS-WEIGHT WOOLENS

Wools
Wool and Worsted Mixtures
Wool and Synthetic Blends
Synthetics That Imitate Wools

Wool and Worsted

Novelty Wool

Wool and Orlon

Synthetic Blend

CRISP WOOLENS	**SOFT WOOLENS**
Thin	
Thin Worsteds	**Thin Wools**
Challis	Wool Challis
Sheer Novelties	Chiffon Flannel
Nun's Veiling	Thin Fur Blends
	Sheer Hopsack
	Fine Jersey
Medium Weight	
Dress-Weight Worsteds	**Chiffon Broadcloth**
Gabardine	**Medium-Weight Jersey**
Homespun	**Dress-Weight Wools**
Poplin	Basket Weave
Serge	Fur Blends
Twill	Homespun
Medium-Weight Blends of	Hopsack
Silk and Worsted	Novelty Weaves
Wool and Worsted	Tweed
Thick	
Suiting-Weight Worsteds	**Bulky Wools**
Gabardine	Homespun
Poiret Twill	Hopsack
Whipcord	Tweed
Double-Knit Jersey	**Pile Fabrics**
Bonded Woolens	Broadcloth
Laminated Woolens	Duvetyn
	Eponge
	Looped Mohair

GENERAL-PURPOSE woolens are adaptable to softly flared or to strictly pleated skirts. They can be gathered, draped, or tailored to a reasonable degree, as the general-purpose dresses on this page illustrate. Woolens are expensive, and general-purpose woolens are widely used because they are less expensive than the special-purpose types shown on the facing page.

Crisp, Springy Woolens. These woolens (at the near right) get their distinctive dry, crisp hand from the worsted content of the fabric. Worsted is high-twist yarn made from long, high-quality wool fibers. Wool yarn is a softer twist that utilizes the shorter, weaker fibers. Pure worsted is very crisp and very expensive. A blend of silk and worsted has become popular because it pro-

322

CRISP WOOLENS	SOFT WOOLENS

Thin

Worsted Sheer   Nun's Veiling

Fur Blend   Sheer Hopsack

Medium Weight

Worsted Gabardine   Alaskine

Argyle Plaid   Chiffon Broadcloth

Thick

Bonded Jersey   Poiret Twill

Duvetyn   Bulky Tweed

duces a crisp hand that wool blends cannot duplicate. Bonded dress woolens (a lining is "bonded" to a thin tweed, jersey, or similar fabric) represent another development in the woolen market that is geared to cutting down costs. All types of fabric with enough substance to shape and mold a silhouette without actual "fitting" owe their popularity to the trend toward casual dress and simplicity of style.

Soft Woolens. The weight of flannel and other plain-surface wools has been decreased in order to compete with the soft, draping quality of jersey. Tweeds and homespuns have been combined with mohair or have used springy bouclé yarns to produce almost weightless bulk that is the woolen counterpart of the cotton workclothes trend. Woolen fabrics, to a great extent, furnish the base on which fashion is built.

Bibliography

Allen, Agnes, *The Story of Clothes,* London: Faber, 1955.

Ballard, Bettina, *In My Fashion,* New York: McKay, 1960.

Barr, E. D. Y., "Psychological Analyses of Fashion Motivation," *Archives of Psychology,* No. 171.

Beaton, Cecil W. H., *The Glass of Fashion,* Garden City, N. Y.: Doubleday, 1954.

Boehn, Max von, *Modes and Manners,* London: Harrap, 1932.

Bradley, Carolyn G., *Western World Costume,* New York: Appleton-Century-Crofts, 1954.

Brooklyn Museum, *The House of Worth,* Brooklyn, N. Y., 1962.

Chambers, Bernice G., *Fashion Fundamentals,* Englewood Cliffs, N. J.: Prentice-Hall, 1947.

Crawford, Morris D. C., *The Ways of Fashion,* New York: Putnam, 1941.

Dior, Christian, *Talking about Fashion,* New York: Putnam, 1954.

Garland, Madge, *Fashion,* Baltimore, Md.: Penguin, 1962.

Hurlock, E. B., "Motivation in Fashion," *Archives of Psychology,* No. 111.

Jarnow, Jeannette A., and Beatrice Judelle, *Inside the Fashion Business,* New York: Wiley, 1965.

Köhler, Carl, *A History of Costume,* New York: Dover, 1963.

Latour, Anny, *Kings of Fashion,* London: Weidenfeld and Nicolson, 1958.

Laver, James, *Taste and Fashion,* London: Harrap, 1945.

Morton, Grace M., *The Arts of Costume and Personal Appearance,* 3rd ed., New York: Wiley, 1964.

Palmer, Robert R., *History of the Modern World,* New York: Knopf, 1961.

Picken, Mary Brooks, and Dora Miller, *Dressmakers of France,* New York: Harper, 1956.

Poiret, Paul, *King of Fashion,* Philadelphia: Lippincott, 1931.

Roach, Mary Ellen, and Joanne B. Eicher, *Dress, Adornment, and the Social Order,* New York: Wiley, 1965.

Saunders, Edith, *The Age of Worth,* London: Longmans, Green, 1954.

Schiaparelli, Elsa, *Shocking Life,* New York: Dutton, 1954.

Snow, Carmel, and Mary Louise Aswell, *The World of Carmel Snow,* New York: McGraw-Hill, 1962.

Train, Arthur K., *The Story of Everyday Things,* New York: Harper, 1941.

Wilcox, Ruth T., *The Mode in Costume,* 2nd ed., New York: Scribner, 1958.

Worth, Jean Philippe, *A Century of Fashion,* Boston: Little, Brown, 1928.

Young, Agnes B., *Recurring Cycles of Fashion, 1760–1937,* New York: Harper, 1937.

Index

Index

Index